The Return of the Ring

Proceedings of the Tolkien Society Conference 2012

Volume II

Edited by
Lynn Forest-Hill

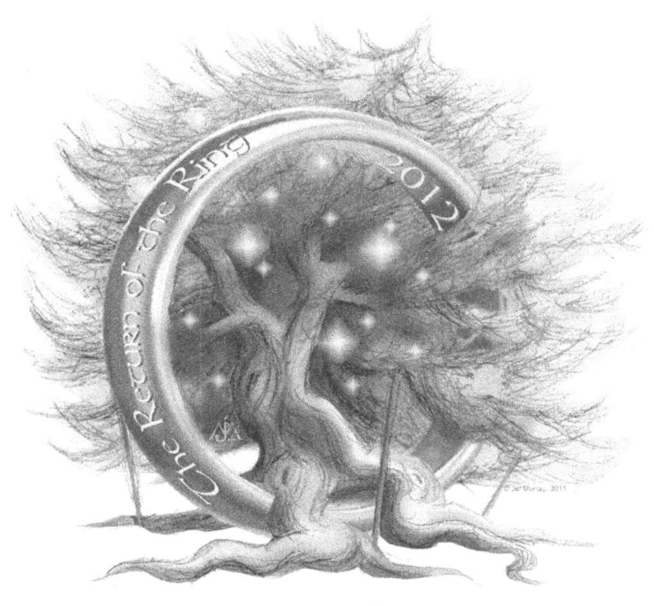

First published, 2016 by Luna Press Publishing™, Edinburgh

ISBN-13: 978-1-911143-03-1

Cover photograph by Pamela Chandler © Diana Willson
Cover design © Jay Johnstone 2016
Return of the Ring logo by Jef Murray

www.lunapresspublishing.com

Contents

Introduction

These proceedings are a record of papers presented at the Tolkien Society's most recent major conference 'The Return of the Ring: Celebrating Tolkien in 2012', which was held at Loughborough University from the 16th to the 20th August 2012. The number of papers collected here, and their range of subject matter has resulted in two volumes. Volume I covers Biography, War, Philosophy and Ethics, and further considerations of Tolkien's use of mythology. Volume II (this volume) covers Medievalism, Fantasy, and Diversity.

The themes presented in this volume are those most frequently associated with scholarly approaches to Tolkien's work, but within each theme new topics extend our appreciation of the richness of those works. Yoko Hemmi offers a welcome reading of one of the less well-known poems 'The Lay of Aotrou and Itroun', while Jamie McGregor analyses the use of heraldry in the major works. Nick Groom turns his attention to the Gothic elements, spanning the use of 'Gothic' to include its eighteenth-century manifestation as these are inflected by its medieval origins. Constance Wagner deploys a medieval handbook on knightly conduct to illuminate the actions of the hobbit and the Gondorian warrior, and as a byproduct of this research illuminates the extent to which Peter Jackson's *Lord of the Rings* adaptations retains the chivalric theme.

Two papers tackle the topic of fantasy from different perspectives. Anna E. Thayer reconsiders Tolkien's influence on later writers of fantasy fiction while Troels Forchhammer looks at attitudes to the fantasies of old stories within the societies Tolkien creates.

It is no surprise that the final section of this volume is the longest because diversity is the keynote of both Tolkien studies and the response of non-writing fans. Maureen Mann takes a serious look at nonsense, Anna E. Thayer considers Tolkien's engagement with the Romantic genre and Reuven Naveh sets 'The Ainulindalë' in the context of modern classical music. Jim Clark exposes the problem of plagiarism but reveals it as a pathway to politically informed alternative versions of Tolkien's work. Murray Smith finds a heightened sense of commercial law infusing *The Hobbit* while Janet Brennan Croft sets out to consolidate the elusive topic of Faerian drama. Chris Barclay investigates the depiction of female characters, with special consideration of Erendis. Christopher Kreuzer reveals the significance of Tolkien's use of colours. It is not by accident that Nancy Martsch's paper on 'Fandom' rounds off this volume because fans are the foundation of the Society, giving it a particular vibrancy, contributing greatly to widening knowledge of Tolkien through their participation on websites, social media, and fan-based events such as WorldCon. Nancy's paper reminds us of how diverse fan participation can be, and that out of it have emerged many of the contributors to the Return of the Ring conference at Loughborough, England, and thus to these proceedings.

Where contributions included in this volume have already been published elsewhere, acknowledgements are given in immediate proximity to those essays. Their inclusion here reflects the comprehensive scope of the Return of the Ring conference, its value as a forum for honing research, and demonstrates yet again the extent to which Tolkien's works encourage diverse critical approaches and breadth of participation.

I would like to record my thanks to Troels Forchammer, Olga Akroyd for help with the editing process. I must also pay tribute to Daniel Helen and Francesca Barbini for managing the production, design and lay out of these volumes - without their hard work these proceedings would not exist. As always, I owe grateful thanks to my family for their tolerance and understanding during the editing process.

Lynn Forest-Hill
Editor

Abbreviations

The Lord of the Rings	*LotR*
The Fellowship of the Ring	*FotR*
The Two Towers	*TT*
The Return of the King	*RotK*
The Hobbit	*TH*
The Silmarillion [when unitalicised refers to the unpublished variants]	*TSil*
Unfinished Tales of Númenor and Middle-earth	*UT*
On Fairy-Stories	*OFS*
Farmer Giles of Ham	*Giles*
Smith of Wootton Major	*Smith*

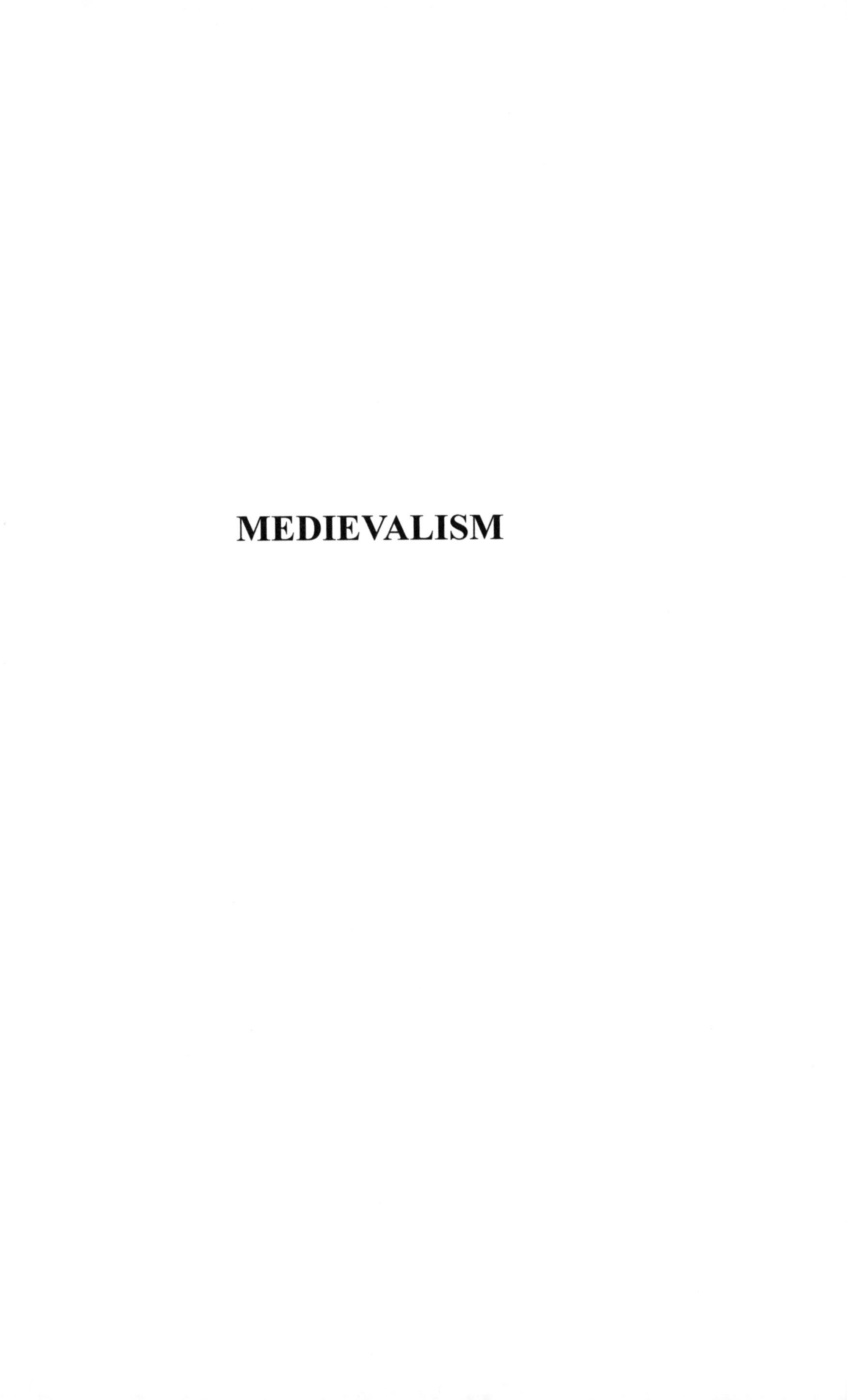

MEDIEVALISM

'Tolkienesque Transformations: Post-Celticism and Possessiveness in '"The Lay of Aotrou and Itroun"'

Yoko Hemmi

Tolkien, as can be seen from his lecture/essay English and Welsh, was among the earliest to criticise Romantic Celticism which even in his day pervaded popular images of things Celtic. When depicting the forest of Brocéliande in 'The Lay of Aotrou and Itroun', however, he seems to exploit the very qualities of what Matthew Arnold called 'Celtic Magic'. This paper attempts to demonstrate how Tolkien, by adopting the viewpoint of post-Celticism, transformed the Breton source of 'The Lay of Aotrou and Itroun' so as to imbue it with the theme of possessiveness which dominates The Silmarillion and The Lord of the Rings.

Tolkien's 'The Lay of Aotrou and Itroun', published in 1945 in the *Welsh Review*, is modelled on Breton *lais*, the typical format of which is generally held to contain 'besides the story proper, a prologue and epilogue, in which either a Breton source is claimed or the setting is given as Brittany', and to be written 'in octosyllabic couplets, in the vernacular rather than Latin'.[1]

Whereas the oral Breton sources, upon which are based 'authentic' medieval Breton *lais* (for example, those of Marie de France), have not survived, with the result that their nature remains obscure, the Breton source that Tolkien used is extant and has been identified as the 'Aotrou Nann hag ar Gorrigan'. This Breton ballad was recorded by la Villemarqué in his *Barzaz-Breiz*,[2] a copy of which Tolkien purchased in 1922 and is now housed in Tolkien's library at Oxford.[3]

1. Mortimer J. Donovan, *The Breton Lay: A Guide to Varieties*, University of Notre Dame Press, Notre Dame and London, 1969, p. 64.
2. For the controversy over, and the reassessment of Théodore Claude Henri, vicomte Hersart de la Villemarqué's *Barzaz-Breiz*, see Mary-Ann Constantine, *Breton Ballads*, CMCS, Aberystwyth, 1996, pp. 10–16.
3. In both my unpublished MA thesis and my article in Japanese (Hemmi [*née* Hiraoka], 1984 and 1985), I compared Tolkien's lay with an English ballad 'Clerk Colvill' along with its analogues (as listed by F. J. Child). Yoko Hiraoka, '*The Lord of the Rings*: A Fairy-Story of J. R. R. Tolkien', unpublished Master's thesis, Keio University, Tokyo, 1984; and Yoko Hiraoka, 'Tolkien's "The Lay of Aotrou and Itroun" and its sources', *The Round Table* 1 (1985), 65–79. Furthermore, I identified Villemarqué's 'Aotrou Nann hag ar Gorrigan' and its translations by Thomas Keightley and Tom Taylor as Tolkien's source and wrote to both Humphrey Carpenter and Christopher Tolkien to inquire if Tolkien owned a copy of *Barzaz-Breiz* but neither of them

Tolkien's lay is set in the forest of Brocéliande in Brittany,[4] or, in 'Britain's land' or 'Britain' – terms Tolkien employs interchangeably with Brittany. The latter, because of its geographical and political peripherality, was associated in the Middle Ages with wonders and marvels, and medieval romances employed Brocéliande as a *topos* for knights' encounters with the enchanted world of fées.[5]

Tolkien's 'Lay of Aotrou and Itroun' tells the story of a lord and a lady (*aotrou* and *itroun* in Breton) whose lives were ruined by a 'Corrigan',[6] a fairy who presided over a fountain in the forest of Brocéliande. The lay may be regarded as heir to Chrétien de Troyes's *Le Chevalier au lion (Yvain)* in the sense that both belong to a tradition of romantic fantasising of the forest of Brocéliande and its fountain. Indeed, Chrétien used one of the tales of wonder circulating in the twelfth century concerning the fountain of Barenton in Brittany, to which Gerald of Wales referred: '[i]f you drink its water out of the horn of an ox and happen to spill any of it on a nearby rock, a shower of rain will fall on you immediately even though the sky be ever so clear from rain'.[7] While Chrétien's twelfth-century contemporary, Wace, in his *Le Roman de Rou* (Part III, ll. 6393–98),[8] attempted to deprive Brocéliande of its enchantment by expressing his disillusionment with it and heaping reproach upon himself for being a fool in going there in search of marvels,[9] Chrétien set *Yvain* in the Arthurian past and incorporated the fountain of Barenton into a sophisticated literary fantasy about an enchanted forest. It is also interesting to compare the spirit and treatment of magic and the supernatural in *Yvain* with that of the Welsh *Owein* (*The Lady of the Well*), which is considered

---

responded. In 1991, Jessica Yates published 'The Sources of "The Lay of Aotrou and Itroun"', in Trevor Reynolds, ed., *Leaves from the Tree: J. R. R. Tolkien's Shorter Fiction*, Tolkien Society, London, 63–71.

4. See Nora K. Chadwick, *Early Brittany*, University of Wales Press, Cardiff, 1969, pp. 292–93.

5. See C. Foulon, 'Enchanted Forests in Arthurian Romance', *Yorkshire Celtic Studies* 5 (1949/52), 3–18; Corinne J. Saunders, *The Forest of Medieval Romance: Avernus, Broceliande, Arden*, D. S. Brewer, Cambridge, 1993, pp. 204–205.

6. A Breton word used as a synonym of *fée* or fairy. See W. Y. Evans Wentz, *The Fairy-Faith in Celtic Countries*, Colin Smythe, Gerrards Cross, 1971, p. 210.

7. Gerald of Wales, *The History and Topography of Ireland*, trans. John J. O'Meara, Penguin Books, London, 1982, p. 63; Gerald of Wales, *Giraldi Cambrensis Opera*, ed. J.S. Brewer, James F. Dimock, and G.F. Warner, vol. 5, Longmans, London, 1867, pp. 89–90.

8. *Le Roman de Rou de Wace*, ed. A. J. Holden, Tome II, Picard, Paris, 1971, p. 122; *The History of the Norman People: Wace's Roman de Rou*, trans. Glyn S. Burgess, Boydell, Woodbridge, 2004, p. 162.

9. As for Wace's intentions, see Yoko Hemmi, 'The Marvel of the Forest of Brocéliande in a Colonial Context: Chrétien de Troyes and Wace', in Fleur Vigneron and Koji Watanabe, eds, *Voix des Mythes, Science des Civilisations: Hommage à Philippe Walter*, Peter Lang, Bern, 2012, 179–93, pp. 187–93.

to share a common source with, or to be derived from, *Yvain*.[10] For example, if we compare the stone beside the spring described in *Yvain* as being 'of emerald / pierced through like a cask, / and it sat upon four rubies, / brighter and redder / than the morning sun / when it first appears in the east',[11] with the simple 'marble slab' in *Owein*,[12] it is obvious that the imaginative quality in the treatment of the marvellous is intensified in *Yvain*. In short, Chrétien endowed the forest with an aura of mythic marvels[13] and Tolkien's lay follows this tradition, which had been enriched through a series of products, both literary and visual, of medievalism in the nineteenth century such as Alfred Lord Tennyson's 'Merlin and Vivien' and Edward Burne-Jones's 'Beguiling of Merlin'.

However, Tolkien's attitude towards the forest of Brocéliande should not be lumped together with the prevailing trend of 'Celticism', that is, the romanticised, stereotypical depictions of the Celtic lands, their people and culture. 'Celticism', which was closely linked to Romanticism as well as medievalism[14] and was advocated foremost by Ernest Renan and Matthew Arnold, remained prevalent in the popular consciousness well into Tolkien's times (and even our own).[15] Renan, for instance, perceived in the mythology of the 'Celtic races', by which he mainly meant the Welsh *Mabinogion*, a 'transparent naturalism … the love of nature for herself, the vivid impression of her magic' which he thought explained

10. R. L. Thomson, 'Owain: Chwedl Iarlles y Ffynnon', in Rachel Bromwich, A. O. H. Jarman, and Brynley F. Roberts, eds, *The Arthur of the Welsh: The Arthurian Legend in Medieval Welsh Literature*, University of Wales Press, Cardiff, 1991, 159–69, pp. 167–68. *Owein or Chwedyl Iarlles y Ffynnawn*, ed. R. L. Thomson, Dublin Institute for Advanced Studies, Dublin, 1986; 'The Lady of the Well' in *The Mabinogion*, trans. Sioned Davies, Oxford University Press, Oxford, 2007.

11. *The Knight with the Lion or Yvain (Li Chevalier au Lion)*, ed. and trans. William W. Kibler, Garland, New York and London, 1985, p. 19; 'Li perrons ert d'une esmeraude / Perciee ausi com une boz, / Et s'a quatre rubiz desoz, / Plus flanboianz et plus vermauz / Que n'êst au matin li solauz, / Quant il apert en oriant', lines 422–27; p. 349. *Yvain ou Le Chevalier au lion*, Texte établi par Kar D. Utti, traduit, présenté et annoté par Philippe Walter, in *Chrétien de Troyes OEuvres completes*, Gallimard, Paris, 1994, pp. 339–503.

12. 'And I came to the tree, and I could see the well beneath the tree, and the marble slab beside it, and the silver bowl fastened to the chain. And I took the bowl and threw a bowlful of water over the slab. And at once the noise came … and after the noise the shower...' *Mabinogion*, op. cit. [10], p. 120.

13. See op. cit. [9], pp. 182–87.

14. Cf. Gerard Carruthers and Alan Rawes, 'Introduction: Romancing the Celts', in Gerard Carruthers and Alan Rawes, eds, *English Romanticism and the Celtic World*, Cambridge University Press, Cambridge, 2003, 1–19.

15. See Joep Leerssen, 'Celticism', in Terence Brown, ed., *Celticism*, Rodopi, Amsterdam-Atlanta, 1996, 1–20; D. Ellis Evans, 'Celticity, Celtic awareness and Celtic Studies', *Zeitschrift für celtische Philologie* 49/50 (1997), 1–27; Patrick Sims-Williams, 'Celtomania and Celtoscepticism', *Cambrian Medieval Celtic Studies* 36 (1998), 1–35.

the pre-Christian worship of forests, fountains, and stone still observed in Brittany.[16]

As can be seen in his lecture, *English and Welsh*, Tolkien was among the earliest critics of the fallacy of Celticism, which promoted the popular image of 'Celtic' literature being 'full of dark and twilight, laden with sorrow and regret'.[17] Indeed, he tried to demonstrate the invalidity of popular images of things 'Celtic' by presenting the genuine 'Celtic' text, that is, the actual Middle Welsh text from the first branch of the *Mabinogi*. He quoted the opening scene of the hunt of the Lord of Annwfn/the Underworld and notes the practicality and keen appreciation of bright colours that the text exhibits.[18]

It should be noted that Tolkien's attitude corresponds exactly with that of contemporary Celtic linguist Kenneth Jackson. Jackson, in his *Celtic Miscellany*, published in 1951 (i.e. four years prior to Tolkien's *English and Welsh* lecture), defines *Celtic literature* as a 'convenient abbreviation for 'the literatures composed in the Celtic languages'',[19] thus asserting that the umbrella-term 'Celtic' is fundamentally linguistic in nature. It is certain that Jackson was aware of the fact that the term was adopted by Edward Lhuyd in 1707 to encompass, for the first time, Irish, Breton, Cornish, Welsh and Gaulish as one language group. As Patrick Sims-Williams pointed out later,

> [b]ecause scholars agree that the concept of 'Celtic' is fundamentally a matter of language, and because the distance between the medieval Celtic languages is so great, the modern tendency to treat medieval Irish and Welsh culture as fundamentally the same seems anachronistic.[20]

Tolkien, when he asked the audience, after quoting from the *Mabinogi*, if the writer could have been a 'Celt', and answered for them that '[h]e had never heard of the word, we may feel sure; but he spoke and wrote with skill what we now

16. Ernest Renan, 'La Poésie des Races Celtiques', in Henriette Psichari, ed., *OEuvres Complètes de Ernest Renan*, vol. 2, Calmann-Lévy, Paris, 1854, 252–301, pp. 269–70; Ernest Renan, *The Poetry of the Celtic Races, and Other Studies by Ernest Renan*, trans. William G. Hutchison, Walter Scott, London, 1896, pp. 22–23.

17. J.R.R. Tolkien, 'English and Welsh', in Christopher Tolkien, ed., *The Monsters and the Critics and Other Essays*, George Allen & Unwin, London, 1983, 162–97, p. 172.

18. Op. cit

19. Kenneth Hurlstone Jackson, *A Celtic Miscellany*, Penguin, London, 1951, rev. edn, 1971, p. 7.

20. Patrick Sims-Williams, 'Some Celtic Otherworld Terms', in A. T. E. Matonis and Daniel F. Melia, eds, *Celtic Language, Celtic Culture: A Festschrift for Eric P. Hamp*, Ford and Bailie, Van Nuys, 1990, 57–81.

classify as a Celtic language: Cymraeg, which we call Welsh',[21] demonstrates that his perception was consistent with those of the leading Celticists of his day (and ours).[22]

Tolkien's wry joke that '[s]hould you wish to describe the riding to hunt of the Lord of the Underworld in 'Celtic' fashion (according to this view of the word), you would have to employ an Anglo-Saxon poet'[23] reminds us of Jackson's criticism of the widely held idea that the Celts were 'full of mournful, languishing, mysterious melancholy, of the dim 'Celtic Twilight' (Yeats's term), or else of an intolerable whimsicality and sentimentality'. In fact, Jackson observed both that it was MacPherson who was primarily to be blamed for exploiting 'Celtic sources to provide a public eager for Romantic material with what they wanted', and that the 'Celtic Revival' movement had played a considerable role in fostering 'this preposterous' idea.[24] He attributed such 'gross misrepresentation' to these writers' ignorance about Celtic literatures, stating concerning Yeats and others that 'most of them could not read the languages at all'.[25] Jackson's complaint, in turn, reminds us of Tolkien's indignant declaration in a letter addressed to Stanley Unwin that he himself did know 'Celtic things (many in their original languages, Irish and Welsh)'.[26] Jackson's irritation regarding the gap between popular perceptions and those of Celticists (i.e. specialists in the field) can be seen from his remark that 'scholars have long known, and all educated people really acquainted with the Celtic literatures now know, that this is a gross misrepresentation'.[27] Similarly, we can detect that Tolkien shared the same

---

21. Op. cit. [17], p. 173.
22. Further discussion of this can be found in my paper 'A Looming Luminary: Kenneth Jackson's invisible presence in Tolkien's "English and Welsh" lecture', which was presented in Kalamazoo at the 48th International Congress on Medieval Studies (9 May 2013).
23. Op. cit. [17], p. 172.
24. Op. cit. [19], p. 12.
25. Op. cit.
26. Humphrey Carpenter, ed., *The Letters of J.R.R. Tolkien*, with the assistance of Christopher Tolkien, George Allen & Unwin, London, 1981, Letter 19, p. 26. Tolkien complained about a reader who criticized his *Quenta Silmarillion* for being too 'Celtic'. On Tolkien's use of 'Celtic things' in his works, see Verlyn Flieger, *Interpreted Music: The Making of Tolkien's Mythology* Kent University Press, Kent OH and London, 2005, pp. 121–36; Marjorie Burns, *Perilous Realms: Celtic and Norse in Tolkien's Middle-earth*, University of Toronto Press, Toronto, 2005. See also Dimitra Fimi, '"Mad" Elves and "elusive beauty": some Celtic strands of Tolkien's mythology', *Folklore* 117 (2006), 156–70; Dimitra Fimi, 'Tolkien's "Celtic Type of Legends": Merging Traditions' *Tolkien Studies* 4 (2007), 51–71; Dimitra Fimi, *Tolkien, Race and Cultural History: From Fairies to Hobbits*, Palgrave Macmillan, Basingstoke, 2009. See also Yoko Hemmi, 'Tolkien's *The Lord of the Rings* and His Concept of *Native Language*: Sindarin and British-Welsh', *Tolkien Studies* 7 (2010), 147–74.
27. Op. cit. [19], p. 12.

sentiment when he states that:

> To many, perhaps to most people outside the small company of the great scholars, past and present, 'Celtic' of any sort is, nonetheless, a magic bag, into which anything may be put, and out of which almost anything may come.... Anything is possible in the fabulous Celtic twilight, which is not so much a twilight of the gods as of the reason.[28]

In a famous letter addressed to Milton Waldman, Tolkien referred to another quality deemed 'Celtic' in the popular imagination, that is, 'the fair elusive beauty that some call Celtic', though, he reminds us, '... it is rarely found in genuine Celtic things'.[29] This particular quality may correspond to what Arnold coined 'Natural Magic', or elsewhere 'Celtic Magic', which he defined as 'a gift of rendering with wonderful felicity the magical charm of nature'.[30] Arnold's examples of this Natural/Celtic Magic are mostly drawn from what he called 'Celtic romance', that is, *The Mabinogion*, which he quotes using Charlotte Guest's translation: for example, to list but two examples, the description of Olwen in *Culhwch and Olwen*, and of how Math and Gwydion made a wife for Lleu out of the blossoms of the oak, the broom, and the meadow-sweet in 'Math son of Mathonwy'.[31] More significantly, Arnold discerns 'the very same note' as these in a passage from Keats's *Ode to a Nightingale*:

> ... magic casements, opening on the foam
> Of perilous seas, in faery lands forlorn.[32]

Arnold also discerns 'the sheer, inimitable Celtic note' in *A Midsummer Night's Dream*[33] which was also one of Keats's favourite plays by Shakespeare.[34] What

28. Op. cit. [17], pp. 185–86. Tolkien was, however, referring to some extreme linguistic etymologies here and his words were not meant to be all embracing.
29. Op. cit. [26], Letter 131, p. 144.
30. Matthew Arnold, 'On the Study of Celtic Literature', in R. H. Super, ed., *The Complete Prose Works of Matthew Arnold, III, Lectures and Essays in Criticism*, University of Michigan Press, Ann Arbor, 1962, 291–395, p. 120.
31. Op. cit., p. 121. Arnold's quotation of 'Math the Son of Mathonwy' is from *The Mabinogion from the Llyfr Coch o Hergest and other ancient Welsh manuscripts, with an English Translation and Notes by Charlotte Guest*, vol. 3, Longmans, London, 1849, p. 239; 'Kulhwch and Olwen or Twrch Trwyth', vol. 2, pp. 275–76.
32. Lines 70–71, quoted in op. cit. [30], p. 126. Arnold employed the spelling 'fairy' instead of 'faery'.
33. Op. cit. [30], p.127.
34. Christine Gallant, *Keats and Romantic Celticism*, Palgrave Macmillan, Houndmills, 2005,

Tolkien meant by 'the fair elusive beauty that some call Celtic', with which he imbued the forest of Brocéliande, its magic fountain and stony caves in 'The Lay of Aotrou and Itroun', seems to be comparable to Keats's Romantic Celticism, which is evident in the passage quoted above.

Thus, it is intriguing to observe, when we take into account Tolkien's critical attitude, how he drew on images and an atmosphere promoted by Celticism, in spite of his awareness that such features were not quintessentially Celtic. Indeed, Tolkien's strategy of consciously utilising 'the fair elusive beauty that some call Celtic' can perhaps be viewed as constituting post-Celticism, which, as will be examined below, can be discerned through a comparison between Tolkien's lay and his source, la Villemarqué's 'Aotrou Nann hag ar Gorrigan', which is classified as 'Breton D' by F. J. Child.[35] 'Breton D', it should be noted however, comprises eighty-five lines, whereas Tolkien's lay is five hundred and six lines long.

Tolkien's lay begins with a refrain that is repeated seven times, and each time with a slight variation in accordance with the mood of the scene. 'Breton D', on the other hand, contains no such refrains. Tolkien's use of refrains therefore may serve as a good example of his post-Celticism functioning as a means of emphasising his own theme. The first refrain sings about 'the wind that blows ever through the trees' in Brittany, and of its 'stony shores and stony caves'. The seventh and last refrain employs almost identical phrases to the first one, closing the circle of the story. According to la Villemarqué, the cave of a Corrigan is called in the Breton language '*ti ar Gorrigan*' (house of Corrigan) or 'Dolmen' (stone-table).[36] On the outskirts of the forest of Brocéliande, there is a large dolmen called 'The Fairy's Rock', and the 'stony shores and stony caves' in Tolkien refer to megalithic stone monuments such as Carnac and Locmariaquer that are found along the Brittany coast. These stones are typically exalted by Renan who declares that 'the stone, in truth, seems the natural symbol of the Celtic races. It is an immutable witness that has no death'.[37] Tolkien was no doubt aware that such an 'ancient' landscape, which is composed of forest, a fairy's fountain, and megalithic stones, was associated with Celtic mysticism in the popular imagination, although he himself knew that such an association

---

p. 109.

35. F. J. Child, *The English and Scottish Popular Ballads*, vol. 1, Folklore Press, New York, 1957. Child lists seven Breton versions of an English ballad titled 'Clerk Colvill' (no. 42, pp. 371–89). These Breton versions are listed with comments on pp. 378–79.

36. Th. Hersart de la Villemarqué, *Barzaz-Breiz: chants populaires de la Bretagne*, 3rd edn, Didier et cie, Paris, 1867, pp. 28–29.

37. Renan, 'La Poésie des Races Celtiques', op. cit. [16], p. 270; Renan, trans. Hutchison, op. cit. [16], p. 23.

was fanciful. Tolkien's tactical employment of post-Celticism, discerned in the refrains, proves very effective therefore in presenting a perspective that far transcends a single mortal's life span.

'Breton D' tells the news of the birth of twins, a boy and a girl, in its opening lines, 5 to 7. Tolkien's lay, in contrast, spends about one third of the whole lay, nearly 180 lines, recounting how a childless lord, out of fear of 'lonely age and death', sought the evil help of a 'witch' in the forest and obtained a fertility potion, by which efficacy his wife gave birth to twins the next spring. It is obvious that this first part of the lay, the content of which is original to Tolkien, being found neither in 'Breton D' nor in any other versions, is crucial to our understanding of the theme which Tolkien incorporated into his lay. This opening section of Tolkien's lay draws our attention to the fact that the lord's attempt to escape a lonely death ended in vain, and that it was his desire both to possess an heir and to retain within his bloodline the material possessions he had accrued (i.e. the hoard) that drove him to enlist the services of the 'witch':

> his pride was empty, vain his hoard.
> without an heir to land and sword.
>
> ....
>
> his darkened mind would visions make
> of lonely age and death;
>
> ....
>
> Thus counsel cold he took at last
> his hope from light to darkness passed. (The Lay of Aotrou and Itroun', ll. 17-18, 20-21, 25-26)[38]

The words 'pride' and 'hoard' bear ominous implications reminding readers of the fact that in Tolkien's works, pride and possessiveness can only lead to catastrophe.

As if to reflect the lord's own view of the witch before his actual encounter with her, Tolkien depicts her alongside images stereotypically connected with witches in folktales, such as spiders, bats, owls, cats, a magic cauldron and a magic potion. However, a refrain which follows this stanza leaves enough implications for us to perceive that the lord made a bargain not with a mere mortal 'witch', but with an immortal being, one ancient and much more powerful.

The stanza depicting the first meeting of the 'Briton lord' and the witch is filled with adjectives associated with Death ('cold', 'stony', 'hoar', etc.), to

---

38. J.R.R. Tolkien, 'The Lay of Aotrou and Itroun', *The Welsh Review* 4 (1945), 254–66.

which the 'crone' is intimately connected. Though Tolkien does not name her yet, her true identity as a fay, Corrigan, is betrayed by the very beauty of a phial of glass given him by the witch, which evokes wonder with its 'cold and gleaming grace' (l. 72) :

> And therewithin a philter lay
> as pale as water thin and grey
> that spills from stony fountains frore
> in hollow pools in caverns hoar. ('The Lay of Aotrou and Itroun', ll. 73-76)

In the conversation between the lord and the lady after the birth of the twins, which constitutes the third to the fifth stanzas of 'Breton D', Lord Nann, eager to reward his wife who has borne him twin babies after just a year of their marriage, asks, 'Now, say what is thy heart's desire, / for making me a man-child's sire?',[39] to which the lady answers that her 'heart's desire' is 'dainty food', 'the meat of the deer' (l. 13). Tolkien too uses the same phrase, 'heart's desire', but differently, to denote the couple's desire to produce an heir. However, even after their 'heart's desire' was fulfilled, they were both consumed by 'a longing strong and sharp' (l. 234):

> ... for water cool and clear,
> and venison of the greenwood deer,
> for waters crystal-clear and cold
> and deer no earthly forests hold. (The Lay of Aotrou and Itroun', ll. 235-39)

Tolkien here subtly combines the desire for venison with that for water, the latter not being present in 'Breton D', and then insinuates that their 'longing strong and sharp' in fact has been instilled in them by the Corrigan. This Tolkien does by slightly changing the wording to enhance the Otherworldly association; that is, from 'water cool and clear' to 'waters crystal-clear and cold' as well as from 'venison of the greenwood deer' to 'deer no earthly forests hold'.

The hunting of a white doe, a motif found only in 'Breton D' among all the versions and analogues of the 'Clerk Colvill' ballad, is also known to have appeared in *Guigemar*,[40] a Breton *lai* by Marie de France, as well as in a later

39. Tom Taylor, *Ballads and Songs of Brittany*, George Routledge and Sons, London, 1865, lines 7–8. Thomas Keightley, *The Fairy Mythology*, new edn, George Bell and Sons, London, 1892, uses 'heart desire' ('What doth thy heart desire, loved one, / For giving me so fair a son?').

40. Guigemar, in Philippe Walter, *Marie de France, Lais, préface, traduction nouvelle et notes:*

anonymous Breton *lai of Graelent*,[41] and hence may be considered a typically Breton or 'Celtic' element.[42] The lord sets off in pursuit of the white doe, vigorously in 'Breton D' and recklessly in Tolkien, ignoring the 'dim laughter in the wood he heard' (l. 264). The 'dim laughter' confirms that the white doe is a psychopomp, leading the lord to the domain of the supernatural. Owing to the connection Tolkien has created adeptly between the hunger/thirst for 'waters crystal-clear and cold' and for 'deer no earthly forests hold', as observed above, it seems a natural consequence that his hunting of a white doe led the lord to 'the fountain of the fay, / before a cave, on silver sand, / under dark boughs in Broceliande' (ll. 284-86). Here, Tolkien may be regarded as reconstructing and restoring what he called, referring to 'Celtic things,' a 'broken stained glass window reassembled without design'.[43] Given this, it is interesting to note that Tolkien, who famously claimed that he felt a certain distaste for 'Celtic things', 'largely for their fundamental unreason',[44] elected in his own Breton lay to reassemble those broken-up pieces found in a Breton ballad with the design of illustrating his own theme, thereby removing the element of fundamental unreason.

After chasing a white doe all day, in 'Breton D' Lord Nann comes to a stream near the Corrigan's grotto[45] and tries to drink water to quench his thirst, whereas in Tolkien's lay, the lord, whose thirst is not of a physical nature, bathes his face in the fountain of the fay. Interestingly, a folk-tale type 'witch' as described earlier in the lay is here transformed into a fay, whose immortality is revealed by her voice that is 'cold / as echo from the world of old, ere fire was found or iron hewn, / when young was mountain under moon' (ll. 297-300). In both 'Breton D' and Tolkien, the lord is accused of disturbing her water, is demanded that he marry her, and is cursed to death upon his refusal. While there is no hint in 'Breton D' of any former sexual relationship between the Corrigan and Lord Nann, thus making her demand and curse look abrupt as well as unreasonable, the English 'Clerk Colvill' ballad, which is an analogue of 'Breton D', seems to imply the underlying motif of a mortal man punished by his fairy lover for

---

édition bilingue, Gallimard, Paris, 2000, p. 42, lines 90–94.

41. Graelent, in Russell Weingartner, ed. and trans., *Graelant and Guingamor: Two Breton Lays*, Garland, New York, 1995, p. 12, lines 211–19.

42. See John D. Rateliff, *The History of The Hobbit*, HarperCollins, London, rev. and expanded one-vol. edn, 2011, pp. 400–402 for Tolkien's use of a white doe in this lay, as well as in *The Hobbit*, along with medieval instances which Tolkien was undoubtedly familiar with.

43. Op. cit. [26], Letter 19, p. 26.

44. Op. cit.

45. 'ti eur Gorrigan': la Villemarqué (op. cit. [36]), translated it as 'la grotte d'un Korrigan'; Keightley (op. cit. [39]) as 'a Korrigan's abode'; Taylor (op. cit. [39]) as 'the grot of a Corrigaun'.

betrayal.[46] In Tolkien's lay, the Corrigan demands that 'With love thou shalt me here requite, / for here is long and sweet the night; | in druery dear thou here shalt deal, / in bliss more deep than mortals feel.' (ll. 317-20). However, the Corrigan's promise of 'druery dear' is not what drove the lord to seek her out; rather, it was his desire to escape a lonely death and keep worldly wealth in the hands of his heirs, which culminated in his obsession with propagating an heir.

The Corrigan in 'Breton D' is described as sitting by the 'fountain fair, / A-combing her long and yellow hair' (ll. 32-33) with a 'comb of gold' because, as is explained in a prosaic manner, 'those maidens' are 'not poor' (ll. 34-35). Tolkien's Corrigan also uses a comb of gold but he imbues it with an image of Death and reinterprets the typical gesture of a water-fay so as to illuminate his own theme:

> The moonlight falling clear and cold
> her long hair lit; through comb of gold
> She drew each lock, and down it fell
> like the fountain falling in the dell. (ll. 293-96)

The image of Death conveyed by the Corrigan's gesture anticipates the lord's imminent death, and later in the lay, when she reappears in the dream of the dying lord, she is described as if to reflect his disillusionment:

> the Corrigan now shrunk and old
> was sitting singing; in her claw
> a comb of bony teeth he saw,
> with which she raked her tresses grey,
> but in her other hand there lay
> a phial of glass with water filled
> that from the bitter fountain spilled. (ll. 370-76)

The lady follows him soon afterwards to 'their long home beneath the clay' (l. 488) and they are thus deprived of the joy of seeing their children grow: 'they saw it not, nor found it sweet / their heart's desire at last to meet' (ll. 491-92). The line, 'His pride was ended, vain his hoard' (l. 472), a variation of the earlier line, 'his pride was empty, vain his hoard' (l. 17), pronounces the lord's fall and constitutes a conclusion to his *adventure* in the forest of Broceliande with a fountain presided over by a fairy.

Although 'The Lay of Aotrou and Itroun' is neither a part of Tolkien's

---

46. Op. cit. [35], p. 372.

legendarium nor of any of his stories set in Middle-earth, it can be noted that the same theme of 'fall caused by possessiveness' is found in many of Tolkien's works. For example, Fëanor's fall was caused by his possessive attitude towards the Silmarils, and in a similar way, as is noted by Rateliff, Thorin Oakenshield's demise was due to his coveting the Arkenstone;[47] so too, Ar-Pharazôn became possessive regarding earthly glory and power, hence his desire for immortality that resulted in the downfall of Númenor. Finally, the effect of the One Ring on mortals is also always described with reference to their ominously possessive attitude towards it: Isildur, Gollum, Boromir, the Ring-bearers Bilbo and Frodo, and even Sam, however fleetingly, suffered from the torment caused by their possessiveness towards the Ring.

By way of a conclusion, Tolkien's 'Lay of Aotrou and Itroun', as noted earlier, may be regarded as heir to Chrétien's *Yvain* in the sense that both belong to a tradition of romantic fantasising concerning the forest of Brocéliande. Chrétien explored the theme of *adventure* and offered his French audiences the enchanting literary world of a magical forest where the Arthurian knights encountered marvels and successfully conquered the marvellous and the unknown.[48] In that sense, Chrétien's *Yvain* may be regarded as tinted with colonial implications.[49] Tolkien's lay, in contrast, depicts the fall of a mortal who, out of his possessiveness towards life and worldly wealth, tried in vain to exploit the marvellous and the unknown, represented by the Corrigan and her fountain. If Tolkien contributed to the romantic fantasy-making of the forest of Brocéliande, by deliberately utilising the images popularised by Celticism, itself an offshoot of colonialism, he showed no desire to depict the marvellous and the unknown being conquered by a mortal lord. Rather, Tolkien's lay can be viewed as an attempt to create a world in which the fairies and the enchanted forest are far more powerful and dominant than mortal Men. In this way, Tolkien's post-Celticism seems to be a literary device which he employed to transform the Breton original into a story that shares the theme of 'fall caused by possessiveness' which dominates his *legendarium* and other stories of Middle-earth.

47. See op. cit. [42], 'The Arkenstone as Silmaril', pp. 603–609.

48. Cf. Patrick Sims-Williams, 'The Visionary Celt: The Construction of an Ethnic Preconception', *Cambridge Medieval Celtic Studies* 11 (1986), 71–96, p. 93.

49. Op. cit. [9], p. 187.

'Tolkien's Devices: The Heraldry of Middle-earth'

Jamie McGregor

This paper claims that what one might call the national flags of Middle-earth –the heraldic devices or emblems representing the various lands, powers or armies in the field in The Lord of the Rings – have a significance, both singly and in relation to one another, that resonates with, underscores and clarifies some of the novel's central themes. Through a brief survey of the more notable examples, the paper seeks to demonstrate how their respective symbols and colours, far from being merely decorative, serve to amplify the text itself. Where the White Tree of Gondor and the White Horse of Rohan (as well as the Silver Swan of Dol Amroth) are wholesome natural images reflective of the positive qualities of the cultures represented, the Red Eye of Mordor and the White Hand of Isengard are curiously disembodied, thereby revealing the essentially maimed and self-defeating nature of evil. In addition, the roles played by such relatively minor examples as the Black Serpent of Harad, the disfigured moon of Minas Morgul and the plain white banner of the stewards, are also considered in relation to the overall pattern.

Chief among the banners of the Men opposing the Enemy is without doubt the 'great standard' of Aragorn that plays so prominent a role at the battle of the Pelennor fields, and that combines the White Tree of Gondor with the Seven Stars and the high crown that are 'the signs of Elendil that no lord had borne for years beyond count' (*RotK*, 'The Battle of the Pelennor Fields', 1109),[1] though it is also worn, as if in memory and reverence of the kings, by the Guards of the Citadel Pippin sees when he first comes to Minas Tirith. The evident majesty of these royal emblems derives in no small part from their ultimately mythic associations. The tree in particular is intimately bound up with the fortunes of the royal house, suggesting an implicit parallel between them, based on an underlying motif of unbroken growth and continuity across vast spans of time. Just as the house of Elendil claims descent via the Númenórean kings from the blended bloodlines of Men and Elves, and even from the semi-divine race of the Maiar, so the tree is a scion of Telperion, one of the two Trees of Paradise. Both human and arboreal strains are thus linked to the beginning of the world and an

1. J.R.R. Tolkien, *The Lord of the Rings*, HarperCollins, London, 1991, 50th anniversary edn, 2004. All quotations from *LotR* are taken from this edition.

authority sanctioned by divinity itself.

All this moreover evokes the Norse Yggdrasil: the world-tree that grows through, unifies and symbolises the entire cosmos. With its roots in the nether hells and its branches soaring to the highest heavens, bringing forth worlds like fruits, Yggdrasil takes the natural attributes of any tree to their logical limits; beginning with the buried seed and growing to limitless bounds, its slow growth unites time as well as space, embodying the oneness of all creation. That the emblem of Gondor shares similar qualities makes it no mere arbitrary badge but an apt and impressive expression of the grandeur, antiquity, divine authority and organic wholeness of the true kingship as Tolkien conceives it.

The heraldic colours employed are also strikingly apt. That the tree is white marks its descent from Telperion, and lends it ethereal associations that are further strengthened by the jewel-like stars and shining crown, while the choice of a sable field offsets the argent emblems to maximum advantage by deepening the contrast, and suggests the effect of celestial light against the backdrop of a deep night sky – all of which reflects Tolkien's consistent alignment of stars and starlight with 'Elvishness'. It is also evidence that the Enemy does not enjoy a monopoly on the use of black – recalling both Tom Bombadil's memories of 'the dark under the stars when it was fearless – before the Dark Lord came from Outside' (*FotR*, 'In the House of Tom Bombadil', 172) and the 'glinting stars' Frodo sees in Mirrormere 'like jewels sunk in the deep' (*FotR*, 'Lothlórien', 435). The implications are of a primordial darkness immanent with mystery, profoundly awe-inspiring, and untainted by the shadow of evil.

While less exalted, both the White Horse of Rohan and 'the silver swan of Dol Amroth' have similar attributes (*RotK*, 'Minas Tirith', 1103). The latter in particular shares with the tree distinctively Elvish associations; in contrast to the deep black background of its royal cousin, however, this emblem is set against a clean aquatic blue appropriate to Dol Amroth's estuarine setting. By contrast, the associations of the White Horse are essentially English. As 'Men of the Twilight', the barbaric Rohirrim lack any Elvish influence and their cultural emblems are correspondingly 'Mannish'; their relative youth as a people, love of freedom and the rolling plains of their country are all embodied in the stirring image of the horse running over sunlit grass – an image literally embodied in Shadowfax, of whom Gandalf says that he 'might have been foaled in the morning of the world' (*FotR*, 'The Council of Elrond', 342.). Taken together, all three emblems – horse, swan and tree – have a clear kindred resemblance, though each enjoys its distinct identity, and they are also increasingly presented in alliance with one another, initially on the battlefield, ultimately – and with heightened effect – on the field of Cormallen, when Sam and Frodo are ushered into their presence, allowing them to be seen by fresh eyes on an exalted occasion:

> Behind the seat upon the right floated, white on green, a great horse running free; upon the left was a banner, silver upon blue, a ship swan-prowed faring on the sea; but behind the highest throne in the midst of all a great standard was spread in the breeze, and there a white tree flowered upon a sable field beneath a shining crown and seven glittering stars. (*RotK*, 'The Field of Cormallen', 1248–49)

In total opposition and contradistinction to these there stands the sinister sign of the Great Eye, one of the most important symbols of the text. Apart from anything else, this is evident simply from the frequency with which it is used as a synecdoche for Sauron, just one of numerous examples being Gandalf's warning: '[t]he Eye of Barad-dûr will be looking impatiently towards the Wizard's Vale, I think; and towards Rohan. The less it sees the better' (*TT*, 'The Palantir', 769).

Firstly, the black background, as noted, is a given for the servants of the enemy and connotes not the sublime primal night of Gondor's banner but the terrifying blackness of the void. Against this the redness of the Eye suggests its fiery wrath, the same infernal quality one associates with the 'dark fire' of the 'flame of Udûn' as contrasted with the 'Secret Fire' of Gandalf's celestial 'flame of Anor' in their confrontation on the Bridge of Khazad-dûm (*FotR*, 'The Bridge of Khazad-dûm', 430). The underlying sense-image is of a dull brooding glow of burning amid the murky smoke or shadows of the underworld. And in this context, essentially established by the colour combination, the particular function of the Eye is to suggest something hostile hidden in the darkness but nonetheless watching the observer, a secret lurking threat recalling Blake's Tyger.

This is all especially apt to the nature and behaviour of Sauron throughout the *LotR*. It is indeed clear to the reader that the Eye is not even merely a metaphor for the Dark Lord but a real presence in itself. The most memorable and vivid instance of this presence manifesting is in the vision Frodo sees in Galadriel's Mirror:

> But suddenly the Mirror went altogether dark, as dark as if a hole had opened in the world of sight, and Frodo looked into emptiness. In the black abyss there appeared a single Eye that slowly grew, until it filled nearly all the Mirror. So terrible was it that Frodo stood rooted, unable to cry out or to withdraw his gaze. The Eye was rimmed with fire, but was itself glazed, yellow as a cat's, watchful and intent, and the black slit of its pupil opened on a pit, a window into nothing. (*FotR*, 'The Mirror of Galadriel', 474)

This is, of course, a passage of great power and significance in the novel, and it is also the clearest visualisation of the Eye that either Frodo or the reader is vouchsafed. But although it represents a 'real' version of the figure reproduced on the shields and banners of Mordor's armies, there is no indication either here or elsewhere in the text that Sauron is *literally* incarnate in this form. This is all the more necessary to stress after the widespread influence of the film adaptation, in which it became necessary to visualise the Eye as a vast searchlight operating from the summit of Barad-dûr. By contrast, the text almost always presents the Eye from Frodo's point of view – and on most of these occasions he feels its gaze rather than actually seeing it himself.

The first of many compelling instances occurs during the scene upon Amon Hen, when Frodo, sitting on the Seat of Seeing, and wearing the Ring, is able to look all the way into Mordor:

> And suddenly he felt the Eye. There was an eye in the Dark Tower that did not sleep. He knew that it had become aware of his gaze. A fierce eager will was there. It leaped towards him; almost like a finger he felt it, searching for him. Very soon it would nail him down, know just exactly where he was. (*FotR*, 'The Breaking of the Fellowship', 523)

And the nearer Frodo gets to Mordor, the more intense this awareness becomes. One of the most vivid examples of the full power and terror of the experience occurs when he has come within just a few days' journey of the Black Gate:

> But far more he was troubled by the ... horrible growing sense of a hostile will that strove with great power to pierce all shadows of cloud, and earth, and flesh, and to see you: to pin you under its deadly gaze, naked, immovable. So thin, so frail and thin, the veils were become that still warded it off. Frodo knew just where the present habitation and heart of that will now was: as certainly as a man can tell the direction of the sun with his eyes shut. He was facing it, and its potency beat upon his brow. (*TT*, 'The Passage of the Marshes', 824)

In this instance, the nature of the Eye becomes more ambivalent: on the one hand, it is the 'sense of a hostile will', an evidently *mental* experience; on the other, it has *physical* effects – Frodo feels it as a distinct and specifically localised emanation. But the only occasion on which it *seems* to become physically visible, is as the hobbits are climbing the final road to the Sammath Naur and swirling clouds part for a moment to reveal the summit of the Tower, at which point: 'as from some great window immeasurably high there stabbed northward a flame of red, the flicker of a piercing Eye' (*RotK*, 'Mount Doom', 1233). But it is no more than a flicker, and it may not even be there, its possible physical position being qualified by the likelihood of its being a 'terrible vision' accessible to the Ring-bearer alone.

The text's detailed engagement with tropes of sight, seeing and the unseen is a subject far surpassing the scope of this essay. Suffice to note that the Eye of Mordor, even more so than the other heraldic devices in the novel, corresponds to a definite reality within its fictional world – and prompts an immediate emotional response, in this case one of unalloyed terror. I have already noted the role the colour symbolism plays in creating this effect, as well as the overt suggestion of an intent unnerving gaze. But there is a further feature of this image that contributes significantly to the impression it makes, particularly in relation to those of the banners described above. Where the Tree, Swan and Horse, as noted, are all complete, wholesome and healthy living beings, the Eye is curiously disembodied, detached from any natural context and consequently conveys an impression of atrocity or violation. This is entirely consistent with Tolkien's conception of evil in general as a disease, a corruption, a malformation, something that strikes one at an almost intuitive level as just plain wrong. It is also in keeping with a widespread pattern in Tolkien's work as a whole that his principal evil characters are somehow maimed, that as they tend to grasp after worldly power they simultaneously sacrifice their native virtue, becoming increasingly winnowed of personality, of individuality, in effect of their souls. Sauron represents this nonentity in its furthest degree in that he never appears in person, is probably a disembodied spirit, though confined to haunt his tower, controls vast forces from afar, remains at all times remote, mysterious and invisible, and is in many ways an absence, as is indicated by one of his titles being 'the Shadow'.

This impression of maiming, then, of dismemberment, is implicit in the image of the single fiery eye gazing from the darkness of the void, suggesting a lurking paranoia diametrically opposed to the free-spirited, robust organic emblems of Gondor and of Rohan. It is all the more notable then that the other principal emblem of an enemy power is likewise disembodied – the White Hand of Isengard. This, it may be remembered, is first noted by Aragorn with some surprise, as the renegade wizard Saruman's emergence as an aspiring power is a relatively recent and unforeseen event, and his heraldic badges have not been noted before. But that the Hand, like the Eye, appears in isolation betrays a similar unnaturalness, as well as that Saruman has – probably unconsciously – modelled his political and military organisation on that of Mordor. Indeed this point is made explicitly and with telling emphasis on one occasion, when the narrator comments of the wizard's stronghold that

> A strong place and wonderful was Isengard, and long it had been beautiful; and there great lords had dwelt, the wardens of Gondor upon the West, and wise men that watched the stars. But Saruman had slowly shaped it to his shifting purposes, and made it better, as he thought, being deceived – for all those arts and subtle devices, for which he forsook his former wisdom, and which he fondly imagined were his own, came but from Mordor; so that what he made was naught, only a little copy, a child's model or a slave's flattery, of that vast fortress, armoury, prison, furnace of great power, Barad-dûr, the Dark Tower, which suffered no rival, and laughed at flattery, biding its time, secure in its pride and its immeasurable strength. (*TT*, 'The Road to Isengard', 724)

The satirical point thus made is that all earthly dictators, however they may delude themselves to be original and benevolent reformers are in truth no more than echoes of an impulse both ancient and diabolical. But this also reinforces the likelihood that the White Hand thinly disguises a kindred resemblance to the Red Eye. The parallel is further underlined by the way both badges have been used to fashion grandiose signposts leading to their respective domains. At the crossroads leading to the Morgul vale, Frodo and Sam encounter a once majestic Númenórean monument now defaced by the enemy:

> a huge sitting figure, still and solemn as the great stone kings of Argonath. The years had gnawed it, and violent hands had maimed it. Its head was gone, and in its place was set in mockery a round rough-hewn stone, rudely painted by savage hands in the likeness of a grinning face with one large red eye in the midst of its forehead. (*RotK*, 'The Journey to the Cross-roads', 919)

Corresponding to this is the 'tall pillar [that] loomed up before' the company riding to Isengard: 'It was black; and set upon it was a great stone, carved and painted in the likeness of a long White Hand. Its finger pointed north' (*TT*, 'The Road to Isengard', 722).

But the differences between the two are likewise significant. Where the Eye is straightforwardly sinister, the Hand is ambiguous and only faintly unsettling, implying either a threat or an offer, combining the qualities of potency, craft and wisdom as well as a potential for benevolence or even generosity. And this is entirely in keeping with the differing natures of the Dark Lord and his treacherous ally. Where the former is openly evil, a Satanic figure motivated solely by undisguised malice and the lust for domination, the recently corrupted Saruman still attempts to delude both others and himself that he is motivated by a greater good. In a speech that evidently expresses Tolkien's opinion of Neville Chamberlain's policy of appeasement, he has Saruman justify his alliance with the Enemy by saying,

> We can bide our time … deploring maybe evils done by the way, but approving the high and ultimate purpose: Knowledge, Rule, Order; all the things that we have so far striven in vain to accomplish, hindered rather than helped by our weak or idle friends. There need not be, there would not be, any real change in our designs, only in our means.

To which Gandalf, voicing Tolkien's allegiance to an uncompromisingly stern morality, replies 'I have heard speeches of this kind before, but only in the mouths of emissaries sent from Mordor to deceive the ignorant' (*FotR*, 'The Council of Elrond', 338). The emblem of the Hand, then, can easily be seen to perform the same function as Saruman's rhetoric – to persuade others that his cause is just. In this the choice of white plays an important role.

I have already attempted to show how Tolkien both conforms to, and questions, the traditional association of black and darkness with danger, fear and evil. The same can also be said of his treatment of white. The symbols of the good powers we have considered, the use of white stone in the construction of Minas Tirith, and the fact that the principal organisation formed to oppose the Dark Lord is named the White Council provide abundant evidence of conformity to a corresponding association of white, light, purity, vision and moral goodness. But the White Hand subverts this easy identification and upsets the pattern. One of the reasons why Aragorn deduces the badge to be Saruman's is because Sauron 'does not use white' (*TT*, 'The Departure of Boromir', 541), suggesting again his deliberate rejection of goodness as such.

But in Saruman's case white is a natural choice and in fact references the history of his corruption and treachery. As chief of the order of wizards and elected head of the Council of the Wise, white is originally his distinctive colour, as grey is that of the Odinic wanderer Gandalf and brown of the Franciscan nature-lover Radagast. But in changing his allegiance, he changes his wardrobe too, becoming 'Saruman of Many Colours' so that 'his robes, which had seemed white, were not so, but were woven of all colours, and if he moved they shimmered and changed hue so that the eye was bewildered'. When Gandalf comments 'I liked white better', his sneering response is that 'It serves as a beginning. White cloth may be died. The white page may be overwritten; and the white light may be broken'. The last image in particular recalls Shelley's 'Dome of many-coloured glass', as does Gandalf's prompt rejoinder 'In which case it is no longer white … And he that breaks a thing to find out what it is has left the path of wisdom' (*FotR*, 'The Council of Elrond', 337). The sequel to this debate is Gandalf's sacrificial death and resurrection as a glorified figure in 'gleaming white' like 'snow in the sunshine', who announces that he is in a sense 'Saruman as he should have been' (*TT*, 'The White Rider', 645), and who now has the 'power and authority' to depose his former master with the ringing declaration 'I am not Gandalf the Grey, whom you betrayed. I am Gandalf the White, who has returned from death. You have no colour now, and I cast you from the order and from the Council' (*TT*, 'The Voice of Saruman', 761).

With this in mind, it becomes evident that the White Hand conceals Saruman's betrayal and desertion of his true colours, so to speak, just as his benevolent appearance disguises his inner corruption. Furthermore, one should not ignore the choice of background; like those of Mordor and Gondor, the emblem of Isengard appears against a black background. In fact, the combination of white on black is identical in the last two cases – and yet where the royal standard of Gondor evokes a profound night sky, that of Isengard is curiously abstract, as if aiming at nothing more than a pretentiously stylish contrast. Since the only real difference is the emblem itself, this must be the deciding factor. And here the dismembered quality it shares with the Evil Eye is clearly significant, but to this is added a further incongruity. Where the whiteness of the Horse or the Swan, or even that of the Tree, is entirely naturalistic, that of the Hand suggests an unwholesome ghostly pallor. So here again, the maimed and tainted nature of evil is referenced, only this time with an added effect of self-deceiving masquerade.

'Tolkien and the Gothic'

Nick Groom

Critics such as Sue Zlosnik have written on Tolkien's use of the Gothic in contemporary and theoretical terms; my own approach, however, is driven by an historical understanding of the term. I argue the Gothic is a characteristically English style of literature, architecture, art, and folklore that derives from representations of the Sack of Rome and the Reformation. The Gothic imagination is therefore a reminder of progress and simultaneously a lament for the past. I understand the Gothic as a way of coming to terms with the processes of English history. This paper begins with a concise account of the Gothic before analysing examples drawn from Tolkien's scholarship, criticism, and Middle-Earth writings. In doing so, I will argue that placing Tolkien's work within an English Gothic tradition reveals his ongoing examination of the nature of identity in relation to the past and the suppressed horrors of historical change.

This paper sets the work of J.R.R. Tolkien in the context of the English Gothic: an approach driven by an historical understanding of the term. Accordingly, I will not be introducing Sigmund Freud in order to discuss the 'Uncanny' or 'transgression' or other forms of 'psychological trauma'; instead, as I argue in *The Gothic: A Very Short Introduction* (2012), my understanding of the Gothic is that it is a characteristically English style of literature, architecture, art, and folklore that draws on cultural memories of the Sack of Rome and the Reformation (and Counter-Reformation) – events that despite being over a thousand years apart were both perceived as rebellions against tyranny, and which were both extremely bloodthirsty. From these founding events a distinctive imaginative response to the past developed in which antiquity was seen as haunted and ruinous – remote from modern society, and yet responsible for it and indeed potentially present everywhere. The Gothic imagination is consequently a reminder of historical progress and simultaneously a lament for the lost past: a guarded suppression of the carnage of history that has nevertheless led to the present day.

Such a conception of the Gothic seeks therefore to go beyond the familiar (and somewhat tired) motifs of the macabre and the mysterious, beyond the monstrous and the magical. Rather, I argue that the Gothic was – and still is – a way of coming to terms with the processes of English history, which is why in the seventeenth, eighteenth, and nineteenth centuries it had a strong political, social, and theological significance. It is from this perspective that I will approach Tolkien's work, beginning with a concise account of the history of the Gothic before analysing examples drawn from Tolkien's scholarship, criticism, and Middle-earth writings. In doing so, I will argue that placing Tolkien's work within the English Gothic tradition casts new light on his preoccupations with national identity, its relation to the past, and the suppressed horrors of historical change.

Most people today would associate the Gothic with eighteenth or nineteenth-century terror fiction, and the Goths with a thriving subculture and musical style that has been around since about the 1980s. If pressed further, some would suggest that the Gothic is also a form of mediaeval architecture, and that the Goths, Visigoths, and Ostrogoths were ancient barbarian races who had overrun the Roman Empire and who may be associated with Attila the Hun and possibly the discoveries at Sutton Hoo. All of these answers are broadly correct, but I will concentrate on the middle of this history – the eighteenth and nineteenth-century connotations of Gothic and the Goths.

The meaning of 'Gothic' was highly perplexed in the eighteenth century – it was a semantic minefield – but nevertheless three strong threads are discernible. First, the Goths were defined as a Teutonic tribe in the period of late antiquity – the declining years of the Roman Empire; secondly, Gothic referred to a political theory derived from the anti-classical values of these Goths; and thirdly, the term referred to the literature and especially the architecture of the Middle Ages and its revival in the cult of medievalism.

The Teutonic tribal Goths crossed the River Danube in AD 376, and within a generation had sacked Rome (AD 410). By the sixth century, the historian Jordanes, himself a Goth, had provided his people with a rich past that originated outside the Mediterranean, and which described their racial migrations to Scythia and their subsequent victory over the Romans. Following Jordanes, historians and chroniclers used 'Goth' as a general term covering the Germanic tribes, including the Angles and Saxons, and also perhaps the Jutes ('Jute' may be a corruption of 'Goth'), who had landed in England in AD 449 under the 'horse lords' Hengist and Horsa. In this version of ancient history, the Goths were therefore imagined to be part of genesis of English nation – and this is how the word 'Gothic' would later develop its political implications.

The Goths were barely mentioned throughout the Middle Ages, but by the Renaissance, Italian painters and architects began to denounce as 'Gothic' everything not built in the Roman style: from Neolithic standing stones to Norman churches to medieval cathedrals. Gothic was, in effect, an alternative to classical civilisation, and interest in it correspondingly grew. Some sixteenth-century antiquarians followed Jordanes, and indeed various Roman writers, in arguing that the Goths not only originated in the north, but were the purest northern race and exemplified hardy northern values. They displayed an instinctive love of liberty, and it was this that had enabled them to overcome the tyranny of the oppressive and decadent Roman Empire. Further examples of the Gothic championing of freedom were evident in English history, and thus the 'Gothic spirit' was identified with great moments in the progress of the nation where the people had demonstrated their Gothic (Anglo-Saxon-Jutish) roots by rebelling against imposed – especially foreign – authority. The presentation of the constitutional rights of Magna Carta to challenge the tyranny of the Norman Yoke after 1066 was construed as a central instance of the Gothic temperament exercised in England, as was the English Reformation. Indeed, the Reformation was pronounced to be a repeat of the original fifth-century Gothic rebellion against Roman tyranny, although obviously as a stand against Catholic as opposed to Imperial Rome.

By the seventeenth century, then, the Gothic had developed into a theory of politics and history: emphatically anti-classical and anti-Catholic. One consequence of this growing emphasis is that much political spin-doctoring in England in the sixteenth and seventeenth centuries was rooted in antiquarianism. Not only did this research seek to establish the routes of prehistoric tribal migrations, the origins of racial identity, and thereby the foundations – topographical, climatic, or otherwise – of national character, but also focused particularly on key historical events such as the coronation of William in 1066 to assess whether the Norman 'Conquest' was an invasion by a tyrant or simply the incorporation of a usurper into a pre-existent Saxon constitution. Theories of Gothic polity were consequently deployed extensively by Protestant Parliamentarians in arguing against the absolutist pretensions of the Catholic-leaning monarch, Charles I. The Gothic subsequently formed the ideological core of the eighteenth-century Whig party in validating the constitutional powers of Parliament over the sovereign, and in justifying the Act of Settlement to secure a Protestant succession.

Yet at the same time as this positive Gothic ideal of liberty and freedom was being expounded as a political credo, it was directly countered by a negative version of the same history. The whole idea of the 'Dark Ages' was proposed in the seventeenth century. This version of events deplored the fall of Rome to the Goths, seeing history as a displacement of classical genius by the barbarians, who had instigated a millennium of ruin from the fifth century to the fifteenth century. So, repeating the attitudes of the Renaissance – which was the great revival of Roman culture – neo-classicist taste, favoured by the Tory aristocracy, reviled the Goths as barbaric, crude, destructive, obscure, and dark. And this condemnation extended to the medieval period, which was despised for its ridiculous Gothic taste. Hence Royalist enthusiasm for classical architecture in the seventeenth and eighteenth centuries, seen most notably in the Duke of Buckingham's London town house (1705), which was acquired by George III in 1761 and was thereafter known as Buckingham Palace.

So a strong anti-Gothic narrative of degeneration was put forward at the same time as the pro-Gothic models of progress. But, as already indicated, there is a third strand to this thinking. The determined revival of classical culture throughout the eighteenth century as 'neo-classicism' or 'Augustanism' as a response to seventeenth-century political Gothicism coincided with a renewed interest in the Middle Ages: what we would today call 'medievalism'. This cultural tendency is seen in architecture, literature, and social manners. Medieval cathedrals and castles inspired interior decoration, furniture, and gardens as well as whole building projects. Gardening was central to the culture of the Gothic: little wild patches of an estate were permitted as a sort of domestic version of freedom from the tyranny of the gardener as a little bit of liberty and subversion, while also tying the Gothic aesthetic to natural wilderness. Architectural Gothic accompanied this trend in the building of follies or even ruins in the gardens of country houses, before Horace Walpole commenced work in 1748 on his 'little cottage': the vast, rambling cod-medieval mansion of Strawberry Hill at Twickenham. There was fresh interest in early English writers from Geoffrey Chaucer to Edmund Spenser, notably in Thomas Warton's critical study *Observations on the Faerie Queene of Spenser* (1754) and Thomas Percy's ballad collection *Reliques of Ancient English Poetry* (1765). Moreover, Richard Hurd outlined the significance of medieval romance and especially the virtues of chivalry for contemporary conduct and masculine behaviour in his *Letters on Chivalry and Romance* (1762).

The English Middle Ages could provide the template for a polite life in the eighteenth century – although not all agreed. Gothic literature was popularly described by John Newbery in *Art of Poetry on a New Plan* (1762) as 'absurd and unmeaning tales of giants, champions, enchanted knights, witches, goblins, and such other monstrous fictions and reveries, as could only proceed from the grossest ignorance, or a distempered brain'. Despite the disparaging tone, this is a clear agenda for Gothic writing as rooted in anti-Enlightenment medievalism. It also effectively summarises Tolkien's own interests: 'giants, champions, enchanted knights, witches, [and] goblins'; only dragons and elves (and hobbits) are absent. Two years after Newbery's dismissal, Horace Walpole of Strawberry Hill published what is popularly considered to be the first Gothic novel, *The Castle of Otranto*, and supernatural Gothic fiction joined the mainstream.

Otranto has all the features we have come to associate with Gothic novels and indeed later movies. It is set in an ancient castle riddled with secret passages, haunted by old prophecies, bizarre supernatural events, and the walking dead – much of which was taken from Elizabethan and Jacobean drama such as Shakespeare's *Hamlet*. If *Otranto* and the Gothic literary genre can be said to have influenced Tolkien, there seems to be plenty of evidence here: Middle-earth is littered with ancient and ruined architecture; there are many subterranean tunnels and passages under mountains, from Moria to the Paths of the Dead; the prophecy of 'Isildur's Bane' motivates the Council of Elrond; the dead walk in the shape of Barrow Wights, Ringwraiths, and Oathbreakers; and there is a strong influence from Elizabethan and Jacobean drama: notably the supernatural Revenge Tragedy *Hamlet*, characterised as it is by northern doom rather than classical tragedy and infused by dreams and self-doubt; and *Macbeth* which, among other scenes and images, provided the inspiration for the March of the Ents. Only in the manifestation of supernatural events do Tolkien's stories fall short of the outlandishly bizarre incidents that pepper *Otranto* – such as the sudden appearance of a gigantic helmet that crushes the hapless Conrad. Such extreme happenings were understandably toned down by Walpole's host of imitators.

If Walpole's profligacies can be excused, it was that he claimed that his new supernatural medievalism was stimulated by the dreams he experienced in Strawberry Hill. This imaginative source was innovative in itself, but Walpole had already explained how this emergent Gothicism differed from classical culture in *Anecdotes of Painting in England*, (1762):

> It is difficult for the noblest Grecian temple to convey half so many impressions to the mind, as a cathedral does of the best Gothic taste ... a proof of skill in the architect and of address in the priests who erected them. The latter exhausted their knowledge of the passions in composing edifices whose vaults, tombs, painted windows, gloom and perspectives infused such sensations of romantic devotion; and they were happy in finding artists capable of executing such machinery. One must have taste to be sensible of the beauties of Grecian architecture; one only wants passions to feel Gothic.

In this explanation, Walpole was developing on the concept of the sublime, as defined by Edmund Burke in *A Philosophical Enquiry into the Origin of our Ideas of the Sublime and Beautiful* in 1757. This theory best expresses the impulse behind these Gothic 'passions'. For Burke, the sublime experience was typified by the experience of terror and immense power heightened by obscurity – obscurity stirring the mind to imagine eternity and the infinite: 'An immense mountain covered with a shining green turf, is nothing in this respect, to one dark and gloomy; the cloudy sky is more grand than the blue; and night more solemn and sublime than the day.'[1] Drawing on examples from English literature, Burke famously quoted Milton's description of Death in Book II of *Paradise Lost*:

> The other shape,
> If shape it might be called that shape had none
> Distinguishable in member, joint, or limb,
> Or substance might be called that shadow seemed,
> For each seemed either; black it stood as Night,
> Fierce as ten Furies, terrible as Hell,
> And shook a dreadful dart; what seemed his head
> The likeness of a kingly crown had on.[2]

In this description all is dark, uncertain, confused, terrible, and sublime to the last degree. And while this passage evokes Tolkien's descriptions of palpable darkness, and indeed the Witch-King of Angmar, I am not arguing that Tolkien was directly influenced by Milton (although he may well have been), but rather, that his version of the sublime – as seen in the unnerving tangibility of shadows – is recognisably Burkean.

The sublime for Burke, Walpole, and later writers signalled the limits of rationality – the 'sleep' of reason – and was best communicated by obscurity. The profoundly suggestive obscurity of terror and power therefore became the crucial activity of the Gothic imagination. Indeed, Burke's work reads almost like a manifesto for later Gothic writers (not to mention film-makers), and elsewhere I have proposed seven types of obscurity of meaning and comprehension that exemplify Gothic aesthetics. For current purposes, these forms of obscurity are nearly all instantly familiar in Tolkien's work:

- Meteorological obscurity (mists, clouds, wind, rain, storm, tempest, smoke, darkness, shadows, gloom). Instances in Tolkien would be, for example, the Misty Mountains, Weathertop, and the Great Darkness on the Pelennor Fields.
- Topographical obscurity (impenetrable forests, inaccessible mountains, chasms, gorges, deserts, blasted heaths, icefields, the boundless ocean). In Tolkien, Mirkwood, Caradhras, the Dead Marshes, and Thangorodrim.
- Architectural obscurity (towers, prisons, castles covered in gargoyles and crenellations, abbeys and priories, tombs, crypts, dungeons, ruins,

1. Edmund Burke, *A Philosophical Enquiry into the Origin of our Ideas of the Sublime and Beautiful* (1757), 2nd edn, R. and J. Dodsley, London, 1759, p. 250.
2. John Milton, *Paradise Lost*, book 2, lines 666–73, quoted in op. cit., p. 232.

graveyards, mazes, secret passages, locked doors). Many examples, such as Dol Guldur, Minas Morgul, Barad-Dûr, Moria, Angband, the Paths of the Dead, the Barrows, and so forth.

- Material obscurity (masks, veils, disguises, billowing curtains, suits of armour, tapestries). The Nazgûl, obviously, as well as Frodo as 'Mr Underhill', Strider/Aragorn, the unfurling of Arwen's standard, Éowyn's disguise as Dernhelm.
- Textual obscurity (riddles, rumours, folklore, unreadable manuscripts and inscriptions, ellipses, broken texts, fragments, clotted language, polysyllabism, obscure dialect, inserted narratives, stories-within-stories). Invented languages and philological cruces are at the heart of Tolkien's Middle-Earth; in addition there are textual artefacts such as Thorin's Map, the inscription on the Ring, and the Book of Mazarbul. More complex examples would be the unfinished and lost poems (not to mention *Tales*) in the *legendarium*, the different languages and dialects of Middle-earth, and the references in *The Lord of the Rings* not only to the First Age but also to Anglo-Saxon poetry and other historical sources.
- Spiritual obscurity (religious mystery, allegory and symbolism, Roman Catholic ritual, mysticism, freemasonry, magic and the occult, Satanism, witchcraft, summonings, damnation). This is a staple of Gothic fiction (and film-making), but offers little for the reader of Tolkien. While there is certainly damnation and forms of magic being exercised, as well as some limited attention to burial rites, the supernatural is surprisingly downplayed and there is little religious mystery and very few accounts of forms of worship. Even The Silmarillion lacks this dimension (Númenor's temple to Melkor and sacrifices being perhaps the prominent exception). Religious belief is a tricky area that I will return to later in this paper.
- Finally, psychological obscurity (dreams, visions, hallucinations, drugs, sleep-walking, madness, split personalities, mistaken identities, doubles, derangement, ghostly presences, forgetfulness, death, hauntings). In contrast, there is plenty here: prophetic dreams, visions of the palantíri, the Mirror of Galadriel, the shift in perception caused by the Ring, split identities (Gollum/Sméagol) and multi-named characters, doubles (the Nazgûl), derangement (the effects of the Ring), and forgetfulness (Niënor).

All of these forms of obscurity aim at sublimity through mystification in order to probe the consequences of history and the telling of secrets. To take, for instance, the last example of psychological obscurity: the unravelling of the plot in *The Children of Húrin* is driven by exposure and revelation.

However, this catalogue of incomprehensible murkiness is of course only part of the story. Because of its fascination with gloom and ineffability, the license allowed to the imagination, and the tendency of the sublime to engage with power and violence, terror and horror, the Gothic became a way of exploring taboo subjects such as confronting the ferocity and cruelty of the French Revolution, giving voice to panics over scientific advance and their challenges to the integrity of humanity, and expressing revulsion over racism and slavery. And Tolkien's own concerns fit these deeper paradigms as well in his heartfelt anxieties over irrevocable rural and industrial change, deep struggles over national identity, and the dreadful and dehumanising effects of mechanised warfare – the major experience of the twentieth century.

The explosion in popularity of the Gothic genre at the end of the eighteenth century is a familiar chapter in English literary history. Hundreds of novels were published, the most noteworthy authors being William Beckford, Ann Radcliffe, Matthew 'Monk' Lewis, Charles Maturin, and Mary Shelley. The genre deeply influenced Romantic poetry as well in the supernatural dreams of Samuel Taylor Coleridge, and the medievalist fantasies of John Keats. Subsequent generations saw a domestication of the genre, in, for instance, the novels of the Brontë sisters (*Wuthering Heights* and *Jane Eyre*, both 1847), and in the second half of the nineteenth century the Gothic featured in work as varied as *The Woman in White*, *The Strange Case of Dr Jekyll and Mr Hyde*, *The Picture of Dorian Gray*, and the 'Sherlock Holmes' stories. In 1897, Bram Stoker's *Dracula* thoroughly overhauled the Gothic brew of legendary history and modernity in a plot that combined folklore and Catholic ritualism with contemporary fears of the city, colonialism, and social degeneration, in a plot driven by state-of-the-art technological sophistication.

But other things were happening in the nineteenth century as well, and the Gothic was not simply a repressed cry of horror at social changes: it was also a mainstream style, and offered the opportunity for a more systematic opposition to urbanisation and industrial capitalism. The Victorian Gothic Revival movement was a deliberate return to medieval architecture and culture, society and values. It is seen most vividly in huge building projects such as the Palace of Westminster (1830s-40s, designed by Charles Barry and Augustus Welby Pugin), the Pre-Raphaelite Brotherhood (from the 1850s), and William Morris's Arts and Crafts movement (from the 1870s). This wide-ranging movement combined the researches into chivalry and modern manners of Thomas Warton and Richard Hurd (which memorably blossomed in the Eglinton Tournament of 1839, a recreation of medieval knighthood) with the extravagant architectural ambitions of Walpole and Beckford. These elements were integrated into a visionary medievalism that produced not only structurally sound buildings, but also offered a social and theological ideal for Christian living. The Gothic therefore became the model for reforging community relations in a Christian society, and the building practices of medieval craftsmen in what became recognised as the three phases of Gothic architecture (based on the pointed arch, ribbed vaulting, and flying buttress) received an enthusiastic new lease of life.

In *Contrasts* (1836) and *Principles of Pointed or Christian Architecture* (1841), Pugin proposed that the social relations that made possible the greatest achievements of medieval Gothic architecture – cathedrals and abbeys – were the epitome of Christian culture, and inculcated virtue. If corrupt societies, such as that of nineteenth-century Britain, produced dismal architecture that alienated the people, Christian Gothic architecture could in contrast reverse this trend and foster morality – the medievalist built environment would actually discourage sin by raising the soul. Thus Gothic became the preferred architectural style for civic buildings, schools and universities, and of course the Anglican Church.

Pugin's religious zeal was given further impetus in the 1850s by the art critic and social reformer John Ruskin, who delineated the elaborate architectural symbolism of Gothic and defined its 'characteristic or moral elements' in The Stones of Venice (1851-3):

1. Savageness.
2. Changefulness.
3. Naturalism.
4. Grotesqueness.
5. Rigidity.
6. Redundance.

These characters are here expressed as belonging to the building; as belonging to the builder, they would be expressed thus: 1. Savageness or Rudeness. 2. Love of Change. 3. Love of Nature. 4. Disturbed Imagination. 5. Obstinacy. 6. Generosity.[3] For Ruskin, Gothic is an expression of individuality, passion, and creativity. As the later architectural historian Nikolaus Pevsner put it: 'To Horace Walpole Gothic is a sophisticated game, to [the Romantics] it is a high flight of creative imagination, to Pugin it is a Christian duty.'

Considering Tolkien's Middle-earth in this tradition reveals, I suggest, that *LotR* is a work of the Gothic Revival, and more especially a work of the Puginian Gothic Revival. Tolkien was, like Pugin, a Catholic, and Pugin deplored the English Reformation and the havoc it had enacted upon medieval architecture, society, and culture. Pugin's aim was therefore to revive medieval social structures not as an expression of repressed guilt at the sometimes brutal course of progress, but because they were consistent with his faith, which was itself continuous with the Middle Ages.

---

3. John Ruskin, *The Stones of Venice*, vol. 2, Smith, Elder and Co., London, 1852, in J. G. Links, ed., *The Stones of Venice*, Da Capo, New York, 1960, p. 152.

The Gothic was a way of coming to terms with the processes of English history, which is why in the seventeenth, eighteenth, and nineteenth centuries it had such strong social, political, and theological significance. But this approach to understanding progress is itself a Whig historical narrative that has at its basis the defeat of the Catholic Middle Ages. For Tolkien this was doubly troubling – he was both a Catholic and a medievalist. So Tolkien does not write as did Protestant Gothic writers of the eighteenth and nineteenth centuries, examining the formation of national identity in relation to the suppressed horrors of historical change, but as an active medievalist – and an actively anti-Enlightenment medievalist – purposely to reconnect with and revive medieval identities. In this he is in the tradition of Catholic Gothicists such as Richard Verstegan, author of *A Restitution of Decayed Intelligence*, a philological national epic first published in 1605, as well as the Catholic sympathiser Edmund Burke in the eighteenth century, and the Roman Catholic Augustus Welby Pugin in the nineteenth century. So although Tolkien might have adopted many of the characteristics of *The Castle of Otranto*, he is not a Walpolean Gothicist. Tolkien does not write novels of terror, still less of horror; instead, he investigates hospitality, chivalry, courage, social responsibility, and the challenges of progress in anxieties over rural and industrial transformation, the culture and fate of England, and industrialised warfare. In this, his work is really more in the tradition of what I would describe as the first Gothic novel: not *The Castle of Otranto*, but *Longsword*, by Thomas Leland (1762) – the first historical romance, heavily influenced by the emerging eighteenth-century cult of medievalism, which itself in due course influenced Walter Scott.

Tolkien's Catholic Gothicism is also then perhaps the reason for his reluctance to engage in his Middle-earth writings with Gothic superstition: spiritual obscurity, allegory and symbolism, ritual, mysticism, the occult, and the practices of religion. Faith and observance are present, but buried: they are implicit throughout Tolkien's Middle-earth work in the same way that they are implicit in Pugin's architecture. In this way, *LotR* is a work of the Gothic Revival, suggesting how community relations in a Christian society can be reforged. Tolkien is describing the emergence of a society founded on hospitality and community; those values are grounded in medieval Catholicism, but they remain as deep, anchoring roots – and are not made manifest. Thus it is that perhaps the closest we come to communion is at the table of Tom Bombadil.

'Frodo and Faramir: Mirrors of Chivalry'

Constance G.J. Wagner

In discussions of Tolkien's The Lord of the Rings, much is often made of Frodo's knightly qualities as Ringbearer and also those displayed by Faramir, second son of Denethor, Ruling Steward of Gondor. In this paper I take that observation to a deeper level by illustrating the chivalric qualities of both characters as required of a knight of the realm according to Geoffroi de Charny, a knight of France during the Hundred Years' War. A Knight's Own Book of Chivalry, a handbook for working warriors written by Charny for France's Company of the Star, reveals what every good knight must know and do. This paper shows how both Frodo and Faramir reflect that, becoming in essence 'mirrors of chivalry' and kindred souls. It is illustrated with examples drawn from the epic novel and the celebrated films, in addition to citing Charny's guidebook for chivalric behavior as framework for the discussion.

He who does best is most worthy. – These simple yet laudatory words come down to us from the fourteenth century, voiced by Geoffroi de Charny, knight of France.[1] In his Book of Chivalry, he lays out his philosophy of knighthood, telling the members of the Company of the Star what it means to follow the chivalric ideal as a life's work. Most likely written at the behest of Jean II of France when the Company was created in 1352, Charny's work gives the reader an intimate view of how best to become – and remain – a worthy warrior.

Though this unique tome was meant to be a guide for chivalric behaviour for knights of medieval France, echoes of Charny's ideal chivalric knight, the *preudomme* (i.e. the worthy man) survived into the twentieth century in Tolkien's epic *LotR* (and in the twenty-first century film trilogy incarnation of the story as well) in the characters of Frodo Baggins, Ring-bearer, and Faramir, Captain of Gondor's guard. Both heroes, committed as they are to the greater good and willing to sacrifice all to preserve it, epitomise in this classic work of fiction what Charny was attempting to promote and preserve among the knightly class.

'I think at last we understand one another, Frodo Baggins,' Faramir says to Frodo at a definitive moment in the filmed version of *The Two Towers*.[2] Having

1. Geoffroi De Charny, *A Knight's Own Book of Chivalry*, trans by Elspeth Kennedy, University of Pennsylvania Press, Philadephia, 2005, p. 52.
2. Peter Jackson, director, *The Lord of the Rings: The Two Towers*, Extended Edition, DVD, New

witnessed something of Frodo's physical and psychological suffering under the burden of the Ring, including the pursuit of the Ring-bearer by the dreaded Nazgûl, Faramir at last sees Frodo not as a pawn used and pursued by Powers greater than Man or Hobbit, but as a warrior worthy, and so a kindred spirit in the lists of knighthood. The unassuming hobbit is here revealed as part of a select company who, according to Charny, 'double the good to be found in them, when from their own instinct and the will for good which God has given them, … know what is right and spare neither themselves nor what they own in their effort to achieve it.'[3] With this statement, Charny identifies 'How the Highest Standard in Deeds of Arms is Achieved',[4] and while he is here essentially praising physical prowess and piety in such a knight, Frodo, over the course of the Quest, becomes enlarged enough in spiritual prowess in fighting his internal battle with the Ring to qualify.

Indeed, before he even sets out from the Shire at Gandalf's urging, Frodo states:

'I suppose I must keep the Ring and guard it, at least for the present, whatever it may do to me' (*FotR*, 'The Shadow of the Past', 60).[5] And upon deeper reflection, he adds, 'I should like to save the Shire, if I could …' (*FotR*, 'The Shadow of the Past', 61), announcing his willingness to serve a higher cause. In the film, the same moment is captured even more compellingly by a Frodo who stands in his comfortable parlour at Bag End and with a simple closing of his hand over the Ring offers himself to Middle-earth with the words: 'What must I do?'.[6] Surely Charny would extol such words as emblematic of one possessed of 'pure simplicity of heart … (one who) would scarcely know how to do wrong, even if (he) wanted to do so, for (he is himself) so innocent'.[7]

And while Faramir, battle-weary Captain of Gondor, may not generally be seen as innocent to the ways of the world, he embodies the ideal of being 'pure of heart' when in the book he proclaims of Isildur's Bane (i.e., the Ring):

> I would not take this thing, if it lay by the highway. Not were Minas Tirith falling in ruin and I alone could save her, so using the weapon of the Dark Lord for her good and my glory. No, I do not wish for

Line Home Entertainment, 2003, scene 60.

3. Op. cit. [1], p. 56
4. Op. cit. [1], p. 55.
5. J.R.R Tolkien, *The Lord of the Rings*, Houghton Mifflin, New York, 1994. All quotations from *LotR* are taken from this edition.
6. Peter Jackson, director, *The Lord of the Rings: The Fellowship of the Ring*, Extended Edition, DVD, New Line Home Entertainment, 2002, scene 10.
7. Op. cit. [1], p. 80.

> such triumphs, Frodo, son of Drogo. (*TT*, 'The Window on the West', 656)

Such a declaration places Faramir in vivid contrast with his older brother Boromir, a member of the Fellowship who falls prey to the lure of the Ring and tries to take it from Frodo, despite having vowed to protect the Ring-bearer. Faramir, who would recognise himself (though modestly) in Charny's depiction of a 'True Man of Worth, Brave and of Good Counsel',[8] and so marked to be a captain of other men-of-arms, still knows his brother to be of a deeper martial vein than he, more overtly heroic, and so, ironically, more prone to the Ring's allure:

> If it were a thing that gave advantage in battle, I can well believe that Boromir, the proud and fearless, often rash, ever anxious for the victory of Minis Tirith (and his own glory therein), might desire such a thing and be allured by it. Alas that ever he went on that errand! (*TT*, 'The Window on the West', 656)

Faramir might instead sense a kinship with the Englishmen of Agincourt, whom Shakespeare's Henry V named 'warriors for the working day,' ready to defend their own but not kin to those who *forever* seek the field of battle. Certainly Charny would agree, noting that those who 'serve their friends and kinsmen … and have done well in this art of war – even if it were only in their own district -- should be honoured among all men in their own locality.'[9]

In desiring to protect their kith and kin, Faramir and Frodo are alike, but there is irony to be found in the fact that the cosmopolitan Faramir, raised in the splendor of an ancient capital of might and learning, should actually have less experience of the wider world than does Frodo, the country-bred hobbit who has been marked by Fate to go a-questing. Both are bookish and curious; indeed both are known to have been a certain 'wizard's pupils' (*RotK*, 'The Siege of Gondor', 795), but only Frodo proves a different kind of knightly mettle by 'undertaking distant journeys' and so would win Charny's additional praise.

'We should … honour those who have been on distant journeys to foreign parts,' Charny notes, 'for no one can travel so far without being many times in physical danger.'[10] Certainly Frodo's relentless march to Mount Doom, a flight out of safety and into savagery, qualifies. Indeed, such experiences as those that sear Frodo's heart and soul, are indicated by Charny as part and parcel of the

8. Op. cit. [1], p. 82.
9. Op. cit. [1], p. 49.
10. Op. cit. [1], p. 51.

'Heavy Responsibilities ... of Rank and Power'.[11] All can learn, *must* learn, much from the:

> great achievements and honorable deeds of valour ... which they have accomplished through suffering great hardship, making strenuous efforts and enduring fearful physical perils and the loss of friends whose deaths they have witnessed ... these experiences have often filled their hearts with great distress and strong emotion.[12]

With each step of the quest, Frodo becomes more like Charny's ideal of the *preudomme*, growing more resolute, determined, and even stoic than his idyllic days in the Shire would ever have predicted he could be. His simple report of the death of Gandalf: 'One, we lost in Moria ...',[13] while succinct, is yet filled with hidden layers of emotion known only to those who have seen War.

When taking each other's measure, Frodo and Faramir allow us to see knightly courtesy come to life. Initially, each has very little reason to trust the other. Frodo, fearing that Faramir may prove to be as warlike and ambitious as the brother who tried to kill him for the Ring, instinctively holds back his secrets. Faramir, with the finely-honed intuition of a seasoned captain, senses that this Halfling, a being out of legend and prophecy, is more than what he appears to be. And yet, the two deal well together, displaying discretion and courtesy toward each other, even in Faramir's circumspect interrogation of the Ring-bearer.

Charny notes that 'the wise know how to hold their peace until it is time to speak,'[14] and in the flickering light of the campfire, Frodo is careful to tell 'no lies, and all of the truth (he) could' (*TT*, 'The Window on the West', 654). Faramir appreciates this, judging it to be the proper chivalric conduct for the situation. When Sam, ever the impatient squire and equally ever quick to rise to his master's defense, accuses Faramir of suspecting Frodo of murder, this Captain of Gondor is a model of Charny's 'Good Ruler,'[15] honest and just, telling Sam:

> 'Patience!' said Faramir, but without anger. 'Do not speak before your master, whose wit is greater than yours. ...I spare a brief time, in order to judge justly in a hard matter. Were I as hasty as you, I might have slain you long ago.... But I do not slay man or beast

11. Op. cit. [1], p. 60.
12. Op. cit. [1], p. 61.
13. Op. cit. [2], scene 40.
14. Op. cit. [1], p. 71.
15. Op. cit. [1], p. 79.

needlessly, and not gladly even when it is needed. Neither do I talk in vain. So be comforted'. (*TT*, 'The Window on the West', 650)

Here certainly is proof of Frodo's estimation of Faramir in relation to Boromir: that this younger son who now detained him in a military camp, though much like Boromir in looks, 'was a man less self-regarding, both sterner and wiser' (*TT*, 'The Window on the West', 650). Charny would praise the Gondorian as a knight rightly placed in authority over others, for Faramir behaves at all times 'with due humility and without arrogance … showing mercy, without excessive pride and ferocity.'[16]

The ability – indeed, the willingness – to employ pity and mercy is one of the key qualities found in Charny's model of the Worthy Man as Ruler.[17] Nowhere is this more in evidence in *LotR* than in Frodo's treatment of Gollum, whom he attempts to reform as best he can, even to restoring the creature's birth name (i.e., Sméagol) – and therefore some dignity – to him.

Though ever-wary Sam feels justified in tying up this 'wretched gangrel creature' (*TT*, 'Of Herbs and Stewed Rabbit', 643), with Elven rope and leaving him to the elements, Frodo belays the attempt, stating, 'Maybe he does deserve to die. But now that I see him, I do pity him'.[18] Thereafter, at every twist and turn in the tale before the baleful influence of the Ring consumes him, Frodo, knowing Sméagol to be a dark mirror of what he himself could yet become, tries valiantly to be less 'eager to deal out death in the name of justice … for even the wise cannot see all ends' (*TT*, 'The Taming of Sméagol', 601). Even in the face of danger, this best of hobbits personifies the true and deep qualities of the chivalrous knight, echoing in his behaviour Charny's words of litany: 'He who does best is most worthy'.[19]

Frodo's inherent chivalrous nature is also displayed in his honouring of the bonds of fealty, revealed, ironically enough, through his connection to Gollum, who 'swears to serve the master of the Precious.'[20] Stepping between the threat of a deadly accurate Gondorian arrow and his Ring-poisoned doppelganger, Frodo pleads for Sméagol's life, knowing that 'the servant has a claim on the master for service' (*TT*, 'The Forbidden Pool', 672). 'This creature is bound to me,' Frodo reveals to a shocked Faramir, 'and I to him. He is our guide. Please … let me go down to him.'[21] In this way does Frodo, the True and Worthy Knight, display

16. Op. cit. [1], p. 78.
17. Op. cit. [1], p. 77.
18. Op. cit. [2], scene 3.
19. Op. cit. [1], p. 52.
20. Op. cit. [2], Scene 3.
21. Op. cit. [2], scene 42.

his awareness of chivalric obligation to those in his care – even a creature as repellant as Gollum. This is in keeping with Charny's precept that the Good Ruler 'should not despise any poor people (or, in Frodo's case, the wretched in his care) … nor disdain to listen to them.'[22] Faramir, noble son of his city's Ruling Steward, understands such obligations and, in the book in an extensive scene heavy with ceremonial language, releases the accursed hobbit back into Frodo's keeping: 'Faramir sat for a moment in thought. 'Very good' he said at last. 'I surrender you to your master, to Frodo son of Drogo. Let him declare what he will do with you!'' (*TT*, 'The Forbidden Pool', 675)

Another ceremonial mark of One Worthy and of high rank, according to Charny, is that such a personage 'should make sure that God be feared, loved, served and honoured in word and deed wherever they are.'[23] This maxim is readily illustrated by Faramir when he and his men turn and face west in a moment of silence and direct Frodo and Sam to do likewise. Noting the hobbits' confusion, Faramir explains: 'So we always do.… We look towards Númenor that was, and beyond to Elevenhome that is, and to that which is beyond Elvenhome and will ever be' (*TT*, 'The Window on the West', 661).

Faramir here alludes to the Valar, the high angelic Powers that watch over Middle-earth in a kind of stewardship for Eru (i.e., the One) or as the Elves name him, Ilúvatar (Father-of-All). But Frodo has his moment of piety as well when he is confronted with the primal horror of Shelob, last and most dread daughter of Ungoliant, a dark demon from the Elder Days of Middle-earth. A bloated she-devil in spider form, Shelob lives in darkness, breathes darkness, vomits darkness, is darkness. And Frodo does battle by brandishing a star-glass, the Phial of Galadriel, in which the light of the star Eärendil (i.e., Venus) is captured in the purest of water. *Aiya Eärendil Elenion Ancalima!* (Hail Eärendil, brightest of stars!), he cries as a blaze of starlight pierces the darkling depths of Shelob's Lair (*TT*, 'Shelob's Lair', 704).

This Elvish cry, a spontaneous, inspired invocation to the powers of heaven for deliverance, would have met with Charny's approval as an example of true religious fervour in battle. The weapon, a gift from the Elven Queen Galadriel (who has oft been identified even by Tolkien as a Mary figure), is a sacred object infused with light and grace. Thus is Frodo so identified with the worthies of Charny's world 'who love, serve, and honour God and His gentle Mother',[24] knowing that not by themselves but '*by God's grace*, they perform well.'[25]

22. Op. cit. [1], p. 78.
23. Op. cit. [1], p. 79.
24. Op. cit. [1], p. 80.
25. Op. cit. [1], p. 56.

'He who does best is most worthy'.[26] And what is the highest act of service a worthy knight can perform? What can he give to show the Truth at his core? The answer is: *everything*. This Faramir offers when he rides out to do battle on the Pelennor Fields, despite Gandalf's entreaties to stay.

'Where does my allegiance lie if not here?' Faramir asks of Gandalf, of himself. 'I will gladly give my life to defend her beauty, her memory, her wisdom.'[27] And in this riding forth, leading a charge, a very tidal wave of knights a-horseback, Faramir is the epitome of a Worthy who would defend his people, who would accept the 'hard martyrdom' of the chivalric ideal.[28]

But what of Frodo? Faramir, Son of Númenor, Captain of Gondor's guard, may gallop o'er a storied battlefield, shield and sword blazing in the sun, to give his all for his people. Frodo, however, in crawling up the face of Mount Doom, his very life essence seeming to pour into the earth, gives *himself* for *all* people.[29]

And at the penultimate moment when Frodo stands above the fiery abyss of the Cracks of Doom, he is become the sacrifice on the burning altar of the Quest. Hard martyrdom, indeed.

'He who does best is most worthy'.[30]

And is rewarded, Charny would say, 'with honour in this world, leading the soul into paradise in the next to take (his) place in that glorious company which will continue for ever in bliss without end.'[31]

Indeed, the Blessed Realm awaits the Ring-bearer at the end of the tale, offering him a place of repose to better understand 'his position in littleness and in greatness',[32] of sacrifice and salvation for all.

Yes. It is so. *He who does best is most worthy.*[33]

Amen.

26. Op. cit. [1], p. 52.
27. Peter Jackson, director, *The Lord of the Rings: The Return of the King*, Extended Edition, DVD, New Line Home Entertainment, 2004, scene 28.
28. Op. cit. [1], p. 35.
29. Op. cit. [27], scene 65.
30. Op. cit. [1], p. 52.
31. Op. cit. [1], p. 105.
32. Humphrey Carpenter, ed. *The Letters of J.R.R. Tolkien*, with the assistance of Christopher Tolkien, Houghton Mifflin, New York, 2000, Letter 246, p. 328.
33. Op. cit. [1], p. 52.

FANTASY

'An Old Light Rekindled: Tolkien's Influence on Fantasy'

Anna E. Thayer (née Slack)

The fantasy genre has long been the subject of awe, adoration, revulsion and repulsion in equal and discriminatory measures. The genre has been present as long as mankind has told tales, and brings with it a collection of expected tropes, topoi, stereotypes and themes. Considering the nature and roots of the genre, the literary climate in which Tolkien was received and the 'master of fantasy's' own aims from the perspective of a critic and writer, this paper asks what expectations Tolkien has bound upon the genre and how far it is possible for his literary descendents to write in (or away from) his shadow. It traces the links between influence and originality, examining Tolkien's goals of sub-creation and eucatastrophe, asking whether these are the lynch-pins of fantasy and what, ultimately, constitutes Tolkien's legacy to the genre that he re-ignited.

> The first qualification for judging any piece of workmanship from a corkscrew to a cathedral is to know what it is – what it was intended to do and how it was meant to be used. (C. S. Lewis, A Preface to Paradise Lost)[1]

The term 'fantasy' has a disconcerting plurality of meaning with, it seems, as many semantic facets as the worlds and subgenres it has spawned. Certainly, the term is contemporarily associated with the 'faculty or activity of imagining improbable things' (OED) and is as much suggestive of 'an idea with no basis in reality' (OED) as it is a genre of fiction.

To address the question of Tolkien's influence on the genre we must first find our way through the ghost lights of awe, adoration, revulsion and repulsion that surround it – a quest well suited to the genre's scope – to ascertain something of what it is.

FANTASY: PENNING THE BLACK SHEEP

The Oxford Dictionary of Literary Terms is intriguingly brief on the matter of fantasy, advising the reader to seek a more detailed exploration of the term

1. C.S. Lewis, *A Preface to Paradise Lost*, Atlantic Publishers and Distributors, Dehli, 2005, p. 1.

in other sources. Indeed, it is almost as eloquent on the subject of 'ficelle'[2] as it is this troublesome genre. Critically speaking, fantasy is the black sheep of literature, sharing the fate that has befallen fairy tale's countless dispossessed princes and youngest daughters - it has often been overlooked and disinherited from the literary canon, deemed as of no more worth than 'juvenile trash'.[3] We might say that it is difficult to pen, both in terms of writing and containment.

So, what is fantasy? In his work *Other Worlds: The Fantasy Genre*, John H. Timmerman gives a handy list of six attributes that can be said to characterise a work of fantasy: 'the use of traditional *Story*, the depiction of *Common Characters and Heroism*, the evocation of another *World*, the employment of *Magic and the Supernatural*, the revelation of a *Struggle between Good and Evil*, and the tracing of a *Quest*'.[4]

For Timmerman, these elements and motifs grant the genre a position at centre-stage of the literary tradition. They are certainly the elements which we would associate with Tolkien, Lewis, Williams, LeGuin, and other fantasists. Mark any work of 'fantasy' against these posts - from Sedgewick's *My Swordhand is Singing* to Hearn's *Tales of the Otori*, from George R.R. Martin's *A Game of Thrones* series to my own recently published novel, then the reader will find that these six attributes are generally unfailingly addressed.

We discern these elements, and their consequent concerns with morality, reality and truth, at the heart of the genre. W.H. Auden was in agreement that the quest played a central role in Tolkien's work, using it as a link between *The Lord of the Rings* and forbear texts such as Malory's *Morte D'Arthur*; C.S. Lewis weighed Tolkien against the imaginative scope of Ariosto. The link to writers like Ariosto and Spenser leads us suggestively to the moral complex of allegory and parable, but Tolkien argued that the genre's value here was not in its allegory but its 'applicability'.

Most readers would be hard pressed to deny the weight of this argument. Though, when taken to excess, applicability may lead to obsession (a fanaticism which the fantasy genre overtly attracts) through the temptation to completely absorb oneself in a fictional reality, the inherent applicability of fantasy to our own lives seems to be a crucial element of the genre's success – we might add it as a seventh element to Timmerman's six.

The question of applicability is relevant not only to Tolkien but to more

2. A term used by Henry James to describe a fictional character whose role as a confidante is exploited as a means of providing the reader with information while avoiding direct address from the narrator.

3. Edmund Wilson, 'Oo, Those Awful Orcs!', *The Nation* 182 (1956), 312–14.

4. John H. Timmerman, *Other Worlds: The Fantasy Genre*, Bowling Green University Press, Bowling Green OH, 1983, p. 3.

modern works. Weighing boy wizard against high school teen, Robin Brown observes that: '*Harry Potter* is about confronting fears, finding inner strength and doing what is right in the face of adversity. *Twilight* is about how important it is to have a boyfriend'.[5] The concerns of one text pale in applicability compared with the other. Perhaps this is why Rowling's fantasy abides whilst Meyer's popularity only really soars with a limited and specific audience – the fantastic world of Harry Potter is imminently more applicable to the lives of its readers, whatever their age.

Putting aside all the subgenres of fantasy – high fantasy, sword and sorcery, urban fantasy, the marvellous, the uncanny, the fantastic – it seems that the universally recognisable structure of fantasy makes it a genre onto which we can – and desire to – project ourselves and our lives, applying our experience to the imaginary and the experience of fantasy's heroes to our own reality in a kind of didactic exchange. It is a liminal genre with immense power, opening the doors between faerie and reality.

Of course, these have been the attributes of the genre as long as we have told tales: as Tolkien would write in a letter to *The Observer* in 1938, fantasy in general (and his own writing in particular), is 'derived from (previously digested) epic, mythology and fairy-story'.[6] The key elements of fantasy can be traced back through the same illustrious literary heritage that produced the visionary scope of *Paradise Lost*, the fairy-tale redemption of Leontes in *The Winter's Tale* and the questioning of Chanticleer's digestive tract; we see them in the adventures of Odysseus, the founding of Rome, the battles of Beowulf, the journey of Gawain, the splintering of Camelot, the solitary way from Eden. Elements of fantasy are embedded in the foundations not only of the western narrative tradition but, as Joseph Campbell has identified, mythologies from across the world.[7]

It seems that we are hard-wired for this kind of storytelling – and it could be argued that no writer, not even the most post-modern or counter-cultural, can escape the themes and influence of fantasy: work from the trenches echoes the titanic clash of classical titans and struggle of man with destiny; Angela Carter's The Bloody Chamber and The Magic Toyshop operate on common cultural memory and expectations – crossing, like many fairy-tales and darker or gothic works of fantasy, into the macabre – and still Bettelheim's theory holds.[8] We read these stories to learn about ourselves and the world we live in.

---

5. R.B. Durham, *Twilight: An Unofficial Companion*, Lulu.com, Online, 2015, p. 6.
6. Humphrey Carpenter, ed., *The Letters of J. R. R. Tolkien*, with the assistance of Christopher Tolkien, HarperCollins, 1995, London, 1995, Letter 25, p. 31.
7. Joseph Campbell, *The Hero with A Thousand Faces*, New York, 1949.
8. Bruno Bettelheim, *The Uses of Enchantment*, London, 1976.

ON THE BRINK: TOLKIEN'S PLACE

We have grappled for an understanding of the weave of this genre. Let us shift the shuttle towards Tolkien, and his particular place in it. Tolkien's passion, as a reader and storyteller, was 'ab initio for myth... and for fairy-story, and above all for heroic legend on the brink of fairy-tale and history' of which he perceived there is 'far too little in the world'.[9] He was the ideal audience for fantasy, recognising in his statement the composite elements of the genre. He believed throughout his life that fairy story 'is really an adult genre, and one for which a starving audience exists',[10] lamenting the 'false and accidental... connexion in the modern mind between children and 'fairy stories' '.[11] It might indeed be true to say that much of the antagonism towards Tolkien's work, and the fantasy genre in general, is the belief that it is 'inferior' and only suitable for children. Hand in hand with this goes the belief that fantasy is somehow a genre in which an author 'indulge[s] himself in developing the fantasy for his own sake'.[12]

Like many works of fantasy to follow it, Tolkien's work has polarised readers; many take a judgement on the genre based on one novel. When 'types' of readers and fantasy literature are so divergent, it is little wonder that the genre can come into ill-repute; a reader hungering after the masculine world of *Conan the Barbarian* may find little to attract them in *LotR*; the reader that adored the religious and moral themes woven into the Narnia stories may find the much more pagan archipelago of Earthsea difficult to swallow. As Tolkien observed, 'something of the teller's own reflections and 'values' will inevitably get worked in[to their tale]',[13] and, perhaps more than any other genre, the bounds of fantasy are so broad that there is as much to repel as enthral its readers.

GENRE-MAKER: TOLKIEN'S INFLUENCES

It should be noted, at this juncture, that Tolkien himself never called his work a work of fantasy – always (in a reflection of his own 'values') of fairy-story. He had felt called, from his earliest youth, to 'kindle a new light, or, what is the same thing, rekindle an old light in the world ... to testify for God and Truth'.[14] As his work On Fairy-Stories was to explore at length, for him 'fairy story' – what we might now call high fantasy – was the most exquisite vehicle of expression

9. Op. cit. [6], Letter 131, p. 144.
10. Op. cit. [6], Letter 159, p. 209.
11. Op. cit. [6], Letter 163, p. 216.
12. Op. cit [3].
13. Op. cit. [6], Letter 181, p. 233.
14. Op. cit. [6], Letter 5, p. 10.

available to him for this purpose: it has 'its own mode of reflecting 'truth', different from allegory or sustained satire, or 'realism', and in some ways more powerful'.[15] Tolkien saw his own work as a continuation of a literary tradition that had been growing for hundreds of years.

And his influence? Influence, a word deriving from a Latin root meaning 'flowing into something', intends ways in which a writer has wrested an idea or genre in a particular direction. Some elements of Tolkien's influence on fantasy are clear and obvious not just in literature but also in media as diverse as art, film-making, role-playing games and MMO RPGs like *World of Warcraft* – where you can meet dwarves, elves and tree-people.

It doesn't just stop with the stock characters – Tolkien's influence is so pervasive that he has even altered our perception of the correct plural of 'dwarf'; a glance at dictionaries in circulation before *LotR* gained popularity (in my case, a dictionary from 1816) shows that the canonical plural was 'dwar***fs***'; now, the OED lists 'dwar***ves***' as an acceptable alternative and this is due to Tolkien's own 'private piece of bad grammar'.[16] Just imagine if he had had his wish, and gone with the delightful word 'dwarrows'.

Bringing dwarves and Elves – not as dainty, sylvan creatures but as formidable and powerful beings – to the fore of the genre, Tolkien directly challenged the prevailing Victorian views of fairies, and the overtly 'lavish ... fantastical, incoherent and repetitive' faerie he felt was portrayed in Arthurian romances.[17] He took these creatures straight back to their mythical northern roots, returning to them something perilous about their stature, something threatening to mankind. A reflection of this can be seen in Smith's encounter with the terrifying dark Elves in *Smith of Wootton Major*.

Perhaps modern fantasy writers have not always preserved the grandeur and terrifying enchantment of characters like Galadriel, but elements of the power and mystique that Tolkien gave them have trickled into later fantasy in the common portrayal of Elves as aloof and alluring. And, certainly, we expect to meet elves and dwarves in works of fantasy. Another stock character introduced by Tolkien is the orc – prior to his work, goblins and gnomes were about as close as you could get (and gnomes now seem to be merging into the trope of 'hobbit' that Tolkien introduced, as a race of generally innocent creatures attuned to nature and more concerned with the mundane than the concerns of the 'higher' fantasy races). The orc has been stewed in the public consciousness long enough that it is moving beyond its Tolkienian type, and beginning to make outings as a protagonist in its own right – as, for example, in the novel *Orcs*, or as a character

15. Op. cit. [13].
16. Op. cit. [6], Letter 17, pp. 23–24.
17. Op. cit. [6], Letter 131, p. 144.

class in the game 'Munchkin'.

Go into any bookshop to the fantasy section, and you will see another area of influence: maps. While Robert E. Howard had a rudimentary map at the beginning of his *Conan* novels, after Tolkien a map at the beginning of your work of fantasy is almost a prerequisite of the genre - and many examples of this *sine qua non* have the good guys in the western part of the landmass. Closely linked to this as a way of building a believable secondary world is the concept of sub-created languages – after Tolkien, any self-respecting fantasy author cannot simply talk about over-hearing a 'barbarian tongue', or scribble down some gibberish words and hope that the reader will suspend their disbelief. There is an expectation of (and perhaps a tolerance for) invented languages that was not present before Tolkien brought his work to the genre.[18]

An area of key concern in the fantasy genre is the role of women and female characters; Tolkien was annoyed by the criticism that *LotR* had 'no Women'[19] – Peter Jackson's adaptation was similarly raked. Let us not forget who defeated the Witch King at the battle of the Pelennor fields, and who tore down Sauron's stronghold with song where an Elven king had failed. Rather than saying that there are no women in Tolkien's work it would perhaps be fairer to say that there are no women who have been brushed with the values of feminism. In this, Tolkien could be said to differ substantially to those who have followed him in the genre. Tolkien's women are fewer far than men, but this is internally consistent to the pseudo-mediaeval reality he creates. Writers who choose to depict sexually liberated, sword-wielding warrior princesses are dealing with a different kind of sub-creation to Middle Earth; we might wonder whether even this is partly due to Tolkien's influence in the sense that it is a backlash against the more traditional, 'fairy-tale'-like conception of a woman's role.

Another element of Tolkien's influence is the attribution to him of the 'father of fantasy' title – which seems to be another way of saying that his works may be mercilessly pulped and regurgitated. *The Forgotten Realms* and *Shannara* series novels seem to be little more than a shameless ripping-off of their source material: my husband observes that 'they are to *LotR* what MacDonalds is to a restaurant'. Harsh, perhaps, but many Tolkien purists would agree with him.

---

18. For example, in the Conan Chronicles, speakers of other languages speak in 'a barbarian tongue'; it is also the stock of fairy tale and myth that when the protagonists meet a foreigner it may be mentioned that another tongue is spoken, but they do not use it. Perhaps we might look to the *Star Trek* franchise as an interesting modern comparison – Klingon was not developed as a full language until the late 70s, a number of years after Tolkien's work had gained popularity. Prior to this, Klingons always spoke English. In contrast, *Babylon 5*, a science fiction series of the 90s, has alien languages built into its fabric from the outset.

19. Op. cit. [6], Letter 165, p. 220.

There is a fine line to be trodden here between the pulp-mill fiction that churns out poorly written novels simply because they will sell, and works that genuinely are 'the next J.R.R. Tolkien'. The trouble with these novels, all undoubtedly influenced by Tolkien, is that the question of their quality is down to the taste of the individual reader – returning us neatly to the problem of the audience of fantasy and the impact of that variable on the genre.

Tolkien's influence is also discernable in the way that he, and elements of his work, have been parodied – Terry Pratchett satirises and parodies the tropes of the fantasy genre and the writers who would model themselves too closely on the grand master. Others have not been so subtle – see, for example, the infamous *Bored of the Rings*. Others do away with Tolkien's tropes almost entirely – but even *The Princess Bride* does not move away from its 'fantastic' fairy tale origins.[20]

Perhaps the element of influence that most clearly unifies high fantasy or Tolkien's faerie is the pre-modern concept of the struggle of good versus evil. After the watershed of modernism and post-modernism, notions of a moral struggle founded in a sense of absolute right or wrong were considered unrealistic, disproven by the gritty reality of human experience. Black and white is too simplistic for modernism; fractured narrative and mores become the lynchpin of literature. Consequentially, moral 'greyness' is the shade very much in vogue even in fantasy. Modern works like *A Game of Thrones* seem to be more epic modernist fantasy than fantasy in Tolkien's much older sense. Tolkien's fantasy is high fantasy, a fantasy whose defining feature is an underlying moral matrix played out both macro and microcosmically, personally and universally. Tolkien knew he was the old light, knew that fantasy was shading away from black and white to grey. His work boldly rekindled a fading fascination with war in the heavenlies and the concept of an absolute moral compass. Perhaps contemporary fantasists, whether they echo this system of high fantasy or not, are equally indebted to Tolkien; where one mirrors, the other repulses. The influence remains – and so does the struggle to be noticed in the company of the master.

Combing through the 'good' and 'bad' examples of the fantasy genre – by necessity a subjective activity – it seems that, whether or not the individual work owes a great deal to Tolkien, a distinction emerges whereby influence and originality are balanced. A good piece of literature in any genre will doubtless be influenced by its forbears – such is the nature of human experience – but it will also offer newly-framed insights from a sub-created world. The form may well, like Tolkien's, be in fairy story or high fantasy – but if this is the origin rather

20. Excellent and entertaining material on the tropes of fantasy is available at <http://tvtropes.org/ pmwiki/pmwiki.php/Main/Fantasy> [accessed 12 November 2015].

than the goal, then the genre is taking steps in the right direction – steps on the same path as Tolkien himself.

THE TROPE CODIFIER

Tolkien has certainly become what the TV Tropes website calls the 'Trope Codifier' for high fantasy, 'the template that all later uses of the trope follow'. Did he ever intend this outcome? By desiring to 'rekindle an old light in the world', we could argue that Tolkien's purpose was very much to influence the direction and ideals of a genre. For him, though, this rekindling was not in characters or plot or the supernatural – or in any of the mechanics of fantasy. It was in the intention of it. To rekindle the old light, he brought his concept of eucatastrophe to the fore of his critical theory and his own writing. Fairy story was a way of bringing comfort and renewed vision to its readers, a way of bringing a suggestion of the transcendence and immanence of God back into the primary, historical world. To do this, Tolkien relied on sub-creation – the inner consistency of reality, and the unique conveyance afforded to him by another world. He recognised, however, the perils of this calling. *Leaf by Niggle* and *Smith of Wootton Major* clearly show Tolkien's concerns about being a writer of fantasy: Niggle struggles to balance his sub-creation with his duties to the primary world; Smith must ultimately relinquish the pleasures and perils of faerie to another. The sub-created world must be handled with care, as either a writer or a reader, or it becomes the flight of the deserter and abode of the fanatic.

It is in the element of sub-creation – creating another fantastical world – that many writers are ultimately paralleled to Tolkien. This capacity of envisioning another world is crucial to the concept of fantasy, lying in its Greek roots *phantatastikos*, meaning 'to have visions' or 'make visible'. But perhaps, unless a work of fantasy strives, as Tolkien did, to testify to truth by means of that sub-creation, the work falls vacuous and dead in the reader's hands. The true measure of high fantasy may be in its eucatastrophic quality – and this is in the area in which Tolkien is unparalleled.

THE SAME STORY STILL: WRITING IN TOLKIEN'S SHADOW

At this point, I proceed in my reflections not as a critic, but as a writer. In *LotR*, Samwise comes to the startling realisation that he and Frodo are still in the same, grand story of Middle Earth as Beren and Lúthien and dozens of heroic forbears. When you are a writer of fantasy, being in 'the same story' as Tolkien is something it is desperately hard to avoid.

I was introduced to Tolkien as a child of about seven, when my father read

The Hobbit to my sister and me. I was enthralled – some of my most vivid memories are of my father's delight as he read to us 'Out of the frying pan, and into the fire'. The appeal of Middle-Earth was that it was another world – a world where I experienced joy and fear, grief and renewal. It formed my vision and understanding of the fantastic. My reading diet, from then on, constituted fairy stories, *The Arabian Nights*, *The Chronicles of Prydain*, *The Belgariad*, *The Derynii Chronicles*, *The Chronicles of Narnia*, the *Earthsea* quintet ...

When I first took up the pen at the tender age of eleven, I was reading *LotR*. I was stuck in the middle of Lothlórien (having been traumatised by the death of Gandalf and so terrified of Galadriel and her purposes for Frodo that I could read no further). Despite all my other reading, before and since, it was Tolkien's work that showed the strongest influence on my own, and was certainly foremost in my mind when I began writing. As all children do, I modelled myself on my 'master'. I left no trope un-copied; I had fearsome black riders pursuing a girl and her companions who were on a quest to preserve a magical medallion from the hands of an evil overlord who lived in a grand, black tower. Sound familiar? But you have to learn the craft from somewhere.

Over a number of years, an invented kingdom grew up as a background for these stories. The painfully patent similarities continued: I had elves and dwarves (who hated each other), and my group of heroes travelled the kingdom before being separated and having to continue their quest without the knowledge that their companions were alive. Evil defeated, they would be reunited. There was now, as my reading grew broader, some variation from my master's themes – I experimented with killing off principal characters and *not* bringing them back, and the avenues opened by a powerful and seductive villainess. Even so, these tales of Azzanor never truly removed themselves from Tolkien's shadow – and I was not yet aware that they should do so.

The next incarnation of my writing took me a step further away, and these tales – *The Chronicles of the Demonbane* – while still pitting heroes in a quest of light against dark, took on a more complex hue. Even so, they were the work of a youth still much too much influenced by Tolkien. I wanted to achieve what he had achieved – an internally consistent secondary reality – where I could tell a story about things that really mattered to me.

It was this series of stories that I first tried to publish. When rejected, I did not at first understand why. I ceased writing while I went to university and became a critic – of literature and of Tolkien's work. Through my studies I came to understand the terrible power of his influence – especially over me. He was the tree of fantasy, and I but a stunted leaf. To become truly like my hero of fantasy writing, I perceived that I had to become original – but there was nothing original that I could do. I continued to believe this until, walking to lectures one crisp spring morning, I came across a tree not far from the English department. From the wrung and settled branches, a spry, fresh, green leaf was budding. And I realised then that originality inherently springs from influence.

My ideas and values were turned with the sharpened perspective of adulthood back to the fantasy genre. I made my peace with Tolkien. Through my critical work, for my undergraduate degree and principally for these conferences, I came to understand more and more about the role of fantasy. Like Tolkien, I believe in its inherently eucatastrophic nature – that this genre is a platform where we can explore the issues and events that ultimately matter in the primary world. This was the kind of story I wanted to tell – and there were still stories to be told. I had to understand Tolkien, and acknowledge his influence, before I could focus on taking a step in the genre. My sub-creation has, in its own way, been a way of testifying to the same truth: fantasy is for the adult-minded and sharpens our taste for our own world – lessons that I only really learnt by interacting with 'the master of fantasy', both his imaginative and critical work.

Did I find originality? That is a question best left to my readers. But I believe that I have held true to the principle of fantasy that Tolkien held the dearest – telling a story with applicability. In my sub-created world,[21] the River Realm, a traditional story – the return of a dispossessed king – takes place against the backdrop of a battle of light and dark that is at times supernatural. So far, so fantasy. But there are no elves and dwarves, dragons, orcs, or devilish phantasmagorias. Only humans. The narrative is focalised through an everyman character whose personal journey is not always tied to the fate of the realm – in fact, critics may argue (and some readers have) that he is no hero at all. But who of us are? The fantasy genre is not just the preserve of peasants being unveiled as kings – it is a place where the choices ordinary people face every day can be questioned and explored.

INFLUENCE, OR INFLUENZA?

Whichever way we look at it, Tolkien's works, both academic and imaginative, have had an enormous influence over the unfolding of the genre that has followed him. I attest to that personally, and know many fantasy writers would say the same.

Tolkien was entirely cogent of the possibility of his work influencing others, feeling that: 'the cycles [of his tales] should be linked to the majestic whole, and yet leave scope for other minds and hands, wielding paint and music and

21. Anna Thayer, *The Traitor's Heir: Volume One of The Knight of Eldaran*, Austin and MacAuley, London, 2011.

drama'.[22] Those who consider him to have cast an unalterable shadow over the fantasy genre may feel that his influence is more of an influenza – that there is no place left for the genre to go, that we are destined to endless tales of hobbits and Elves that will never equal the work of the man whose imagination gobbled up every avenue of fantasy left.

But the truth is that Tolkien's overarching influence actually brought key aspects of this genre to the very forefront of study, and in his appeal to so many of us he has forced the academic world to look again at fantasy. His masterful re-weaving of crucial elements of story, and deeply considered theory of the vitality of faerie, is both a challenge and a call to arms to future fantasists. Tolkien's legacy to the genre is, I feel, as he would have wished. He is the piece of kindling that he aspired to be – the spark illuminating fantasy past, and inspiring fantasy yet to come.

22. Op. cit. [6,] Letter 131, p. 145.

'In the memory of old wives': Old Tales and Fairy-stories in Middle-earth

Troels Forchhammer

This essay is an investigation of the role of old tales and fairy-stories in the different cultures of Middle-earth and how Tolkien uses this portray these cultures. Through the optics of Tolkien's essay On Fairy-Stories we may learn a lot about a culture by investigating the role of folk-tales and fairy-stories within the culture. In this talk special attention is given to the primary human cultures encountered in The Lord of the Rings, of the Shire, Rohan and Gondor, but this is also, as far as possible, compared to non-human cultures, in particular the Elvish cultures of Rivendell and Lothlórien. I show how the attitudes towards old folk-tales and fairy-stories constitute an important element in the characterisation of Middle-earth cultures and even individual characters throughout LotR.

Many studies have focused on the metafictional aspects of the transmission history of Tolkien's mythology – from the tales of the *Quenta Silmarillion* to *The Red Book* and further on to Tolkien the translator. Thus Verlyn Flieger speaks of the importance of the concept of a physical book, albeit a fictional one,[1] and the importance to Tolkien of the author of that meta-fictional book,[2] Gergely Nagy investigates the effect on the reader when viewing the many versions of the legendarium as belonging to a metafictional mythological tradition,[3] and Vladimir Brljak invents a fan-meta-fiction in order to connect the Fourth Age with Tolkien the translator.[4] It has also been noted, especially by Verlyn Flieger, how particularly *The Lord of the Rings* and *Smith of Wootton Major* work as exemplars of the kind of fairy-story that Tolkien sets out as the truest form of

1. Verlyn Flieger, 'Tolkien and the Idea of the Book', in Wayne G. Hammond & Christina Scull, eds, *The Lord of the Rings 1954–2004: Scholarship in Honor of Richard E. Blackwelder*, Marquette University Press, Marquette, 2006, 283–99.
2. Verlyn Flieger, 'The Footsteps of Ælfwine', in Verlyn Flieger and Carl F. Hostetter, eds, *Tolkien's Legendarium*, Greenwood Press, Westport, 2000, 183–98.
3. Gergely Nagy, 'The great chain of reading: (inter-)textual relations and the technique of mythopoesis in the Túrin story', in Jane Chance, ed., *Tolkien the Medievalist*, Routledge, New York, 2003, 239–58.
4. Vladimir Brljak, 'The Books of Lost Tales: Tolkien as Metafictionist', *Tolkien Studies* 7 (2010), 1–34.

this genre in his famous essay *On Fairy-Stories*.[5] I have, however, not yet come across a study that focuses on the treatment of fairy-stories and folk-tales within *LotR* – how he uses these to illustrate points he makes in *On Fairy-Stories* and how he uses these stories to characterise the peoples of Middle-earth.[6]

Faërie, Tolkien tells us in his abandoned introduction to MacDonald's *The Golden Key*, was once a 'big word'[7] meaning both 'enchantment or magic, and the enchanted world or country in which marvellous people lived'.[8] In the Middle-earth of *The Hobbit* and *LotR* most people on both sides of the old war live primarily, or even exclusively, by normal, non-magical, means.[9] Thus, though Middle-earth is to us a world of marvellous people (both great and small), there is also to these very inhabitants of Middle-earth, a Faërie – even one that is, so to speak, closer to home than the Blessed Realm, Eldamar, which is in *The Hobbit* called 'Faerie in the West', (*TH*, 'Flies and Spiders', 219)[10] a land populated with the creatures of old tales, now perhaps only half believed, if at all.

My purpose here is to begin an exploration of how Tolkien uses the reactions of his characters to their encounters with this Faërie of Middle-earth, the meta-Faërie if you will, both to illustrate points from his essay and also to tell us important things about his characters. In the on-line discussion that provided the germ for my thoughts here it was asked which were the stories that Gandalf had once been telling the hobbits and which Bilbo remembered fondly in addition to Gandalf's displays of fireworks. Attempts to correlate the sparse information about these tales with stories from *The Silmarillion* were at best speculative (and that is perhaps being generous), and I have since come to believe that this is the wrong question to ask about these stories; instead of asking what the stories actually were, we should rather be asking what they *did*.

And for this, we have some information in Bilbo's reminisces. Bilbo holds

5. Verlyn Flieger, 'Fantasy and Reality: J.R.R. Tolkien's World and the Fairy-Story Essay', *Mythlore* 22 (1999), 4–13. See also Verlyn Flieger, 'When is a Fairy-story a *Faërie* Story? *Smith of Wootton Major*' in her *Green Suns and Faërie: Essays on J.R.R. Tolkien*, Kent State University Press, Kent OH, 2007, 65–73. Verlyn Flieger, 'Tolkien on Tolkien: "On Fairy-Stories", *The Hobbit*, and *The Lord of the Rings*', in her *Green Suns and Faërie: Essays on J.R.R. Tolkien*, The Kent State University Press, Kent OH, 2012, 54–64. Verlyn Flieger, 'The Theorist of the Fairy-Tale', *The Lord of the Rings Fanatics Plaza* <http://www.lotrplaza.com/showthread.php?23777-The-Theorist-of-the-Fairy-tale-Verlyn-Flieger> [accessed 25 August 2013].

6. Many of Flieger's works contain elements of this – e.g. in papers referred to in notes op. cit. [2] – but I am not aware of any paper, or book chapter, focusing on this aspect.

7. J.R.R. Tolkien, *Smith of Wootton Major: Extended Edition*, ed. Verlyn Flieger, HarperCollins, London, 2005, p. 7.

8. See op. cit., p. 74.

9. Humphrey Carpenter, ed., *The Letters of J.R.R. Tolkien*, with the assistance of Christopher Tolkien, HarperCollins, London, 1995, Letter 155, p. 200.

10. Douglas A. Anderson, ed., *The Annotated Hobbit*, HarperCollins, London, 2003.

Gandalf and his stories responsible for 'many quiet lads and lasses going off into the Blue for mad adventures' (*TH*, 'An Unexpected Party', 33–35). The creatures of Gandalf's stories, the dragons, goblins and giants (all of which Bilbo, incidentally will encounter during his own adventure) as well as the topics, rescuing princesses and the unexpected luck of widows' sons, are all reminiscent of traditional folk-tales and fairy-stories, and the effect they have on the hobbits is, in my opinion, akin to a combination of the *recovery* and *escape* that Tolkien mentions in *On Fairy-Stories*: to see things clearly again 'as we are (or were) meant to see them', as 'freed from the drab blur of triteness or familiarity' (*OFS*, 67),[11] and escaping the prison of a drab life to the world outside which 'has not become less real because the prisoner cannot see it' (*OFS*, 69).[12]

With Gandalf's fairy stories to the hobbits these take the forms of a fresh outlook on the world that has the effect of making the hobbit children curious about the world, seeing the white space on the Shire maps as they were meant to see it, wanting to explore it anew, and an escape from the predictability and familiarity of Hobbit life. In the greater context of the later work this becomes, of course, an aspect of Gandalf's efforts to rekindle the hearts of the free peoples of Middle-earth to resistance to Sauron, but I would argue that recovery, of the same kind, but of a different order, is precisely at the very heart of that mission.

Moving, then, on to *LotR*, we meet Gaffer Gamgee down at *The Ivy Bush*, discussing the matter of Bilbo with friends and acquaintances. What we see here is not really related to fairy-stories at all, but shows that whatever their attitude to fairy-stories, the hobbits are quite fond of telling stories about their neighbours (*LotR*, 'A Long Expected Party', 28–31).[13] Seventeen years later, strange things are happening, and we find the sons of the gardener and the miller discussing in *The Green Dragon*, where Ted Sandyman, the miller's son, scorns Sam's speech of dragons, saying that he thinks matters such as dragons to be for children only (*LotR*, 'The Shadow of the Past', 58–59), reflecting precisely the position that Tolkien challenges in his fairy-story essay. Considering Ted's role later in the story when Saruman rules in the Shire it would seem clear that we here have the Shire equivalent of that clerk of Oxenford who declared 'that he "welcomed" the proximity of mass-production robot factories, and the roar of self-obstructive mechanical traffic, because it brought his university into "contact with real life"' (*OFS*, 70). As the mood in the pub seems to be favouring Ted in this discussion we may surmise that the scepticism towards Faërie in and around the Shire is the

11. Verlyn Flieger and Douglas A. Anderson, eds, *Tolkien On Fairy-Stories*, HarperCollins, London, 2008, section 83, p. 67. Subsequent citations to *OFS* refer to this edition.

12. See op. cit. section 88, p. 69.

13. J.R.R. Tolkien, *The Lord of the Rings*, HarperCollins, London, 2005. All quotations from *LotR* are taken from this edition.

norm, going, at least in Ted, so far that he questions the stories about the Elves though he does appear to accept the basic fact of their existence, effectively wrapping up the Elves in his own drab familiarity.

In opposition to Ted, we have Sam, who not only loves Bilbo's stories of the old days, but who also wants desperately to believe them. In this we may see the effects of a chain of events that started, not with Gandalf's 'chance meeting' with Thorin in Bree, but rather with the tales that he told the young hobbits at the Old Took's parties. Bilbo's recovery of a clear view of the world around him, looking again at the world outside the Shire *as he was meant to see it* also means that his neighbours, who had been able to always 'tell what a Baggins would say on any question without the bother of asking him' are forced to look at Bilbo anew (*TH*, 'An Unexpected Party', 30), and the fire that is kindled in Bilbo's heart is mildly contagious – Sam and Frodo have surely caught it, and other hobbits may also be in danger of contamination, but the Shire in general has not yet escaped their own 'mental myopia'.[14]

Speaking of hobbits in general, it is interesting that Gollum appears to have heard 'lots of tales in the evening, sitting by the banks of the Great River, in the willow-lands, when the River was younger too,' of which he particularly mentions 'Tales out of the South about the tall Men with the shining eyes, and their houses like hills of stone, and the silver crown of their King and his White Tree: wonderful tales' (*LotR*, 'The Black Gate is Closed', 838). Gollum's recollections of the old tales he heard in his childhood appear in a context that seems to suggest that these memories offer him some degree of consolation as he moves from 'a pitiable state' to speaking without his usual sibilants and directly to his 'Master' – a lessening of the pain of this tortured soul.

Though this may to some extent be dependent on changes to the chronology of the Third Age between the first drafting and the final book, and particular in the chronology of Gollum, it would nonetheless appear that the river-people in some ways were better informed about ancient lore than the Shire hobbits.

Bree-land is special mostly because we do not know their tales. We are told that they like songs – including one with such fantastic content as 'The Man in the Moon Stayed Up Too Late', that they have their own tales according to which 'they were the original inhabitants and were the descendants of the first Men that ever wandered into the West of the middle-world' (*LotR*, 'At the Sign of the Prancing Pony', 195), but except for this, they seem to be more concerned with the present than the past, telling stories of how dreadful the world is a few miles away (and yet not understanding the real danger). However, the Bree-landers appear no more adventurous than the hobbits of the neighbouring Shire,

14. Op. cit. [9], Letter 246, p. 329.

and despite a liking for tales these seem not to have had the same effect in Bree as Gandalf's stories had in the Shire.

Rivendell is foreshadowed by Aragorn's song of Lúthien and Beren. In the essay, Tolkien asserts that 'The human stories of the elves are doubtless full of the Escape from Deathlessness,' and I suppose I am not the first to be reminded forcefully about the story of Beren and Lúthien when reading this: here, as in many other places in the essay, the fairies that Tolkien speaks of are his own Elves. It is of course remarkable that the same story, when you look at it from a human perspective, is suddenly full of the Escape from Death as both Beren and Lúthien come back from death to live again: thus the story becomes also a fairy story of the humans as much as it is a human story of the Elves.

Aragorn's purpose for telling – or rather singing – the story to the hobbits is to cheer them up, to offer then consolation through a degree of escape from their dark predicament. Curiously this is parallel to the situation in which a pre-cursor to the poem, there named 'Light as Leaf on Lindentree', appears in Tolkien's alliterative *Lay of the Children of Húrin*, where we are told that Halog 'Then a song he made them for sorrow's lightening / a sudden sweetness in the silent wood'.[15] In both cases we see how the song offers the same kind of consolation and escape to the human listeners.

In Rivendell we also meet the enchantment of which Tolkien speaks in his essay *On Fairy-Stories* when, after the feast, Frodo comes under the spell of the Elven-song so that it almost seem to him 'that the words took shape, and visions of far lands and bright things that he had never yet imagined opened out before him' This is emphasised by the tale of Aragorn and Arwen when Aragorn first meets Arwen while singing about Lúthien and he thought 'that he had strayed into a dream, or else that he had received the gift of the Elf-minstrels, who can make the things of which they sing appear before the eyes of those that listen' (*LotR*, 'Here Follows a Part of the Tale of Aragorn and Arwen', 1387).

Frodo's and Aragorn's experiences here are excellent examples of that enchantment of which Tolkien speaks in the essay, which

> produces a Secondary World into which both designer and spectator can enter, to the satisfaction of their senses while they are inside; but in its purity it is artistic in desire and purpose. (*OFS*, 64)

Again, Tolkien is not merely speaking of some generic elves – he is, in *On Fairy-Stories*, speaking specifically of his own Eldar. It may be significant that at

15. J.R.R Tolkien, *The Lays of Beleriand*, ed. Christopher Tolkien, George Allen & Unwin, London, 1985, p. 108.

the first excursion into 'the first and in some ways the most perilous of Tolkien's perilous realms'[16] ends with the four travelling hobbits meeting another character that can also produce this Elvish enchantment, Tom Bombadil.

The songs sung by both Gimli (in Moria) and Legolas (in Lothlórien) have elements of fairy-story or folk-tale told in a lyrical form. As so many other songs in Middle-earth, these songs have the function of preserving history and confirming racial/ethnical unity – this is emphasised when Legolas' song of Nimrodel is mentioned specifically by the Galadhrim guards as one of the reasons for not stopping the company. In both cases the song also has the effect, and is sung precisely for that reason, of offering a degree of consolation and escape – like Aragorn's song of Lúthien and Beren discussed above.

Verlyn Flieger points out that 'Lórien carries more clearly than any other region of Middle-earth the trademark '*Of Faërie*.'[17] Walking in Lóthlorien is in many ways as stepping into a fairy-tale, though to Frodo it seemed 'that he had stepped over a bridge of time into a corner of the Elder Days' into a land where 'the ancient things still lived on in the waking world' (*LotR*, 'Lothlórien', 454–55). So when Frodo's blindfold is removed and he can experience Lothlórien fully, he experiences the recovery of Faërie seeing known colours 'as if he had at that moment first perceived them and made for them names new and wonderful.'[18] To Sam, however, this feels as if he was '*inside* a song' (*LotR*, 'Lothlórien', 457), making this passage relevant for the present study as a description of the feeling of the enchantment of the Elven-songs discussed above.

Along with Aragorn's application of athelas leaves, creating 'an air wholly fresh and clean and young, as if it had not before been breathed by any living thing and came new-made' (*LotR*, 'The Houses of Healing', 1136) this is the clearest example of recovery in *LotR* – of seeing colours and smelling air 'freed from the drab blur of triteness or familiarity' (*OFS*, 67). Note also that this fresh air might have come 'from shores of silver far away washed by seas of foam' referencing the 'Shores of Faery', the shores of Blessed Realm, which is, within the narrative, the ultimate Faërie. It is also significant that Aragorn's healing powers, while clearly inspired by actual medieval beliefs, within the story are attributed to his descent from Lúthien, giving Aragorn the mythic descent that allows him to be himself partially of Faërie and thus justify his ability to offer recovery, consolation and escape as healer and story-teller.

16. Flieger, 'The Theorist of the Fairy-tale', op. cit. [5].

17. Op. cit.

18. The making new names for the colours also recalls Tolkien's statement in *Mythopoeia* that 'trees are not 'trees', until so named and seen' – Frodo is himself experiencing some sense of what Tolkien speaks of in this part of the poem, and which is, within his legendarium, the domain of the first Elves – the Quendi, or 'those that speak with voices'.

The Rohirrim, the ancient Germanic people of Rohan, apparently have some surprisingly modern attitudes. In the essay, Tolkien says that 'the association of children and fairy-stories is an accident of our domestic history.' (*OFS*, 40) In Rohan, however, the old tales and stories, of their nearby Faërie are also relegated to the nurseries and the custody of the old wives, so that Gandalf remarks to Théoden that the Ents could have been recognised by children of Rohan though their king did not.

Even Aragorn had thought the Ents 'only a memory of ancient days, if indeed they were ever more than a legend of Rohan.' The Rohirric view of the legends of hobbits – or halflings – in much the same way:

> 'Halflings!' laughed the Rider that stood beside Éomer. 'Halflings! But they are only a little people in old songs and children's tales out of the North. Do we walk in legends or on the green earth in the daylight?' (*LotR*, 'The Riders of Rohan', 565)

and Aragorn's answer is of course apt as the answer for all that we see here, 'A man may do both' – not least a man talking about a fairy-story within a fairy-story.

In all fairness one should possibly be a little careful about the modernity of the Rohirric attitude towards the old tales. In early manuscript drafts to the fairy-story essay, Tolkien wrote that

> To the nursery or at least the care of children the old women also were (and still sometimes are ~~found~~) appointed, and have been so long before the stories told by ma mère l'Oye and to this they provided the foundation for the tales of Charles Perrault. I wonder if the ~~choice of~~ audience could [be] said to be chosen deliberately by the child/Master Perrault. Both took what they could get. Fairy-stories are primarily associated with children because men ~~or would be [illeg] those~~ father and mothers ordained it so.[19]

If this was the case long before Charles Perrault, then we should, perhaps, not be terribly surprised to see it happen among the Mercian-speaking Rohirrim.

This leads me directly to Gondor, which is at first represented by Boromir, who mirrors, or perhaps rather foreshadows, the attitudes of the Rohirrim,[20] saying that the tales he has heard of Fangorn to him seems 'for the most part old

19. See op. cit. [11], 'Manuscript A', p. 186.

20. Even Éomer saw this, saying about Boromir that 'More like to the swift sons of Eorl than to the grave Men of Gondor he seemed to me' (*LotR*, 'The Riders of Rohan', 567).

wives' tales, such as we tell to our children.' Boromir has little use for the old wives' tales, and the implication is that he thinks that children are the natural audience for such tales because they are the only ones who have the time and patience and gullibility for listening to them. Celeborn's response is important:

> 'Then I need say no more,' said Celeborn. 'But do not despise the lore that has come down from distant years; for oft it may chance that old wives keep in memory word of things that once were needful for the wise to know.' (*LotR*, 'Farewell to Lórien', 487)

Boromir's attitude is offset by his brother, who clearly listened to Gandalf, and supposedly also to the old wives that his brother had no patience for. Faramir not only respected Gandalf, but he also speaks with respect about Lothlórien, which as I have argued above, in itself is in a way a fairy-story (certainly by allowing mortals entry into Faërie), where Boromir almost refused to enter. Faramir, too, speaks of the peril of Faërie (or Lórien, rather), but from another perspective: gone is the dangerous witch of Lórien (whom we also meet in the beliefs of the Rohirrim), and instead his realisation of peril is tempered with his envy that Frodo and Sam 'have spoken with the White Lady.'(*LotR*, 'The Window on the West', 888)

One of the old wives of whom Boromir speaks is, of course, Ioreth. The whole exchange concerning the kings' hands and athelas in the Houses of Healing is also highly illuminating and falls in the same category as the tradition of the Ents: old truths that 'were once needful for the wise to know' that are now just 'old wives' tales such as [they] tell [their] children' – but again circumstances conspire to make these old truths once more needful for the wise to know. Ioreth, however, clearly believes in the verses that she repeats – her desire for a king in Gondor because such a king would certainly be able to heal Faramir is genuine, and Gandalf acknowledges this when naming her 'wise-woman of Gondor'. It is of course also noteworthy that the herb-master, despite his attempt to downplay the rhyme and distance himself from it, actually does know the rhyme about *athelas*, and it is he who repeats it to Aragorn and Gandalf. I would argue that despite the undeniable historicity (to the people within the story) of the days of the Kings in Gondor, the tales of these days are, in very real sense, fairy-stories to the people of Gondor in the run-up to the War of the Ring – most importantly in the sense that these stories, by looking at the Days of the Kings across a vast abyss of time, nonetheless open a door, as Tolkien says in the Fairy-Story essay, to Other Time.[21]

21. Op. cit. [11], section 40, p. 48.

In the Fairy-Story essay, Tolkien speaks about the glimpses of an underlying truth in fairy-stories, in Flieger's quotation:

> Probably ... every sub-creator wishes in some measure to be a real maker, or hopes that he is drawing on reality: hopes that the peculiar quality of this secondary world (if not all the details) are derived from Reality.... The peculiar quality of the 'joy' in successful Fantasy can thus be explained as a sudden glimpse of the underlying reality or truth.[22]

While it is quite easy to come from 'the peculiar quality of 'joy'' to the sense of glimpses of Christian truth, I think the idea of truth in fairy-stories goes further. Flieger comments on this passage, speaking of the recognition:

> that there is a reality or truth that underlies that fact. And if the writer, the sub-creator, is an honest craftsman – and Tolkien certainly was – it will sometimes be 'hard' recognition, for there are some underlying realities or truths that do not always bring joy. And if the secondary world is to reflect the primary one, it must acknowledge that.[23]

In the examples I mention above, we see Tolkien using this in another way. Here there is a quite literal truth to the 'old wives' tales' as there really *are* Ents in the Entwood, just as the hands of the king really do heal, and athelas really does restore life to the dying when lying in the king's hands. In the essay Tolkien mostly deals with authored fairy-stories, not the old folk-lore traditions that are being passed on from old wives to children, and so he speaks of the mode of truth that can be found in a successful authored fairy-story, but in his own work he also shows another way in which fairy-stories may contain glimpses of truth: the stories that have been handed down from generation to generation contain hints of glimpses of historical truth: dare I mention that Danish archaeologists believe that they have, in Lejre, found the remains of Heorot, the mead-hall that Beowulf visited?

This brings me to the last episode from *LotR* that I wish to discuss here. As the three hobbits are climbing the Stairs of Cirith Ungol, Frodo and Sam speak of the great stories, and Samwise connects their own quest with that of Beren and Lúthien asking 'Don't the great tales never end?' He goes on to speculate on future telling of their own story, in essence imagining a future fairy-tale featuring

22. Op. cit. [11], section 103, p. 77.
23. Flieger, 'J.R.R. Tolkien's World and the Fairy-story Essay', op. cit. [5], p. 7.

Frodo's and his struggle to reach the Fire. In this way we see, once more, a way for the idea of Faërie to bring *consolation* to the two hobbits, even to the point where Frodo

> laughed, a long clear laugh from his heart. Such a sound had not been heard in those places since Sauron came to Middle-earth. To Sam suddenly it seemed as if all the stones were listening and the tall rocks leaning over them.' (*LotR*, 'The Stairs of Cirith Ungol', 932)

Consolation is also one of the three effects that Tolkien, in his essay On Fairy-Stories, argues that fairy-stories have:

> And even when men are not facing hard things such as these, there are ancient limitations from which fairy-stories offer a sort of escape, and old ambitions and desires (touching the very roots of fantasy) to which they offer a kind of satisfaction and consolation.[24]

and

> The consolation of fairy-stories, the joy of the happy ending: or more correctly of the good catastrophe, the sudden joyous 'turn' (for there is no true end to any fairy-tale): this joy, which is one of the things which fairy-stories can produce supremely well, is not essentially 'escapist,' nor 'fugitive.' In its fairy-tale – or otherworld – setting, it is a sudden and miraculous grace: never to be counted on to recur.[25]

If Frodo's laughter is not sudden and miraculous (even the *stones* listened!) and if it is not a joyous turn, then I don't know what it is.

So, to conclude: Tolkien's work on his Andrew Lang lecture *On Fairy-Stories* was, according to himself, 'entirely beneficial to *The Lord of the Rings*, which was the practical demonstration of the views that I expressed.'[26] Others have done great work in showing how this connection works – how Tolkien, in *LotR*, provides the reader with recovery, consolation, and escape, and not least a eucatastrophic happy ending. How he successfully applied his theories of sub-creation to produce a work that has a remarkable degree of the 'inner consistency of reality' and which produces – certainly in me – 'secondary belief'. *LotR* is, in other words, according to Tolkien's theories as laid out in *On Fairy-Stories* a

24. Op. cit. [11], section 96, p.73.
25. Op. cit. [11], section 99, p. 75.
26. Op. cit. [9], Letter 234, p. 310.

highly successful fairy-story.

What I have tried to show here is that this does not just work for the reader of Tolkien's book – he also shows these things by letting his characters experience recovery, escape and consolation from fairy-stories, he shows how fairy-stories can contain underlying truths and even 'things that once were needful for the wise to know.' I argue that Tolkien explicates his theories of fairy-stories in *LotR*, not just by making the story itself a good fairy-story, but also by letting his characters interact with metafictional fairy-stories within the greater fairy-story.

Finally I will suggest that Tolkien supports all of this by hinting at a hierarchy of wisdom (or perhaps something that we might call spiritual nobility) within Middle-earth that is somewhat correlated with the reaction to the Faërie in their midst, both in the form fairy-stories, of old wisdom passed down from days of old, and in the form of the inhabitants of Faërie – the Elves. This would work both for individual characters and for peoples – those who are portrayed as the wiser and more noble will also, in general, have a more positive reaction to their Faërie – knowing, accepting and trusting the wisdom of fairy-tales, old folk-wisdom and Elves.

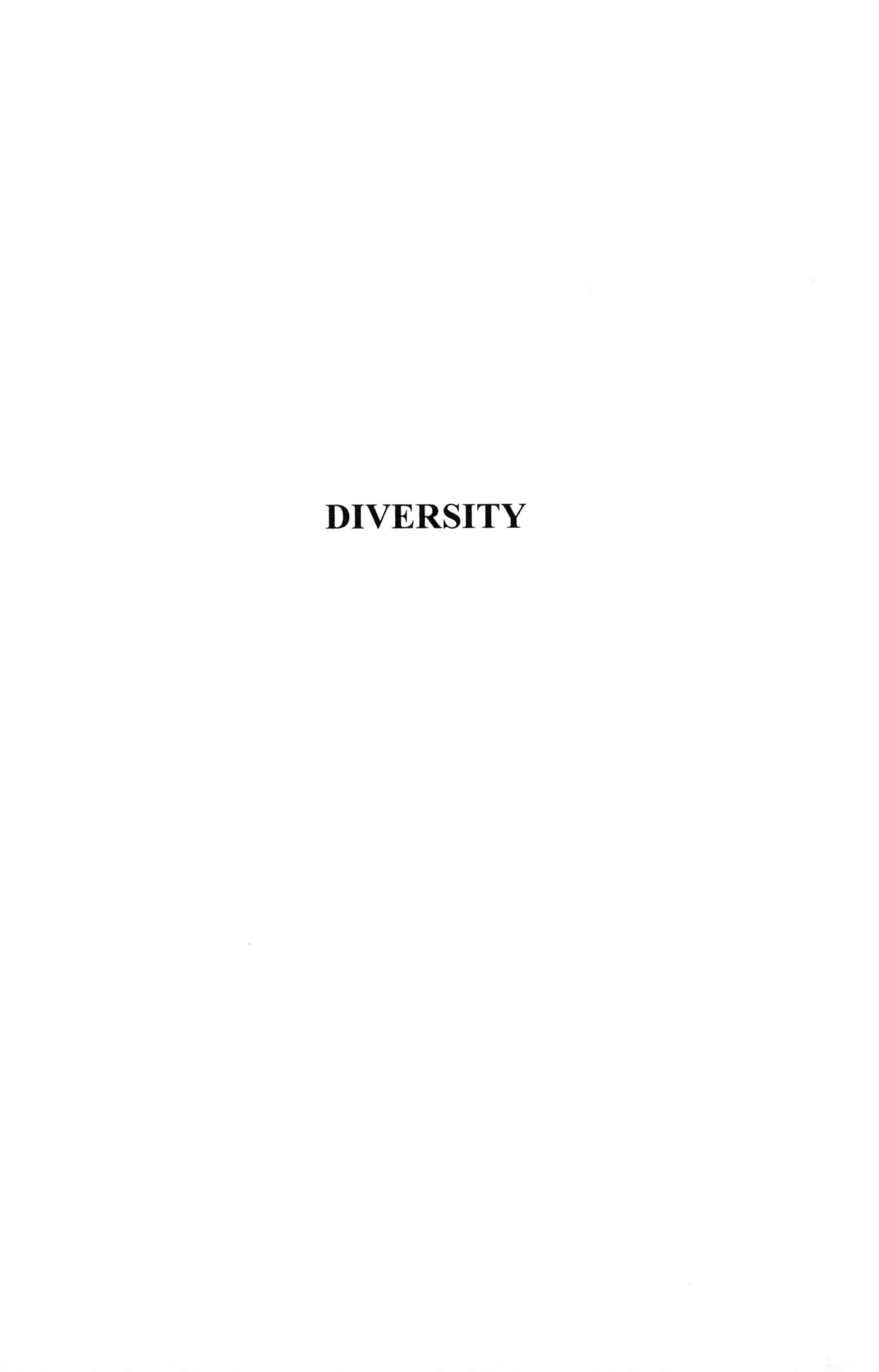

DIVERSITY

'Tolkien and Nonsense'

Maureen F. Mann

This paper considers the nature of Tolkien's nonsense in light of theories on this distinctive type of humour. It examines his use of the word 'nonsense' in his letters and his fiction and his ideas about language invention in the essay 'A Secret Vice' before considering how this theorising of nonsense is applicable to Farmer Giles of Ham, The Adventures of Tom Bombadil, The Hobbit, and The Lord of the Rings. It discovers many cogent similarities with contemporary theorising in Tolkien's work. Just as significantly, it finds important differences from this theorising due particularly to his interest in nursery rhymes and ancient language. The paper demonstrates that Tom Bombadil provides more than simply 'an adventure along the way' imported into the Ring story: he represents an aspect of language significant to Tolkien's thought.

To begin, I would like to consider a few of Tolkien's comments in which he uses the word 'nonsense', in both his fiction and non-fiction. My paper will not be exhaustive by any means, as it is a preliminary excursion into the realm of nonsense.

First some words from Bilbo as he contemplates the possibility he has overslept the dwarves.

> 'Don't be a fool, Bilbo Baggins!' he said to himself, 'thinking of dragons and all that outlandish nonsense at your age.' (*TH*, 'Roast Mutton', 43)[1]

This is the 'Baggins' side of Bilbo speaking, placing dragons, the element of Tolkien's greatest desire in fairie, in the context of things which are foolish or extravagant conduct, or absurd, senseless or worthless stuff (OED) in contrast to propriety, banality, and common sense. Bilbo's thoughts come with the assumption that nonsense belongs to children and is something we must grow out of. This might seem to be a commonplace use of the word, but its association with dragons and fairie will prove important.

My next quotation comes from a letter written to Edith Bratt while Tolkien was in training during World War I.

1. J.R.R. Tolkien, *The Hobbit*, HarperCollins, London, 1998, Chapter 2.

> This miserable drizzling afternoon I have been reading up old military lecture-notes again:—and getting bored with them after an hour and a half. I have done some touches to my nonsense fairy language – to its improvement. I often long to work at it and don't let myself 'cause though I love it so it does seem such a mad hobby![2]

This excerpt reflects Tolkien's unease with yet great desire for his hobby of language invention. Here, clearly, his concept of nonsense is related to his concepts of fairie.

One more example from the *Letters*, written in response to Stanley Unwin's reaction on first reading material of the *legendarium*.

> My chief joy comes from learning that *The Silmarillion* is not rejected with scorn. I have suffered a sense of fear and bereavement, quite ridiculous, since I let this private and beloved nonsense out; and I think if it had seemed to you to be nonsense I should have felt really crushed.[3]

Once again, Tolkien expresses his great desire for his 'mad hobby'. Desire, tension, and loss are all significant aspects of his thought here. What is intriguing about this statement is that Tolkien uses two different meanings of the word 'nonsense' in one sentence. The first is closer to 'silliness' while the later use is closer to 'worthless' – or perhaps simply 'unintelligible', a non-judgmental meaning Tolkien gives to the word 'nonsense' in the Preface to *The Adventures of Tom Bombadil* – a meaning that is absent from the OED. Once again, 'nonsense' is intimately related through his emotional involvement to the mythology which grew out of his invented languages.

These uses of the word 'nonsense' suggest a particular attitude which is not found in contemporary theories about nonsense, as represented by Roderick McGillis's chapter 'Nonsense' in *A Companion to Victorian Poetry*. Tolkien's attitude has more affinity to critics of nonsense such as George Orwell and G. K. Chesterton – yet there are many similarities to contemporary theory nonetheless.

Tolkien was familiar with nonsense as a literary genre and not only as a notion or concept. This familiarity is shown particularly in the essay 'A Secret Vice' (given that title by Christopher Tolkien, from Tolkien's own phrase and use).[4]

---

2. Humphrey Carpenter, ed., *The Letters of J.R.R. Tolkien*, with the assistance of Christopher Tolkien, Allen & Unwin, London, 1981, Letter 4, p. 8.
3. Humphrey Carpenter, *J.R.R. Tolkien: A Biography*, Allen & Unwin, London, 1977, p. 184. Carpenter quotes Tolkien's reply to Unwin from 16 December 1937.
4. Dimitra Fimi, *Tolkien, Race and Cultural History: From Fairies to Hobbits*, Palgrave

The example of *animalic* (his first invented language) which Tolkien admits to is full of ludic fun and a giddy enjoyment of pricking the pomposity of polite decorum: '*dog nightingale woodpecker forty*' means 'You are an ass' he says, the word for 'forty' being 'donkey' but acquiring the 'converse meaning' as Tolkien calls it.[5] It shows a typical adolescent willingness to challenge pomposity but this is a quality common to much literary nonsense. More relevant is what Tolkien called 'one idiotic connected fragment ('A Secret Vice', 203) of his second invented language, *Nevbosh* or 'New Nonsense'. For the purposes of clarity, here is Humphrey Carpenter's translation:

> There was an old man who said 'How
> Can I possibly carry my cow?
> For if I were to ask it
> To get in my basket
> It would make such a terrible row!'[6]

Carpenter's translation makes clear the rhythm and rhyme scheme of a limerick (although Carpenter mistranslates '*bocte*' i. e. pocket – as 'baskets'). Clearly, the Novboshites wrote a traditional five-line *aabba*-rhyming limerick that begins with a specific person (if not a specific place), as Carolyn Wells has observed of limericks.[7] We might wish we had explicit allusions to Edward Lear's limericks, but the Novboshites could have picked up the form from the habit of their Latin lessons.[8] Tolkien claims that *Nevbosh* represented a new level of language invention where the speakers were attempting to '*invent* 'new words' (groups of sounds) to represent familiar notions' ('A Secret Vice', 203). This is the delight in neologisms which McGillis ascribes to nonsense;[9] it demonstrates that the Novboshites were using language with delight in sound and play and with less concern for being serious about meaning or communication.

Macmillan, Basingstoke, 2010, p. 77.

5. J.R.R. Tolkien, 'A Secret Vice', in Christopher Tolkien, ed., *The Monsters and the Critics and Other Essays*, HarperCollins, London, 2006, 198–223, p. 200.

6. Op. cit. [3], p. 36. The original Nevbosh (op. cit., p. 203) is as follows:
   Dar fys ma vel gom co palt 'hoc
   Pys go iskili far maino woc?
   Pro si go fys do roc de
   Do cat ym maino bocte
   De volt fac soc ma taimful gyroc!'

7. Carolyn Wells, *A Nonsense Anthology*, Scribner's, New York, 1905, p. xvii.

8. Op. cit., p. xxii.

9. Roderick McGillis, 'Nonsense', in Richard Cronin, Alison Chapman and Antony H. Harrison, eds, *A Companion to Victorian Poetry*, Blackwell, Oxford, 2002, 155–70, p. 159.

'A Secret Vice' shows other intriguing affinities with theorising about nonsense. For instance, the title fits nicely with Tolkien's claims about desire and pleasure in the invention of language – 'vice' contrasts well with, for example, the 'They' of Lear's limericks, who Orwell describes as 'sober citizens in bowler hats who are always anxious to stop you doing anything worth doing'.[10] Tolkien's essay is replete with statements about the pleasure of language. His claims that the *animalic*-speakers delighted less in the secrecy of the language and more in the fun of the 'linguistic ability' ('A Secret Vice', 201), making 'so-called articulate noises' ('A Secret Vice', 202). For instance, they adopted the word *lint*, meaning 'quick, clever, nimble' ('A Secret Vice', 205)

> because the relations between the sounds *lint* and the ideas proposed for association with them gave *pleasure*.... The instinct for 'linguistic invention' – the fitting of notion to oral symbol, and *pleasure in contemplating the new relation established*, is rational, and not perverted.... Certainly it is the *contemplation* of the relation between sound and notion which is a main source of pleasure. ('A Secret Vice', 205-06)

Tolkien reiterates that this pleasure is separate from the '*communicative* aspect of language' ('A Secret Vice', 208) and is more keenly 'pleasure in articulate sound, and in the symbolic use of it' ('A Secret Vice', 208). He concludes that this 'is an attenuated emotion, but may be very piercing—this construction of sound to give pleasure' ('A Secret Vice', 219). This delight in sound has some relationship with contemporary theory. Roderick McGillis makes the argument that 'Desire is perhaps the secret of nonsense'.[11] In his particular examples, McGillis examines secret codes for sexual desire in Victorian nonsense. However, Tolkien's desire is closer to Roland Barthes' explorations of what we enjoy when reading which he presents in *The Pleasure of the Text*. Tolkien's inventor of language, who sidesteps the limitations of a given language for the delights of creating new relations, is close to Barthes' anti-hero, the reader of the text, who finds bliss in cohabitation with language.[12] Tolkien's concluding remarks on the free adjective, which he claims no language has yet attained, where one may say

10. George Orwell, 'Nonsense Poetry (1945)', in his *Fifty Orwell Essays*, Project Gutenberg, Australia http://gutenberg.net.au/ebooks03/0300011h.html#part29 [accessed 12 November 2015].

11. Op. cit. [9], p. 159.

12. 'Now this anti-hero exists: he is the reader of the text at the moment he takes his pleasure'. Roland Barthes, *The Pleasure of the Text*, trans. Richard Miller, Hill and Wang, New York, 1975, p. 3.

green sun or dead life, are logical contradictions which would possibly also have pleased Barthes.

Tolkien prioritises this delight in sound over the communicative function of language. In comparison, McGillis argues that the intense focus of nonsense upon its own noise and sound is a parody of the desire to communicate, as well as a strategy for dealing with the unpleasant realities of Victorian life. Nonsense, says McGillis, is 'a way of ironising from a distance'.[13] In Tolkien, the invention of language is clearly a distancing from boredom or unpleasantness that may involve irony. The first person Tolkien identifies as a devotee is a fellow soldier 'who revealed himself in a moment of extreme ennui' ('A Secret Vice', 199):

> We were listening to somebody lecturing on map-reading, or camp-hygiene, or the art of sticking a fellow through without (in defense of Kipling) bothering who God sent the bill to; rather we were trying to avoid listening, though the Guard's English, and voice, is penetrating. The man next to me said suddenly in a dreamy voice: 'Yes, I think I shall express the accusative case by a prefix!' ('A Secret Vice', 199)

The last we hear of this fellow is that 'Probably he was blown to bits in the very moment of deciding upon some ravishing method of indicating the subjunctive ('A Secret Vice', 200).

McGillis attributes many subversive traits to Victorian nonsense but perhaps the most predominant one is its ridicule of the 'high seriousness of canonised poetry.[14] The preeminent example of this is Lewis Carroll's *Jabberwocky*. I am not on a source hunt here, but simply want to point out that Tolkien was familiar with the specific characteristics and traits of nonsense as a genre. Tolkien had to have been familiar with Carroll's poem because he used it to chastise critics of *Beowulf*:

> For it is of their nature that the jabberwocks of historical and antiquarian research burble in the tulgy wood of conjecture, flitting from one tum-tum tree to another.[15]

The allusion is all the more powerful because *Jabberwocky*, in the words of Roderick McGillis, 'is a poem about the power of poetry to cut through evasion,

13. Op.cit. [9], p. 155.
14. Op. cit. [9], p. 158.
15. J.R.R. Tolkien, 'Beowulf: The Monsters and the Critics', in Christopher Tolkien, ed., *The Monsters and the Critics and Other Essays*, HarperCollins, London, 2006, 5–48, p. 9.

bluster and huffery-puffery in language',[16] and here Tolkien is ridiculing the short-sightedness of those who claim to understand language well. More evidence that Tolkien was quite well aware of the tendency of nonsense to challenge humbug.

McGillis mentions several other traits of nonsense which we will see in Tolkien's own nonsense, such as its mix of the comic and the morbid, its tendency to lampoon, it's speaking to a dual audience. I will focus on only a few of McGillis' traits. There are two significant differences between his theorising and Tolkien's imaginative writing, amidst the similarities. One is that Tolkien works within a tradition which McGillis does not directly address (it is not, after all, Victorian), the folk tradition of nonsense, particularly as found in nursery rhymes. The other is Tolkien's own vision of ancient language and his desire not to eliminate it but to extrapolate it. The link between Tolkien's ideas about language creation and nonsense lies in the nature of both to push the boundaries of normal or banal communication. Both challenge a sense of reality that is itself too restrictive or mundane. The clue lies in his concept of 'unintelligible'.

I would like to turn now to *Farmer Giles of Ham*. Bilbo Baggins, we learn, is not the only character who associates legends, dragons, nonsense, and childhood delight; so too does the narrator of *Farmer Giles* who talks about Giles' fondness as a child, before he learnt sense, for tales about dragon slaying.[17] Here again, delight, childhood, and escape are connected. For G.K. Chesterton, this is an essential element in nonsense: '... the idea of ***escape***, of escape into a world where things are not fixed horribly in an eternal appropriateness, where apples grow on pear-trees, and any odd man you meet may have three legs'.[18] Giles' story is often regarded as a parody of Arthurian legend and of critics who quarry literature for historical and anthropological information,[19] but there is a great deal in this story which pertains to theories of nonsense as well, not the least of which are two allusions to nursery rhymes. The first is an historical reference to the time of King Coel in the Foreword, who has come down to us as that 'merry old soul who called for his pipe and his bowl and his fiddlers three'. The second occurs when the dragon taunts the King with the refrain from the Humpty Dumpty nursery rhyme, 'All the king's horses and all the King's men' (*Giles*, 159). (In this case, the line becomes a threat to kill them all.)

Like much nonsense, *Farmer Giles* has a mixed readership. Tolkien first

16. Op. cit. [9], p. 168.

17. J.R.R. Tolkien, *Tales From the Perilous Realm*, HarperCollins, London, 2008, p. 125.

18. G.K. Chesterton, 'A Defense of Nonsense', in his *The Defendant*, Project Gutenberg, <http://www.gutenberg.org/files/12245/12245-h/12245-h.htm#A_DEFENCE_OF_NONSENSE> [accessed 12 November 2015].

19. Christina Scull and Wayne G. Hammond, *The J.R.R. Tolkien Companion and Guide*, vol. 2: *Reader's Guide*, Houghton Mifflin, Boston, 2006, pp. 60, 294.

told the story as 'an impromptu tale' to his children.[20] It went through several expansions to satisfy editor's wishes for length. Tolkien himself said that its revision 'has taken on a rather more adult and satiric flavour',[21] although he also noted that children still enjoyed it.[22] As Scull and Hammond have reported, C.A. Furth, the editor, complained that the tale was a selling problem because it was neither a children's story nor a novel.[23] Eventually it was published with Pauline Baynes's illustrations to flesh out its length, but critical reviews commented that it was not quite a children's book.[24] McGillis points out that Lear's and Carroll's works were also written for children, yet have found enduring appeal with adults. He argues that

> nonsense speaks to a dual audience.... [its] appeal to ... both adult and child, is part of its subversive appeal. Nonsense thus breaks the barriers of high art, art that through sophistication and complexity speaks only to a learned and urbane audience.... the adult and child reader share a laugh at pretention and high seriousness'.[25]

The parody of the four wise clerks of Oxenford with their definition of blunderbuss of course does exactly this, suggesting the failure of the kind of scholarship which Tolkien had castigated so humorously in *Beowulf: The Monsters and the Critics*. One could argue that all Tolkien's narratives are devoted to breaking down this barrier, but the quality is particularly strong in his nonsense.

The definition of 'blunderbuss' (to say nothing of its anachronistic presence) exemplifies how nonsense challenges conventional communication. The definition was apparently first included in response to a query from one of the children, but its survival through revisions satisfies another purpose. Nonsense, says McGillis, 'draws attention to the inevitable slippage between signifier and signified'[26] – that is, slippage between a name and the thing it names; if one word has such 'slippage', how much more the attempt to completely explain one word with several words. Chesterton talks about how the shapes of things defy our 'trivial definitions' in his 'Defense of Nonsense'.[27] And Marnie Parsons argues

20. Op. cit., p. 289.
21. Op. cit. [19], p. 291; op. cit. [2], Letter 31, p. 39.
22. Op. cit. [19], p. 291.
23. Op. cit.
24. Op. cit.
25. Op. cit. [9], p. 163.
26. Op. cit. [9], p. 156.
27. Op. cit. [18].

that 'When Lewis Carroll and Edward Lear take definitions and classifications literally, Nonsense is the 'predictable' result.[28] Tolkien himself gave an opinion on definitions in a letter to his aunt Jane Neave:

> As for *plenilune* and *argent*, they are beautiful words *before* they are understood – I wish I could have the pleasure of meeting them for the first time again! – and how is one to know them till one does meet them? And surely the first meeting should be in a living context, and not in a dictionary, like dried flowers in a hortus siccus![29]

Definitions are ripe for ridicule in nonsense. The reality of Farmer Giles' blunderbuss defies the definition offered by the Oxenford Clerks, judging by all the 'nots' in the passage which follows the definition. And if there were any more nonsensical result of its use, it is that the giant goes home thinking he's been stung by a fierce insect and only at the end of the tale does he learn otherwise from the dragon. The giant can no more recognise reality than the definition can reflect it.

Nonsense 'delights in things of the body, including food and drink' says McGillis,[30] and he suggests that the riot in the pleasures of bodily existence in nonsense is almost carnivalesque. Whether that specific quality fits *Farmer Giles* may be argued, but the tale does contain many comic depictions of bodies, physical contortions, and ungainly movements; it delights in frailty and deformity and humiliation (of the dragon and the King, at least, both of whom are characters with inflated opinions of themselves).The giant is almost totally described by his body and its calamitous effects: he is near-sighted and rather deaf, while his head has often 'left his feet to look after themselves' (*Giles*, 105); he doesn't just kill the cow Galatea; he flattens her. Giles's assault on the giant is full of hilarious physicality, for the giant's 'large, ugly face' appears incongruously over the top of a hill and so Giles takes a startled shot with the fully loaded blunderbuss and hits the giant in the eye and nose. The dragon is prone to making bad jokes about the taste of the people he's eaten, while satiation is often his downfall. Giles's wife Agatha is said to become 'a queen of great size and majesty.... There was no getting around Queen Agatha—at least it was a long walk' (*Giles*, 162). 'There is a great deal of drink spilt down throats in the village, particularly Giles'. 'Next market day he got enough free drink to float a boat: that is to say, he nearly had his fill' (*Giles*, 112). It takes several days of ale-quaffing for Giles to find

28. Marnie Parsons, *Touch Monkeys: Nonsense Strategies for Reading Twentieth-Century Poetry*, University of Toronto Press, Toronto, 1994, p. 12.
29. Op. cit. [2], Letter 234, p. 310.
30. Op. cit. [9], p. 163.

his courage to go dragon hunting and he nearly gives up the hunt to return for his dinner before coming upon the dragon unexpectedly (*Giles*, 130). At court there is a good bit of feasting on Dragon's Tail, not the real dragon's tail, but a culinary concoction. Giles' armour is a regaling of details related to the condition of things, which mostly are old, dusty, rusty and second-hand and the butt of the dragon's jokes. The retreat between Giles and the dragon emphasises puffing and blowing, bawling and shouting, as if Giles were watching a mere horse race (*Giles*, 134).Giles's tribute to the king is 'six oxtails and a pint of bitter' (*Giles*, 161) – a comedown from the real dragon's tail of historical legend. And Garm repeatedly contends with the dragon's tail. There are a great many tangible things of the body in the world of Farmer Giles.

McGillis argues that names are important in Nonsense and lists some of them that have become household names in our time: Jumlies, Jabberwocky, Snark. To his list can be added Lear's Pobbles. In Tolkien's tale, names are foregrounded and usually a humorous incongruity between characters and their names prevails. The narrator quickly dispenses with Giles's Latin name, suggesting that the current age has less time for the leisurely pursuit of naming. Then we are told there is both book-Latin and dog-Latin, although of course Garm speaks only the Vulgar tongue and not dog-Latin. As McGillis notes parenthetically, 'Latin has proved a useful vehicle for nonsense' (*Giles*, 165).When the dragon and Giles first meet, each warily refuses to provide his name. When the townspeople encourage Giles to go a-dragon hunting, they invent a plethora of majestically-sounding names for him and for his sword; Giles is given multiple titles and names after his victory and his crowning. The dragon has a preposterously mixed Greek and Latin name; the cow is named for a sea nymph from Greek mythology whose name means 'she who is milk-white'. Giles' wife's name is Agatha, but she is more the nagging shrew than a godly woman or wife. (Her command to 'drown that dog in the morning' has all the arbitrary silliness of the Red Queen's 'Off with her head' as Garm never deserves the slurs and threats flung at him). The blacksmith, the conversely named Sunny Sam, gloomily foretells a bad fate for the meeting on the feast day of two canonised popes: 'Hilarious and Felix! I don't like the sound of them' (*Giles*, 138). The giant has no name while 'Garmr' is a ferocious watchdog at the gate of Hell in Norse mythology. The concluding analysis of place names lampoons philology. '*Must* a name mean something?' asks Alice of Humpty Dumpty.[31] Much of the fun in *Farmer Giles* asks just what meaning belongs in the possible incongruities of a name.

Throughout his essay McGillis argues that parody is a strong element in

31. Lewis Carroll, *Alice's Adventures in Wonderland and Through the Looking-Glass*, Penguin, London, 1980, p. 182.

nonsense, whether parody of the seriousness of the traditional love lyric, or of nature poetry, or of canonical poets. He argues, through a complex argument which I will not rehearse, that 'Jabberwocky' revisions the heroic world of *Beowulf.* (The first stanza of the poem was first published with the title Stanza of Anglo-Saxon Poetry.).Whether Tolkien knew of this stanza in the periodical *Mish-Mash*, and Carroll's accompanying parody of critical interpretation and poetic communication,[32] I cannot say. What does seem plausible is that *Farmer Giles* is a parody of heroic dragon hunting stories. (It was, after all, written roughly in the same years as *The Hobbit.*) The absurd dialogues of Giles and Chrysophylax defeat any expectations of violence and turn their encounters into battles of wits. They lack the riddling perplexities of Alice's conversation with Humpty Dumpty and the Red Queen – Tolkien was a linguist, not a mathematician – but they play with knightly behaviour and courtly civility. They begin with the completely unexpected greetings of 'Good morning' (*Giles*, 131), and the Dragon's 'Then we meet by good luck.... The pleasure is mine' is ironically reiterated on their second meeting by Giles (*Giles*, 148). On both occasions neither characters' words truthfully represent their motivations and the essence of game which surrounds their conversation seems to be one each recognises; the narrator tells us that Chrysophylax licks his lips as 'a sign of amusement' (*Giles*, 131) rather than gustatory expectation. And of course the challenge is made all the more ludicrous by the paradox of his challenger – not a knight but 'a bold farmer' and a ginger to boot (*Giles*, 133). Both eagerly proclaim their desire not to kill each other, a reversal of the expected situation. Giles even taunts Chrysophylax's bargaining with the word 'nonsense' (*Giles*, 135) – an exclamation of disbelief rather than 'absurd', but the incongruity is identified and extends to much of their relationship. The two do manage to communicate, but find a conclusion completely at odds with dragon hunting adventures. This is not quite as serious as McGillis's claim that nonsense through parody targets the privilege of canonised works (Giles, *156*). It is rather, simply, fun, possibly an asterisk version of dragon tales in the same way that Tom Shippey has described Tolkien's philological work with poems and nursery rhymes.

Farmer Giles of Ham is not the only work of Tolkien to open with a playful preface. *The Adventures of Tom Bombadil* also has a preface that imitates scholarly style. It explicitly identifies the contents of its book as nonsense or 'nonsense rhyme'.[33] Of the Red Book we are told that many of the carelessly written verses

32. 'This is an obscure, but yet deeply-affecting relic of ancient Poetry'. Lewis Carroll, *The Annotated Alice: The Definitive Edition Alice's Adventures in Wonderland and Through the Looking-Glass*, Norton, New York, 2000, p. 149.

33. Op. cit. [17], p. 169. Subsequent references to *Adventures* refers to this edition of *The Adventures of Tom Bombadil.*

'are nonsense, now often unintelligible even when legible, or half-remembered fragments' (*Adventures*, 169).This attitude towards nonsense sounds similar not to McGillis's theorising but to comments made by George Orwell. For Orwell, the bulk of English folk nonsense lies 'in nursery rhymes and scraps of folk poetry, some of which may not have been strictly nonsensical at the start, but have become so because their original application has been forgotten'. For instance, Orwell suggests that when Edgar in *King Lear*, disguised as Mad Tom, quotes 'Pillicock sat on Pillicock hill' and other refrains, Edgar is uttering nonsense, that is, fragments coming from largely forgotten ballads. Tom Shippey has suggested that Tolkien 'tried his hand' at two versions of 'The Man in the Moon' in order to 'provide a narrative and semi-rational frame for the string of totally irrational non sequiturs which we now call 'nursery rhymes'.[34] For Shippey, the 'Man in the Moon Poems' are possible reconstructions of a primary text that has been lost. They are an attempt to make meaningful what now appears irrational or incongruous. It is, however, also a sign of 'nonsense's polyphony'[35] that Tolkien can produce two different ur-texts.

It is perhaps also worth noting that 'much nonsense comes with a visual aid', according to McGillis.[36] For him, illustrations such as those with Lear's work complicate the decoding of the limericks. *Alice in Wonderland* is renowned for Tenniel's original illustrations as well as for the great variety of illustrators coming after him who have tried their hand at depicting Wonderland. Pauline Baynes was asked to illustrate the Bombadil book specifically because Tolkien had been so satisfied with her illustrations for *Farmer Giles of Ham*:

> If I dare say so, the things sent to you.... were conceived as a series of very definite, clear and precise pictures – fantastical, or nonsensical perhaps, but not dreamlike! And I thought of you, because you seem able to produce wonderful pictures with a touch of 'fantasy', but primarily bright and clear visions of things that one might really see.[37]

Tolkien clearly had a definite sense of what he was doing with these poems, and that sense included a particular notion of nonsense as something dealing very tangibly with the thingness of things, a quality McGillis argues in his study of nonsense.[38]

---

34. Tom Shippey, *The Road to Middle-earth*, rev. edn, Houghton Mifflin, Boston, 2003, p. 36.
35. Op. cit. [9], p.157. McGillis quotes the theorist Lecercle.
36. Op. cit. [9], p. 160.
37. Op. cit. [2], Letter 235, p. 312.
38. Op. cit. [9], p. 164.

The Preface to the Bombadil book also identifies another quality of nonsense, one which returns us to 'A Secret Vice'. The stanza of Bilbo's 'When winter first begins to bite' is clearly offered as a fragment of nonsense (*Adventures*, Preface, 171) which delights in pleasing, harmonious sound; this quality is identified specifically as hobbit taste. The poem 'Errantry' is described as 'another kind which seems to have amused hobbits: a rhyme or story which returns to its own beginning, and so may be recited until the hearers revolt' (*Adventures*, Preface, 170). We are told, as well, that hobbits

> are fond of strange words, and of rhyming and metrical tricks—in their simplicity Hobbits evidently regarded such things as virtues or graces, though they were, no doubt, mere imitations of Elvish practices. They are also, at least on the surface, lighthearted or frivolous, though sometimes one may uneasily suspect that more is meant than meets the ear' (*Adventures*, Preface, 174).

'Errantry' is replete with rhythm, euphonious sounds, assonance – the kind of qualities that Tolkien enjoined especially in the lecture 'A Secret Vice'. These points suggest that this Preface elucidates an important part of Tolkien's concept of nonsense – a kind that McGillis does not consider because he accepts Noel Malcolm's argument that

> nonsense existed only in a literary culture.... [because it is a genre] deeply self-conscious about form [which] foregrounds such features of language as onomastics, rhythm, rhyme, stanza shapes and rhetorical devices – especially paradox, prosopoeia, repetition, alliteration, and paronomasia'.[39]

Yet formal rhetorical features of language can be found in children's nursery rhyme as well as satisfying hobbits' taste in literature. One need not know the formal rhetorical terms to intuit the music of words. Chesterton again is relevant here:

> Now the old nursery rhymes were honestly directed to give children pleasure. Many of them have genuine elements of poetry, but they are not primarily meant to be poetry, because they are simply meant to be pleasure.The imagery of it is exactly what is wanted for the first movements of imagination when it experiments in incongruity. For it

39. Op. cit. [9], pp. 155–56 and *passim*.

> is full of familiar objects in fantastic conjunction.[40]

Here again is the idea of pleasure in language play, something that for Tolkien can belong to any and all, not only the literary elite. It is particularly appropriate for hobbits to favour such nonsense, because a taste for incongruity in rhyme is a way to avoid incongruity in real life, a trait most hobbits display, except the Tooks. McGillis argues that 'The Victorians' delight in nonsense ... fits with their delight in things simple and straightforward'.[41] True enough of hobbits too.

Orwell addresses another point which the theorists omit but one which very clearly suggests how extensive the landscapes of nonsense can be and how Tolkien can be seen working within that terrain:

> Lear was one of the first writers to deal in pure fantasy, with imaginary countries and made-up words, without any satirical purpose. His poems are not all of them equally nonsensical; some of them get their effect by a perversion of logic, but they are all alike in that their underlying feeling is sad and not bitter. They express a kind of amiable lunacy, a natural sympathy with whatever is weak and absurd.[42]

'Fantasy,' 'imaginary countries,' 'made-up words' are all eminently applicable also to Tolkien's works while 'amiable lunacy' suits Tom Bombadil as well as 'Errantry' and the two Men in the Moon poems. The final three – 'The Hoard,' 'The Sea-Bell,' and 'The Last Ship' – all convey a deeply sad undertone of loss. These are not lighthearted poems about nothing, yet they hint at a world beyond the mundane and banal one we all know. Tolkien and Orwell share a similar understanding of nonsense.

No doubt many of you already are anticipating that the Tra la la lally Elves' song in *The Hobbit* is nonsense. You are right, of course, as that is exactly what the narrator calls it: 'So they laughed and sang in the trees; and pretty fair nonsense I daresay you think it. Not that they would care; they would only laugh all the more if you told them so' (*TH*, 'A Short Rest', 68). Yet there is another similarity as well. The song operates similarly to the function of nonsense to provide escape from the confines of reality into something less predictably constraining, something related to 'ironising at a distance', for the Elves are

40. G. K. Chesterton, 'Child Psychology and Nonsense (1921)', *Illustrated London News*, 15 October 1921 <http://nonsenselit.wordpress.com/g-k-chesterton-child-psychology-and-nonsense-1921/> [accessed 12 November 2015]
41. Op. cit. [9], p. 168.
42. Op. cit. [10].

attempting to lighten the spirits of the travellers by making fun of their travails. So also is the lullaby nonsense that the Elves sing to Bilbo in the final chapter, with its incongruous blossoming stars, flowering moon, and bright windows of Night (*TH*, 'The Last Stage', 358); its gentle cadences are a release into the realm of sleep. Nonsense, not simply humour, is a strong feature of *The Hobbit*.

First, the story is consistent with other works in the nonsense tradition in having a dual audience of child and adult. Second, a constant theme is to play with meaning. Gandalf's first greeting with Bilbo and the jokes about what 'Good Morning!' means can stand beside any of Alice's absurd dialogues in Wonderland (*TH*, 'An Unexpected Party', 14–16; *passim*): 'What a lot of things you do use Good morning for!' said Gandalf. 'Now you mean that you want to get rid of me' (*TH*, 'An Unexpected Party', 16).The greeting involves as well joking about names – 'I am Gandalf and Gandalf means me' (*TH*, 'An Unexpected Party', 16). It is no mistake that Gandalf searches for a thief in the Took family and the extensive explication of the mark on the door provides another bit of zaniness about meaning – in fact, there is quite a bit of meaning given for a single mark. Third, the story of Golfimbul's defeat and the genesis of the game of golf combines a common theme of dismemberment with another joke about a name – and it is about a rabbit hole as well. A fourth example: the dwarves' washing up song lampoons Bilbo's fuss and bother about domestic decorum (*TH*, 'An Unexpected Party', 24) – another example of nonsense deflating high seriousness shown to mundane matters.[43]

Interestingly, nothing in the depiction of the trolls is nonsense – slapstick, I would argue; nor is there any nonsense in the queer lodgings of Beorn, nor in the Laketown events, nor in the scenes with the goblins inside the mountain. The riddle game with Gollum is too sacred to deserve nonsense; it forms the basis for Bilbo's heroism, where word replaces sword; it is an intensely profound game of survival without any pomposity to it; the riddling with Smaug does not rise to the level of absurdity, although again we have play with names, a strategy for which the narrator praises Bilbo. Nor is the goblins' song of taunting and ridicule in 'Out of the Frying-Pan into the Fire' quite nonsense: it is too uncomfortably close to what likely is to happen; there is nothing incongruously pretentious about the situation. This absence is consistent with McGillis's argument that Victorian nonsense 'avoids the overtly serious'.[44]

Yet for all its focus on tangible things and physicality, nonsense, McGillis suggests, 'reminds us that the world we know is perhaps less tangible than we

43. Op. cit. [9], p. 158.
44. Op. cit. [9], p. 163.

might like to believe'.[45] Perhaps this is one reason why Bilbo's loss of reputation does not matter. This characteristic is argued slightly differently by Chesterton:

> So long as we regard a tree as an obvious thing, naturally and reasonably created for a giraffe to eat, we cannot properly wonder at it. It is when we consider it as a prodigious wave of the living soil sprawling up to the skies for no reason in particular that we take off our hats.... Everything has in fact another side to it, like the moon, the patroness of nonsense.[46]

This wonder is also what happens when trees become Ents. Again, Tolkien's nonsense challenges a common sense approach to the world.

This quality of wonder might also explain Tom Bombadil's lack of seriousness. And so I come at last to *The Lord of the Rings* with a few final observations. Tom Bombadil's hat is clearly a runcible hat. His verse obviously reflects the pure pleasure of sound without communicative effect to say nothing of their simple rhymes and refrains and euphonious sounds. His mere words have the power to heal or resolve, as is shown in his defeat of Old Man Willow and the Barrow Wight. Even Tom's prose is rhythmic. McGillis argues that a similar quality is a feature of Victorian nonsense, particularly the style of George MacDonald in *At the Back of the North Wind*, where 'language aspir[es] to the condition of pure sound',[47] and developes an 'incantatory force' such as is found in nursery rhymes.[48] This might be an appropriate time to point out that 'absurd' comes from the Latin, meaning 'out of tune, jarring, inharmonious' as well as 'out of harmony with reason or propriety' (OED).

The word 'nonsense' is used on two occasions to describe Tom and both involve sound. Frodo first hears Tom when he has been calling desperately for help as Merry and Pippin are trapped and swallowed by Old Man Willow:

> He turned around and listened, and soon there could be no doubt: someone was singing a song; a deep glad voice was singing carelessly and happily, but it was singing nonsense: *Hey dol! Merry dol! Ring a dong dillo*....Half hopeful and half afraid of some new danger, Frodo and Sam now both stood still. Suddenly out of a long string of nonsense-words (or so they seemed) the voice rose up ... (*LotR*, 'The

45. Op. cit. [9], p. 165.
46. Op. cit. [18].
47. Op. cit. [9], p. 166.
48. Op. cit. [9], p. 167.

> Old Forest', 116)[49]

This is quite obviously ironising from a distance. The second use occurs as Tom leads them away from the Barrow and on towards their journey to Bree:

> Tom sang most of the time, but it was chiefly nonsense, or else perhaps a strange language unknown to hobbits, an ancient language whose words were mainly those of wonder and delight. (*LotR*, 'Fog on the Barrow Downs', 143)

This is Tolkien's unique point about language, the communication of thought through sound even when 'unintelligible'. This is, after all, the effect on the hobbits of Gildor singing 'O Elbereth':

> It was singing in the fair elven-tongue, of which Frodo knew only a little, and the others knew nothing.Yet the sound blending with the melody seemed to shape itself in their thought into words which they only partly understood' (*LotR*, 'Three is Company, 77–78).

Both Frodo and Sam have recourse to nonsense verse shortly after leaving Tom. Frodo's reciting of the 'Man in the Moon' has calamitous consequences, but nonetheless it provides a clear example of the social context that Tolkien likely thought surrounded the nonsense of nursery rhymes in their ancient form: delight in incongruity. Sam himself, when invited to sing to cheer the group after the frightening conflict with the Black Riders on Weathertop, recites a rhyme of his own invention which he specifically calls 'nonsense' rather than 'proper poetry' (*LotR*, 'Flight to the Ford', 201), the Stone Troll song. Whether this was something he recalls, or something he invents after the influence of Tom, is not clear, but Frodo says it shows a quality in Sam that Frodo has never seen before; Sam is the hobbit most intrigued by Tom. The Stone Troll song features all the traditional characteristics of nonsense, mixing the morbid with the comic, delighting in rhyme and repetition of lines, and retelling an absurd encounter over family bones. In the version of the song which Tolkien sings on YouTube the names are different; in Sam's version, Tom challenges the troll, not John. Sam's singing in this context clearly suggests the value of nonsense McGillis claims:

49. J.R.R. Tolkien, *The Lord of the Rings*, HarperCollins, London, 1995. All quotations from *LotR* are taken from this edition.

> Nonsense for the Victorians was, paradoxically, a means of staying grounded, of returning to the shore after sailing the dark, broad seas.... this eminently loony genre of poetry kept the Victorians sane.[50]

As with *The Hobbit*, nonsense recedes in *LotR* as incongruity disappears and the quest becomes more urgent, but its presence in all of Tolkien's work discussed here provides explicit examples of the inter-relationship of language and nonsense in Tolkien's thought. If only Frodo had been able to enjoy nonsense after the Scouring of the Shire ... but as Tolkien noted in 'A Secret Vice', 'wars are not favourable to delicate pleasures' ('A Secret Vice', 200). 'A Secret Vice' is central to understanding the place of nonsense in Tolkien's enchantment with language.

50. Op. cit. [9], pp. 168–69.

'Stars Above a Dark Tor: Tolkien and Romanticism'

Anna E. Thayer (née Slack)

A profound shift in the West'ss attitudes to art and human creativity, Romanticism's focus was on freedom of self-expression: this found its culmination in the exultation of the spontaneity and originality of the individual imagination. This imagination was to break through the status quo of contemporary literature, turning the Romantic pen back towards myth and legend, the transcendent qualities of nature and a renewed relationship with language. Whether celebrating the sublime ardour of the poet's creative imagination, indulging in the excesses of sensitivity or unleashing the new stirrings of the Gothic, the Romantics were a force of renewal in literature. Tolkien found himself working with the literary legacy of the Romantics. This paper will overview Romanticism in general terms and, with specific reference to The Lord of the Rings, assess in what ways Tolkien's writings can be considered to be the work of a Romantic author. This examination will, in turn, allow a more detailed consideration of how Tolkien both uses and reworks the Romantic impulse.

The beauty of it smote his heart ... and hope returned to him. (*LotR*, 'The Land of Shadows', 957)[1]

Imagine an English Romantic poet. What kind of picture comes to mind? Perhaps an indolent young man, quill in hand, ambling through the countryside? Or something much wilder – a visionary poet with wind-driven hair? Out of barbaric curiosity, I tested this same question on some of my students. Their responses ranged from 'Some wet guy with flowing hair, moping in a field writing' to just two words: 'Oh God!' The latter student was not enamoured with English and its great literary heritage (and ambushing them in the lunch queue probably didn't help). What my students' answers do suggest is that the Romantics are commonly misunderstood; the passing of two centuries sometimes blinds us to what is most fundamental about them.

The Romantics were radicals, thinking and writing about as far outside the contemporary box as it was possible for poets and writers in their time to go. Anti-establishmentarianism could have been their middle name. In every sphere – philosophical, ideological, political, religious and literary – these eighteenth-

1. J.R.R. Tolkien, *The Lord of the Rings*, HarperCollins, London, 1995. All quotations from *LotR* are taken from this edition.

century bad boys represented a threat to the establishment. These were the kind of men that sweet old ladies would shake their heads at. Worse than bad and ugly – they were considered mad and dangerous to know.

Why? The Romantic movement created a profound shift in the West's attitudes to art and human creativity. Classical purity was formal and stiff-necked, and stifling neo-classical imitation seemed to repress the glory of the human spirit. This was not, to use a delightful English idiom, the Romantics' 'cup of tea'. Going entirely against the grain of contemporary literary thought, they turned inwards to unleash their innermost capacities of self-expression, exulting in the spontaneity and originality of their individual imaginations.

It was a Promethean exploit. In fact, we might take the story of Prometheus as a good symbol for what the Romantics were trying to achieve – they were wresting back the fire of the human spirit – imagination – for the use of all mankind. Unlike its classical counterpart, however, this Romantic Prometheus is released – just as he is in Shelley's closet drama *Prometheus Unbound.*

Imagination is the presiding spirit of the Romantic movement. It was the visionary capacity that allowed the Romantic pen to strike back to a realm of myth and legend so as to capture the transcendence of nature and sheer presentness of human existence. More even than presiding spirit, imagination was the Romantics' very lifeblood, and it ran throughout Europe.

THE WILD, THE IMPROBABLE, THE FANCIFUL: ENGLAND'S ROMANTICS

Asked to name the six key figures of English Romanticism, any good student of English Literature will list William Blake, William Wordsworth, Samuel Taylor Coleridge, John Keats, Percy Bysshe Shelley and Lord Byron as the guilty parties. These poets range from the truly visionary to the revolutionary and the outright tragic. They were all prolific writers – any one of them might claim Ozymandias' infamous words: 'look on my works, ye mighty, and despair'. Tigers, albatrosses, daffodils and Grecian urns had perhaps never before enjoyed such notoriety as these poets gave them. And, although they may have differed in opinion on some details, the heart of their theories of poetry was the same: everything resided in the crucial role of the imagination.

William Blake perhaps put it most clearly when he wrote: 'This world of imagination is the world of eternity'.[2] Indeed, for Coleridge, imagination was 'the living Power and prime Agent of all human Perception ... a repetition in the

2. William Blake, *Poetry and Prose of William Blake*, ed. Geoffrey Keynes, Nonesuch Press, London, 1939, p. 639.

finite mind of the eternal act of creation in the infinite I AM'.[3] More personably than his co-Romantics, Keats wrote: 'I am certain of nothing but the holiness of the heart's affections and the truth of the imagination'.[4]

This is what we might, with hindsight, call a eucatastrophic vision of literature. However it is expressed the essential sentiment is the same: there is something about imagination that transcends human experience and puts it back in touch with higher, eternal truths. The city of London, reviled by Blake as a place where 'soldiers' sighs/ Run in blood down palace walls',[5] is mystically redeemed in its reconnection to the glories of creation when Wordsworth finds its smokeless morning sleep as much a thing of splendour as the Edenic first light on valley, rock and hill.

This is linguistically and ideologically powerful stuff. But the Romantic imagination entailed far more than lounging about on London bridges writing sonnets. This notion of imagination was all-encompassing. For the Romantics, imagination meant breaking away from the classical unities of form and structure; spurning the trappings of rationalism in favour of the feeling of individual experience; and rejecting the rapidly expanding grind of urban life so as to return to man's true setting – nature, free from the 'mind-forged manacles' of a mechanistic view of life. It was an ideal vision of the world in so far as it was rooted entirely in ideas.

Needless to say, the Romantics were not very high up on Locke and Newton's Christmas card lists. Romanticism was an 'all or nothing' affair. You could not be half-hearted in this line of literature.

Transposing these ideals of imagination from mind to paper might seem a daunting prospect. But these poets were nonplussed by the challenge. They saw themselves as inheritors of the great romances, those 'wild, improbable ... fanciful' tales that were 'full of wild scenery'.[6] Imagination was the key – and these writers used it to unlock new styles and types of literature.

IMAGINATION: THE DIVINE VISION

It is by now clear that in order to grasp the Romantics we need to grapple with the

3. S.T. Coleridge, *Biographia Literaria*, vol. 1, ed. J. Shawcross, Clarendon Press, Oxford, 1907, p. 202.
4. Quotation from Keats' letter to Benjamin Bailey, 22 November 1817, <http://www.john-keats.com/briefe/221117.htm> [accessed 12 November 2015].
5. William Blake, *William Blake: Songs of Innocence and of Experience*, ed. Richard Wilmott, Oxford University Press, Oxford, 2001, p. 38.
6. S.T. Coleridge, *Letters of Samuel Taylor Coleridge*, vol. 1, ed. Ernest Hartley Coleridge, Houghton Mifflin, Boston and New York, 1895, p. 352.

idea of imagination. The OED defines it, rather dryly, as 'the faculty or action of forming ideas or mental images'. Imagination is a concept that, from our earliest childhoods, is set in stern opposition to reality. Tolkien himself acknowledges this in *On Fairy-Stories*, where he explores how fantastical literature can be condemned as escapist and juvenile. This trend goes back at least as far as Plato's theory of forms – imagination here is considered as a step too far from the true nature of things, leading to the expulsion of poets from the Republic. Even today, imagination is seemingly divorced from any redemptive creative wellspring – its places are the nursery or the business board room. Phrases like 'he has an over-active imagination' or 'you're just imagining things' point to a certain distrust of this human faculty.

For Blake, imagination was 'the divine vision', one that enabled you to see 'a world in a grain of sand'.[7] Tolkien would go on to make this same connection, both in *Mythopoeia* (where he writes to C.S. Lewis that 'we make still by the law in which we're made') and *On Fairy-Stories*. For Tolkien, as for the Romantics, the process of subcreation – a divinely ordained imagining of other worlds – is not only innately but vitally human, connecting us to creation itself in a way that few other processes are capable of doing.

In many ways, we can view Tolkien's minor work *Leaf by Niggle* as a deeply personal and thinly-veiled allegorical dialectic exploring this very issue. Niggle spends as much of his life as he can working on his painting of a tree, but it is only after he leaves the purgatorial Workhouse and goes on to Niggle's Country that the truer nature of his painting is revealed:

> A great green shadow came between him and the sun. Niggle looked up and fell off his bicycle.
> Before him stood *the* Tree, his Tree, finished. If you could say that of a tree that was alive, its leaves opening, its branches growing and bending in the wind that Niggle had so often felt or guessed, and so often failed to catch. He gazed at the Tree, and slowly lifted his arms and opened them wide.
> 'It's a gift!' he said. He was referring to his art, and also to the result; but he was using the word quite literally.[8]

Tolkien clearly aligns himself here with what we might call a Romantic mode of imagination. If we take Niggle's tree as an allegorical expression of the role of imagination in art, then it is a gift, to be used wisely (as the rest of Niggle's tale

7. Op. cit. [2], p. 11.
8. J.R.R. Tolkien, *Tales from the Perilous Realm,* HarperCollins, London, 2009, p. 299 (emphasis mine).

clearly shows). But the tree is only truly finished once its mimetic quality – the way in which its artistry mirrors something definitive and eternal – is revealed. The art brings us a step closer to the high, eternal form. In this way, Tolkien's view of imagination assimilates and inverts Plato's theory of forms:

> 'Niggle's Picture!' said Parish in astonishment. 'Did you think of all this, Niggle? I never knew you were so clever. Why didn't you tell me?'
> 'He tried to tell you, long ago,' said the man, 'but you would not look. He had only got canvas and paint in those days, and you wanted to mend your roof with them. This is what you and your wife used to call Niggle's Nonsense...'
> 'But it did not look like this then, not real,' said Parish.
> 'No, it was only a glimpse then,' said the man; 'but you might have caught the glimpse, if you had ever thought it worth while to try.' (*LN*, 141)

As for the Romantics, imagination is a gift, a divine vision, a subcreative act that can reconnect man to the divine. Rather than removing us from the true nature of things Tolkien argues that it can offer us a heart-shattering glimpse of them. It was an idea that would find academic crystallisation in his concept of eucatastrophe. Pursuing the creative impulse grants us a glimpse of eternity – in Niggle's case, 'an introduction to the Mountains'. C.S. Lewis called the same 'glimpsing' experience 'Joy'. Blake, with his accustomed visionary vigour, likens that moment of transcendent clarity to 'Hold[ing] infinity in the palm of your hand / and eternity in an hour'.[9]

PAINTING NIGGLE'S TREE: IMAGINATION IN ACTION

Imagination is the envisioning of something beyond reality, something which perhaps offers a glimpse of eternity. So far so good – but how do you get a transcendent experience neatly down onto an obliging bit of paper?

The Romantics almost invariably turned to poetry. The choice is an obvious one – it could be argued that few other literary forms offer the writer such an intense vehicle of expression, replete as it is with the subtleties of rhythm, diction and imagery. Poetry is an ancient and aural art, one that forces the listener or reader to open their own imagination to the writer's vocalised vision. Take, for example, the hypnotic power of William Blake's *The Tiger* – a poem which is

9. Op. cit. [2], p. 118.

itself concerned with subcreation:

> Tiger, Tiger, burning bright
> In the forests of the night:
> What immortal hand or eye
> Could frame thy fearful symmetry?
> ....
> When the stars threw down their spears,
> And watered Heaven with their tears,
> Did he smile his work to see?
> Did he who made the lamb make thee?[10]

The tight rhymes and relentless rhythm of Blake's poem convey a sense of awe and urgency in a way that perhaps no prose can. This visionary lyric assaults the senses, forcing an imaginative response in its arresting language and questioning of the reader – we cannot evade it. Blake's choice of poetic form and structure are exact.

Of course, Tolkien's works are not renowned for their poetry – although one can (and I would!) argue for the astonishing, eucatastrophic power of Sam's song in Cirith Ungol or the almost unbearable poignancy of *Bilbo's Last Song.* But that is not to say that we must bar Tolkien from his Romantic heritage on account of his choice of form; we often have a special reverence for poetry, tending to view it as the highest form of literary expression. At times that is well deserved. But we should not forget that our word poetry derives, after all, from the Greek verb *poiein*, to create – and if Tolkien does anything, he creates. The power of poetry perhaps lies in the way that it can linguistically and musically spark the imagination. If that is the case, then Tolkien's prose is at times as poetic as the most startling or breath-taking passages of the Romantic canon:

> And in that very moment, away behind in some courtyard of the City, a cock crowed. Shrill and clear he crowed, recking nothing of wizardry or war, welcoming only the morning that in the sky far above the shadows of death was coming with the dawn.
> And as if in answer there came from far away another note. Horns, horns, horns. In dark Mindolluin's sides they dimly echoed. Great horns of the North wildly blowing. Rohan had come at last. (*LotR*, 'The Siege of Gondor', 861)

10. Op. cit. [5], p. 34

Tolkien's choice and use of language here is every bit as deliberate as that of his Romantic forebears. He weaves together semantic patterns, chosen details and literary allusions to create a moment of eucatastrophe. Tolkien's choice of prose, we might argue, serves as a foil to such moments of lyrical or visionary clarity. In this, perhaps he goes a step further than the Romantics; while they focussed on keeping their sense of imagination in overdrive, Tolkien's prose more closely mimics the experience of reality: our lives are not overflowing with this kind of imaginative, eucatastrophic clarity – what Virginia Woolfe would call 'moments of being'. A prosaic exposition of an imaginary world therefore allows us to integrate more fully with its mundane experience and its moments of being – something that poetry does not always permit us.

Tolkien's prose is littered with such instances; almost invariably, he ties that sense of 'poetry' to the experience of eucatastrophe, as in this example from *The Two Towers*:

> 'Look, Sam!' [Frodo] cried, startled into speech. 'Look! The king has got a crown again!'
> The eyes were hollow and the carven beard was broken, but about the high stern forehead there was a coronal of silver and gold. A trailing plant with flowers like small white stars had bound itself across the brows as if in reverence for the fallen king, and in the crevices of his stony hair yellow stonecrop gleamed.
> 'They cannot conquer forever!' said Frodo. And then suddenly the *brief glimpse* was gone. The sun dipped and vanished, and as if at the shuttering of a lamp, black night fell. (*LotR*, 'The Journey to the Cross-Roads', 727, emphasis mine)

This second passage is perhaps less spine-tingling than the first coming, as it does, not on a field of battle but really just in a field – but the power of imagination and its culmination in eucatastrophic glimpses of something beyond us is nevertheless outspoken. We are presented first with a microcosmic, personal experience of the power of imagination in Frodo's response to the natural world. In fact, his experience is so over-powering that it startles our troubled hobbit hero to speech, the verbs *cried* and *startled* strongly implying a moment of transcendence before we reach its verbal expression in 'The king has got a crown again!'. It is in the imagining of a crown – expressed delicately but evocatively in Tolkien's detailed attention to the natural world, where the flowers become 'small white stars' – that we are led to the moment of clarity: 'they cannot conquer forever'. Like a true Romantic, Tolkien turns to the natural world and infuses it with a sense of the eternal so as to express the power of the imagination to lesson us in eternal things. But Tolkien is at pains to show the temporal nature of this experience: Frodo's 'brief glimpse' is gone as suddenly as it appeared, and a more prosaic diction (with the vanishing sun compared to a shuttered lamp) reinforces our sense that everyday experience always truncates the moments in which our imaginations are liberated to glimpse beyond it. The juxtaposition is heart-rending – but it is chiefly achieved through creative mastery of natural details.

As *LotR* nears its end, Tolkien's engagement with the natural world becomes a *tour de force* of pathetic fallacy. The road to Mordor becomes somewhat of a physical representation of Frodo and Sam's emotional and spiritual journey, heightening our sense of their exhaustion and nigh despair. Against this framework, Tolkien sets the scene for another moment of transcendent imagination:

> Far above Ephel Duath in the West the night-sky was still dim and pale. There, peeping among the cloud-wrack above a dark tor high up in the mountains, Sam saw a white star twinkle for a while. The beauty of it smote his heart, as he looked up out of the forsaken land, and hope returned to him. For like a shaft, clear and cold, the thought pierced him that in the end the Shadow was only a small and passing thing: there was light and high beauty for ever beyond its reach. (*LotR*, 'The Land of Shadow', 957)

C.M. Bowra once wrote that: 'The Romantics ... explore[d] ... the world of the spirit ... each of them believed in an order of things which is not that which we see and know ... They wished to penetrate to an abiding reality ... [and] were convinced that, though visible things are the instruments by which we view this reality, they are not everything and have indeed little significance unless they are related to some embracing and sustaining power'.[11] In this passage, Tolkien does just that.

The artistry and setting of the natural world have again become the vehicle for a powerful epiphany of imagination. Tolkien's language here oscillates, in a way that is delightfully appropriate to Samwise, between the touching tones of the everyday ('peeping', 'twinkle for a while') to the high and poetic modes of romance ('smote', 'forsaken'). Sam is aware both of the transience of the piercing star and the permanence of the idea it represents in his imagination. Tolkien perfectly captures the essence of a moment of divine vision as it occurs, not in the Romantic imagination, but in human experience – and, vitally, this linking of reality and the eternal leads to eucatastrophic renewal: hope returns to

11. C. M. Bowra, *The Romantic Imagination*, Oxford Paperbacks, Oxford, 1976, p. 9.

Sam so that 'his own fate, and even his master's, ceased to trouble him'.

The twinkling white star in every way indicates to us an embracing and sustaining power. This very Romantic capacity of using the natural world to capture the essence of spiritual moments is evident throughout Tolkien's work. The same imagination that conjures up wild worlds uses the very fabric of those worlds to transmit hope and imagination as best it can.

SHELOB'S LAIR: AN ASIDE ON TOLKIEN AND THE GOTHIC

Of course, the Romantic imagination did not simply conjure up instances of revelatory clarity. The movement was experiential and so also indulged in the sensuous and the nightmarish. The idealism of the Romantics gave rise to the thrills of the Gothic – literature so radical that it was deemed unsuitable for women. While many of these works – such as *Frankenstein* or *Wuthering Heights* – are now considered among the classics of world literature, they were sensational and unpredictable.

The link between the monstrous and the world of Romance may well seem evident to us – knights were fighting dragons long before Spenser's Redcrosse knight encountered Errour in her den or Gawain ventured to the Green Chapel – but the radical nature of the Romantics produced an equally radical version of the monstrous. For some, the Gothic quickly became viewed as a distasteful literary expression of excess, calculated to thrill and little else.

And here is another place where Tolkien differs from his Romantic and Gothic forbears: he wrote that 'every romance that takes things seriously must have a warp of fear and horror, if however remotely or representatively it is to resemble reality, and not the merest escapism.'[12] While acknowledging the integral link between romance and horror Tolkien's focus is still clearly that of resembling reality. In the same letter, he adds about the horror he has attempted in his own novel: 'But I have failed if it does not seem possible that mere mundane hobbits could cope with such things. I think that there is no horror conceivable that such creatures cannot surmount, by grace (here appearing in mythological forms) combined with a refusal of their nature and reason at the last pinch to compromise or submit'.[13]

For Tolkien, the purpose of fear and horror is to both render the world of the imagination more life-like, and to produce a platform for the outworking of grace. This is perhaps seen nowhere as clearly as in Shelob's lair:

12. Humphrey Carpenter, ed., *The Letters of J. R. R. Tolkien*, with the assistance of Christopher Tolkien, HarperCollins, London, 1995, Letter 109, p. 120.

13. Op. cit.

> they were in utter and impenetrable dark.... Here the air was still, stagnant, heavy, and sound fell dead ... As they thrust forward they felt things brush against their heads, or against their hands, long tentacles or hanging growths perhaps... and still the stench grew.
> ... from behind them came a sound, startling and horrible in the heavy padded silence: a gurgling, bubbling noise, and a long venomous hiss. They wheeled round, but nothing could be seen. Still as stones they stood, staring, waiting for they did not know what….
> The bubbling hiss drew nearer, and there was a creaking as of some great jointed thing that moved with slow purpose on the dark… .'Master, master!' cried Sam, and the life and urgency came back into his voice. 'The Lady's gift! The star-glass!' (*LotR*, 'Shelob's Lair', 744ff.)

Tolkien does not stint in building up the horror of Shelob's lair and is masterful in his execution of suspense. But where Peter Jackson unashamedly turns to the tropes of the horror-film (itself a genre drawing heavily on the gothic) Tolkien keeps the narrative details concrete and sense-focussed, drawing his readers into the lair itself. Like Frodo and Sam, we are left with only our senses of touch, sound and smell – literal and metaphorical sight only returns with the memory of Galadriel and the use of the star-glass. It is Galadriel's gift – that of light in the darkness – which acts as the grace that permits the hobbits to surmount the horror of Shelob's lair. Keeping his focus on overcoming horror rather than allowing it to overwhelm the narrative sets Tolkien apart from those who first followed in the steps of the Romantics.

THE GREAT INSTRUMENT FOR THE MORAL GOOD

Shelley once wrote that the imagination was 'the great instrument for the moral good'. Although their interpretation of moral was not necessarily uniform the statement is summative of much that the Romantics strove to achieve. Imagination was a tool to enrich human experience.

Tolkien undeniably lived and wrote in the tail of the Romantics' visionary comet, and his work has traits in common. But in Tolkien's case, 'moral' good would perhaps be better read as spiritual good – for him, imagination is a pathway to the integration of the world around us with the world beyond us. It is when the two are imaginatively connected, allowing us through one to catch a glimpse of the other – when we are, as Tolkien puts it, escape and then return to the world able to see green as green again – that imagination has served its highest purpose. He strove to unify the realms of experience and 'being' in a way that encompassed the eternal but enriched, rather than cast aside, the temporal. Standing at the threshold between imagination and faith, Tolkien's romanticism truly is a kind of divine vision.

'The Ainulindale and Tolkien's Approach to Modernity'

Reuven Naveh

When Tolkien first wrote 'The Music of the Ainur' the musical world was in the midst of a revolution: the collapse of tonal music and the rise of new alternatives, the most important being Arnold Schoenberg's concepts of atonality and 'emancipation of dissonance'. Among others, writers such as Thomas Mann and Milan Kundera used Schoenberg as an allegory to the catastrophes of the modern era. The Ainulindale reacts to these concepts, thus being much more than a text about abstract and divine music. In particular, the role of 'dissonance' in tonal and atonal music will be discussed, to reflect the role evil plays in Tolkien's world and in particularly in the Ainulindale. The logic behind western tonal music can symbolise Tolkien's ethics, while atonal music reflects its negation and the rise of evil powers.

INTRODUCTION

This paper is partially based on a previously published article.[1] It discusses the relations of some of Tolkien's writing to western tonal and atonal music, and mainly compares the atonal music of Arnold Schoenberg to Melkor's part in the Ainulindale. The comparison is made from the perspective of Tolkien's negative opinion on Modernism. The paper includes references to concepts and compositions in western music, from the twelfth to the twentieth century. The most important is the concept of tonality, which needs to be defined properly. 'Tonal music' is a term used to characterise the so-called 'western classical music', which reached maturity in the eighteenth and nineteenth centuries. By *tonality* we mean a musical system based on a well-defined scale, which has a clear, agreed-upon hierarchy of possible and impossible progressions and revolves around a single centre commonly known as the *tonic*. The progressions in tonal music are characterised with clear sense of direction, in which unstable moments are 'solved' into more stable ones. The most stable event is the arrival at the tonic. The term 'atonality' refers to music which breaks the tonal rules. Attempts to create atonal music were made in the twentieth century, and we shall get to that at the end of the paper.

1. Reuven Naveh, 'Tonality, Atonality, and the Ainulindalë', in Heidi Steimel and Friedhelm Schneidewind, eds, *Music in Middle-earth*, Walking Tree Publishers, Zurich, 2010, 29–52.

I would like to start with an anecdote. Richard Wagner's masterpiece *The Ring of the Nibelung* drew lots of comparisons to Tolkien's writings because of the references to Norse mythology and the use of a ring of power which brings destruction on its owners.[2] Here is one example which I find relevant. Consider the following comparison between Tolkien's Nazgûl and Wagner's Valkyries, the immortal warriors responsible for delivering dead warriors to Walhala. Brunhilde, the main Valkyrie, is the heroine of the Ring cycle, and the music known as 'The Ride of the Valkyries' is the most famous piece from the cycle. Both the Nazgûl and the Valkyries are Nine, and are riding on flying horses/ beasts; they are fulfilling the absolute will of their master (Sauron or Wotan); they are immortal; and they are invisible to mortals, unless those are dying (in the case of the Valkyries) or enter their world by wearing the ring. However, the comparison which is relevant for this paper is that both the Valkyries and the Nazgûl can be described as crying in terrible voices.

One of the most detailed descriptions of the Nazgûl's cry is: 'A long drawn-wail came down the wind, like the cry of some evil and lonely creature. It rose and fell, and ended on a high piercing note.... it was answered by another cry, fainter and further off, but no less chilling to the blood.' (*FotR*, 'A Shortcut to Mushrooms', 88).[3] It is not hard to imagine that Tolkien had in mind the famous 'Ride of the Valkiries' and the shouts of the Valkyries to each other during the scene. Anyway, Tolkien's description can easily be seen as a mockery of a disliked musical style of singing, and the way the Valkyries sing, with their 'Hoyotoho' cries, demonstrates a very radical example of operatic soprano singing.

Naturally, this point is very speculative. Still, it can reflect Tolkien's opinion of Wagner, or his general opinion of operatic singing. It can also be considered as another example in the long tradition of parodying Wagner, from Debussy to Bugs Bunny. But I think this mockery of the Valkyries' singing can also be interpreted as a criticism of the general style of Wagner's music, which is generally considered progressive and revolutionary among the nineteenth-century composers, leading to the twentieth-century modernity.

In this paper I will show how Tolkien's disdain for modernity fits the way music is portrayed in his writing. The Nazgûl-Valkyrie comparison demonstrates that; but naturally the focus should be on Tolkien's most important text about music – the Ainulindale. If we remember that the first version of the Ainulindale appeared in *The Book of Lost Tales* which dates back to around 1920, the criticism which it reflects becomes a direct criticism of Tolkien's time, since this

2. Christopher MacLachlan, *Tolkien and Wagner: The Ring and Der Ring*, Walking Tree Publishers, Zurich, 2012. See also Renée Vink, *Wagner and Tolkien: Mythmakers*, Walking Tree Publishers, Zurich, 2012.

3. J.R.R. Tolkien, *The Fellowship of the Ring*, HarperCollins, London, 1995.

is exactly the decade in which modern music and its aesthetics had been shaped and became known and controversial.

THE MUSIC OF THE AINULINDALE

An important question is what gives us the legitimacy to discuss the music of the Ainur in terms of actual music, and especially in the terms of western music, which was only developed in recent centuries? I am arguing that while the music of the Ainur was clearly abstract and celestial music, it is described and perceived in the terms of real-life music. Tolkien's description relates to the music of the Ainur in terms and features taken from western classical music.

- Instruments: 'Then the harpists, and the lutanists, the flautists and pipers, the organs and the countless choirs of the Ainur began to fashion the theme of Ilúvatar into great music' (*Lost Tales I*, 53).[4]
- Chords: 'and in one chord … the Music ceased' (*TSil*, 'Ainulindalë', 3–5).[5]
- Harmony: 'and a sound arose of endless interchanging melodies woven in harmony' (*TSil*, 'Ainulindalë', 3–5).
- Themes: 'and a new theme began amid the storm, like and yet unlike the former theme' (*TSil*, 'Ainulindalë', 3–5).
- Discord (dissonance): 'and straightway discord arose about him' (*TSil*, 'Ainulindalë', 3–5).

In the description of the music in the Ainulindale, a special role is reserved for Melkor. Here are some of the quotes describing it:

> But the discord and noise that Melko had aroused started into uproar against it, and there was a war of sounds (*Lost Tales I*, 53).
>
> ...because his secret thoughts had no kinship with the beauty of Ilúvatar's design its harmonies were broken and destroyed. Yet sat Ilúvatar and hearkened till the music reached a depth of gloom and ugliness unimaginable (*Lost Tales I*, 53).
>
> ...it was loud, and vain, and endlessly repeated; and it had little harmony, but rather a clamorous unison as of many trumpets braying upon a few notes. (*TSil*, 'Ainulindalë', 3–5)

4. J.R.R. Tolkien, *The Book of Lost Tales I*, ed. Christopher Tolkien, George Allen & Unwin, London, 1983.
5. J.R.R. Tolkien, *The Silmarillion*, ed. Christopher Tolkien, George Allen & Unwin, London, 1977.

Melkor's music is described in a very negative way. It is also considered as causing discomfort to the rest of the Valar, and it does not combine with their music. Yet, when Ilúvatar talks to Melkor, he states the following:

> 'And thou, Melkor, shalt see that no theme may be played that *hath not its uttermost source in me*, nor can any alter the music in my despite'.
>
> 'And thou, Melkor, wilt discover all the secret thoughts of thy mind, and wilt perceive that they are *but a part of the whole* and tributary to its glory.'[6]

These quotes are of course quite astonishing. How can what is going to be the ultimate evil of Tolkien's mythology be regarded as part of the whole? We can ask this question considering the theological and moral meaning of the Ainulindale, but it is as interesting if we want to regard the Ainulindale as *music*. What does Ilúvatar mean when he says that Melkor's music is part of the whole?

Of all the musical terms, Melkor's music associates with the concept of dissonance, termed 'discord' by Tolkien. A dissonance, the opposite of consonance, is a combination of notes that clash and, when played together, create a feeling of unpleasantness. This is the described effect of Melkor's entrance to the music. The dissonance might describe both Melkor's music by itself, and mainly the result of its being played simultaneously with the music of the other Ainur.

The peculiarity of this use of dissonance as part of the creation process is enlightened by the comparison to other musical descriptions of creation. Wagner's prelude to the *Das Rheingold* portrays a pure and pristine state of the world. The prelude is several minutes of 'pure' harmony, which stays constantly on the E flat major tonal chord, and with no room for dissonance. A different approach is to describe the creation as coming out of the chaos, and let the dissonance represent this chaos. Haydn, in the prelude to the oratorio *The Creation* does this, in a pretty delicate way. A less famous but much more radical example comes from the ballet *Les Elemens* (1737) by the French composer Rebel. The music begins with a very dissonant description of the chaos which preceded the creation.

Tolkien does not follow any of these routes: His creation is described neither by 'pure' consonance nor by chaotic dissonance. Both consonance and dissonance are apparent in the music, and their combination creates the music of the Ainur. Beyond their symbolic meaning, Ilúvatar's words to Melkor show that Melkor's

---

6. Op. cit. (emphases mine).

dissonance is not external to the music (unlike a child who tries to interfere with his father's piano playing, for example) but is inherent in it. Therefore, to understand Melkor's role in the music, we need first to understand the role of dissonance in music theory.

WESTERN MUSIC AND DISSONANCES

Dissonances and the way they are treated have central role in music theory from the beginning of polyphonic music, or music for several voices, and this dates as early as the twelfth century – so dissonances and consonances precede what we call tonality. Along the years, the definitions of dissonance have varied, as well as what is forbidden and what is allowed, but the basic principle remained: consonances are 'good' while dissonances are 'bad'. Even when dissonances are allowed, they are allowed as temporary and passing, always to serve the legitimate consonances.

In the twelfth century the rules were strict, and only consonances (and only those called 'perfect consonances') were allowed. Dissonances were strictly forbidden, and especially the most notorious – the tritone, which has been given the nickname *diabolus in musica*. As we can see, linking music with religion and linking the dissonance with the devil is not Tolkien's invention. It is interesting to mention that an interval which was considered a perfect consonance – the perfect fourth – in later centuries was recognised as dissonance and treated as such.

Later on, dissonances became more legitimate, but were still handled as passing and temporary events. The Renaissance style which is considered very calm and harmonious has produced the set of rules known as 'Palestrina's counterpoint', which establish the combination of several voices, with a focus on handling dissonances properly: through proper preparation and resolution to a consonance. While derived from the Renaissance, these rules became the basis of music theory, and they are actually an obligatory part of any music student program.

When western tonal music had reached maturity, in the eighteenth and nineteenth centuries, the use of dissonance became regular and common. The notorious tritone, for example, has become a part of several very common chords, such as the dominant seventh chord or the diminished seventh chord.

The opening of Pergolesi's *Stabat Mater* is a beautiful example for the use of dissonance within the tonal framework. The two voices (soprano and alto) create a set of dissonances and their consonant resolution. This is again an example of religious symbolism in music, because the way the voices cross each other is interpreted as a sign of the cross, especially in such a religious context. For our matter, both consonance and dissonance are parts of this symbolism. Pergolesi's example also demonstrates a dissonance which is not harsh and causes no discomfort. This example shows that when used properly according to the laws of handling a dissonance, there is nothing diabolical or disturbing in dissonance.

On the other hand, the harsh sound of dissonances makes them good candidates to express shock or surprise, even within the tonal framework. For example, we can mention Beethoven, who commonly uses dissonances, even at the beginning of a musical piece. Nevertheless, even the most radical dissonances still create merely a temporary tension which is eventually solved properly. One of the most radical and well-known examples for such appearance of dissonance in classical music is the development section of the first movement of Beethoven's *Eroica* symphony. This is a fairly dramatic section, leading to a very dissonantic music, only to present a new theme with a completely different mood.

The principle that dissonances must be resolved to stable events, considered to be among the fundamentals of tonality, started to dissolve in the late nineteenth century. It is common to look at Wagner's prelude to *Tristan and Isolde* as a sign of this revolution. The prelude presents a chord, known as 'The Tristan Chord' which does not belong to the typical harmonic language and in addition, is not resolved as one would expect from a dissonant chord (it does *sound* like a regular chord). In addition, the prelude itself avoids any clear tonal resolution and remains in an indefinite state for its entirety.

SCHOENBERG AND MELKOR

Here we come to the protagonist of this paper – Arnold Schoenberg (1874-1951). Schoenberg is only one of the composers within the twentieth-century framework and definitely not all twentieth-century composers follow his principles (we may mention, as a very short list, Stravinsky, Bartok, Hindemith, Prokofiev, and Shostakovich). Schoenberg is also not the only composer whose modernist style was highly criticised in the relevant period of the early twentieth century. A well-known example is Stravinsky's *The Rite of Spring* which caused one of the most notorious musical scandals in its premier. But Schoenberg is still the most prominent figure of the twentieth century musical revolution, and especially in regard to the shift from tonal to atonal music.

Schoenberg's musical career can be divided into three main periods: The first, late-romanticism (till 1906), in which he still wrote romantic tonal compositions; the second, free atonality (1906-1920) in which the tonal system is thrown away, with no clear system to replace it; and the third, the dodecaphonic period (1921 henceforth), in which Schoenberg invented a new composition technique (also known as the twelve-tone system). Unlike the second period, the third represents a very strict set of compositional rules, which are even stricter than those of the tonal system.

The innovations in Schoenberg's free atonal style may be summarised in three main principles:

- Atonality: that is, in addition to avoiding the traditional scales, no tone is more important than the others. As a result, the music loses any sense of directionality and clear hierarchy between the tones.
- New tone clusters: unlike tonal music, which is based mainly on triadic chords, Schoenberg's music presents different kinds of chords and tone clusters. Naturally, they are much more dissonant and 'bothering' than the traditional chords and harmonies.
- The so called 'emancipation of dissonance': the dissonance becomes as important as the consonance, and there is no more hierarchy between them. The dissonance is totally autonomous in the sense that it is not considered to create tension which requires resolution.

A representative composition of the second period is the five orchestral pieces, op. 16 (1909). This composition is not just an excellent example of Shoenberg's free atonal style, but it is also very relevant to this paper, because we have a recorded evidence of its performance in England, shortly before Tolkien started his mythology. At its premiere in London in 1912, it was described by *The Times* as 'an assay in dissonance' and was compared to Tibetan song in terms of their comprehensibility.[7] This may reflect the general opinion in England (and not just in England) about Schoenberg, at that time and ever since.

I believe it is not hard to see the similarities between Melkor's music and Schoenberg's revolution, at least as it was perceived by his critics. Both Melkor and Schoenberg try to invent their own music, partly by innovation and partly by breaking and distorting the norm. Both are fond of free dissonance and the terms used in the Ainulindale to describe Melkor's music can easily be used to criticise Schoenberg's music, or modern music in general. The free atonal period is not just relevant for this paper from the chronological aspect, but also because it represents best the Melkorian approach, which concentrates on the abolishment of the order and logic of the world.

But if we return to Ilúvatar words – 'And thou, Melkor, wilt discover all the secret thoughts of thy mind, and wilt perceive that they are but a part of the whole and tributary to its glory' – we see that the comparison is deeper than mere criticism of the way atonality sounds. Ilúvatar does not condemn Melkor's music, nor does he say that it should have sounded differently. Even after Melkor's

---

7. Hans Heinz Stuckenschmidt, *Twentieth Century Music*, trans. Richard Deveson, McGraw-Hill, New York, 1969.

music has been heard and caused so much discontent among the other Ainur, it is still considered 'a part of the whole'. In this respect, Ilúvatar's approach is similar to the conception of dissonance in tonal music, as we just saw. It is an inherent part of it, sometimes to be used in dramatic or alarming ways, but its existence is used to strengthen the tonality and it is never autonomous.

Therefore, we can see that the main concept the text attacks is the concept of 'emancipation of the dissonance', which is fundamental to Schoenberg's music (of course, I am not suggesting Tolkien knew this terminology – but that he attacked the music derived from it). Atonal music is criticised for taking the 'evil' parts and setting them free, with no coherence or hierarchy. On the other hand, tonality represents an ordered and balanced world, in which even the dark aspects have their function.

THE CRITICISM OF MODERNISM

Finally, I would like to put the discussion in the perspective of Tolkien's negative opinion of modernism in general. Tolkien's negative views of the norms and aesthetics of his period are well known and are reflected also in his literary works: the attribution of modern explosives to the goblins in *The Hobbit* or the character of Ted Sandiman in *The Lord of the Rings* are famous examples. These opinions were also explicitly expressed by Tolkien. Here are some examples:

> It is part of the essential malady of such days— producing the desire to escape, not indeed from life, but from our present time and self-made misery— that we are acutely conscious both of the ugliness of our works, and of their evil. So that to us evil and ugliness seem indissolubly allied. (*OFS*, 57)[8]

> Such is modern life. Mordor in our midst. And I regret to note that the billowing cloud recently pictured did not mark the fall of Barad-dûr, but was produced by its allies – or at least by persons who have decided to use the Ring for their own (of course most excellent) purposes.[9]

> He will rebel against the laws of the Creator – especially against mortality. Both of these (alone or together) will lead to the desire for Power, for making the will more quickly effective, – and so to

8. J.R.R Tolkien, 'On Fairy-stories', *Tree and Leaf*, Unwin, London, 1964, 11–72.
9. Humphrey Carpenter, ed., *The Letters of J.R.R. Tolkien*, with the assistance of Christopher Tolkien, George Allen & Unwin, London, 1981, Letter 135, p. 165.

> the Machine (or Magic). By the last I intend all use of external plans or devices (apparatus) instead of development of the inherent inner powers or talents — or even the use of these talents with the corrupted motive of dominating: bulldozing the real world, or coercing other wills. The Machine is our more obvious modern form though more closely related to Magic than is usually recognised.[10]

It is evident that Tolkien sees the modern era as belonging to and collaborating with the evil and dark sides of his world. There are especially two points we can mention – the relation between evilness and ugliness and the attempt to rebel against God and nature. This is true for Melkor, for Sauron and for the modern heirs of the Orcs with their machinery and sophisticated weapons. These points also reflect Tolkien's opinion on the modern aesthetic and art.

Of all the expressions of modernity in art, modern music is probably the most notorious. The music of Schoenberg raises objections that supersede reactions to the works of Picasso or Kafka, for example. This was true at the time of his compositions (as seen in the *Times* article) and it is still true today. When Tolkien criticises the aesthetics of modernism, it is not unlikely that he had in mind, among other things, music such as Schoenberg's pieces for orchestra.

However, my analysis of the Ainulindale reveals that the criticism against modern music is much beyond its being ugly or hard to hear. The breaking of the tonal frameworks becomes a symbol of breaking a unified and coherent world, to establish a world of chaos. The usual dichotomy of good and evil is replaced, through the symbolism of tonality and atonality, with a concept of balance, which is broken by modernity. Therefore, twentieth-century music is not only directly attacked in the Ainulindale, but it is also used as a symbol for the evil and rebellious nature of modernism.

If Tolkien indeed used the figure of Arnold Schoenberg as a symbol of twentieth-century musical modernism, he was not alone in doing that. The most important example is Thomas Mann's novel *Dr. Faustus*, in which the hero is a fictional composer which invents a musical method which greatly resembles Schoenberg's 12-tone system. The allusion to Schoenberg's music in this modern version of the Faust story configures him again as 'diabolic'.

I would like to finish this paper with another literary example, from Milan Kundera's *The Book of Laughter and Forgetting*. This work is a lament for the writer's homeland Czechoslovakia and the oppression it suffered after the Prague Spring and the Russian occupation. Here, Kundera compares Schoenberg's music and his 12-tone system to the communist ideology and the concept of

10. Op. cit., Letter 131, p. 145–46.

absolute equality, while the tonal system is described as a monarchy with its knights and classes:

> This is what my father told me when I was five: a key signature is a king's court in miniature. It is ruled by a king (the first step) and his two right-hand men (steps five and four). They have four other dignitaries at their command, each of which has his own special relation to the king and his right-hand men. The court houses five additional tones as well, which are known as chromatic. They have important parts to play in other keys, but here they are simply guests.
>
> ...That is what my father told me. What follows is all my own. One day a great man determined that after a thousand years the language of music had worn itself out and could do no more than rehash the same message. Abolishing the hierarchy of tones by revolutionary decree, he made them all equal and subjected them a strict discipline: none was allowed to occur more often than any other in a piece, and therefore none could lay claim to its former feudal privileges. All courts were permanently abolished, and in their place arose a single empire, founded on equality and called the twelve-tone system.[11]

Thinking of the tonal system as a monarchy, as Kundera did, may shed a light not only on the symbolism of the Ainulindale, but also on the ending of *LotR*. I guess most people nowadays will not accept such an authoritative governing system as desired or ideal, and yet Aragorn's crowning is definitely the positive climax of the book.

From the perspective of this paper, monarchy is not viewed just as the rise of an absolute ruler, but also as a well defined stable system, in which everything has a meaning. Giving up such a system, for the sake of absolute freedom or absolute equality, is something which both Tolkien and Kundera, despite their very different points of view, warn against. The abstract nature of music, with its universally recognised rules, is the tool to carry this message.

11. Milan Kundera, *The Book of Laughter and Forgetting*, trans. Michael Henry Heim, Penguin, Harmondsworth, 1981.

'Tolkien, the Russians and Industrialisation'

Jim Clarke

In On Fairy-Stories, Tolkien explains how he finds man to be a supernatural creature, whereas fairies 'are natural, far more natural than he. However, Tolkien's supernaturalism is primarily a pastoral one; the bucolic Shire and arboreal havens are as idealised as the hobbits and Elves which populate them. Tolkien contrasts these with Mordor and Isengard. While Tolkien's pastoralism is compelling, nevertheless it lacks scientific coherence and realistic rigour. I intend to show that, writing within a significant Russian tradition of reworking Tolkien's oeuvre Yeskov seeks to subvert Tolkien's narrative by positing that it is history written by the victor. For Yeskov, it is the Elves and not Sauron who are fascist aggressors, so frightened by the enlightened scientific progress of Mordorian culture that they must manipulate men into destroying it. Yeskov reimagines the War of the Ring from Mordor's perspective and recasts Middle Earth in a hyperrealistic inversion which opens it up to moral and political nuance. I will show how Yeskov's recasting of The Lord of the Rings as the propaganda of the victor illuminates a rare blindspot of Tolkien's.

Middle-earth is not another world; it is our world in another time, in what we might call an alternative history. It is a time in which other sentient races and species co-exist alongside man, and in which both weapons of mass destruction and genetic engineering are prominent, and science and technology have a lengthy history, but yet the musket rifle has yet to be invented. Tolkien insisted 'Middle-earth is not an imaginary world ... The theatre of my tale is this earth, the one in which we now live, but the historical period is imaginary.'[1] As the anthropologist Virginia Luling has suggested, it is a North-West Europe which has not been 'Europeanised', or to use Patrick Curry's term 'modernised'. What both critics perhaps are suggesting is that Middle-earth at the end of the Third Age has not yet been industrialised.

Tolkien was hostile to industrialisation, and this is evident in *The Lord of the Rings* where Mordor is depicted as the sole industrial state. Mordor's industrialisation, which Saruman attempts to emulate at Isengard, has catastrophic consequences for the landscape, nature and the biosphere. Sam

1. Humphrey Carpenter, ed., *The Letters of J.R.R. Tolkien*, with the assistance of Christopher Tolkien, George Allen & Unwin, London, 1981, Letter 183, p. 239.

and Frodo encounter a 'defiled' and 'diseased' land in Mordor, and Treebeard gives an eloquent speech about the loss of his forest and friends to 'orc-work', or 'wanton hewing'. There is effectively a spectrum of pastoralism running from the idealisation of Lothlórien, via the cosiness of the Shire, the decaying grandeur of Minas Tirith, and ultimately to the ecological devastation of Mordor. This spectrum closely parallels the moral and biological order of Middle-earth. Dimitra Fimi has noted the similarities between this hierarchy and the medieval 'Great Chain of Being', especially as it is expressed in Treebeard's poem to Merry and Pippin about 'the lore of Living Creatures'.[2] Within the havens of the Elves, industrialisation is virtually non-existent. Elven technology is entirely in tune with the needs of nature. By contrast, small farming and development marks out the Shire, whereas the realms of men show indications of developed agriculture, trade and architecture, but none of the heavy industry that mars Isengard or Mordor.

This is the Middle-earth we know, Tolkien's Middle-earth. I want to introduce and discuss a different Middle-earth, so as to illuminate some aspects of Tolkien's creation. First we must travel back in time and far to the East. But we must also, temporarily, abandon our acceptance of Tolkien's Middle-earth as the only Middle-earth, and this is perhaps the hardest thing to do.

In *LotR* and elsewhere, Tolkien leaves himself open to criticism of a particularly contemporary kind. The evil beings who emanate from the South and East of Middle-earth are consistently described as 'swart' with 'slant-eyes'. When we map this onto the given geography of Middle-earth, somewhere Tolkien himself described as North-West Europe in a different era, then these swarthy, slant-eyed foreigners transpire to be none other than Asians and Africans. It would be too simplistic to accuse Tolkien, a man who grew up in an era of imperialism and who experienced a war originating from the East, of casual racism. After all, he famously rejected what he called 'the wholly pernicious and unscientific race-doctrine.'[3] Nevertheless, it is a useful thought experiment to ponder what those evil beings from the east and the south might themselves make of such a characterisation, or indeed of Tolkien's inextricable link between evil and industrialisation. By extension, this calls the entire War of the Ring into question. What happens if we think of the war not as a binary battle between good and evil, but the more nuanced kind of conflict we are more familiar with, where no one side has a monopoly on being right? What ramifications would such a thought experiment have for Tolkien's position on industrialisation?

Fortunately, an Easterner, the Russian scientist Kyrill Yeskov has performed

---

2. Dimitra Fimi, *Tolkien, Race and Cultural History: From Fairies to Hobbits*, Palgrave Macmillan, Basingstoke, 2009, p. 141.
3. Op. cit. [1], Letter 29, p. 37.

this very experiment. He entitled it *The Last Ringbearer*, or *Последний кольценосец* in Russian.[4] Let me map out the very unusual circumstances in which Yeskov's novel came into being. Until the fall of the Soviet Union, Tolkien had a sporadic and inconsistent publishing history in Russia. As Olga Markova and Maria Komenkovich have revealed, his writings were, for various reasons, considered inappropriate by the Soviet authorities.[5] As Markova notes, Tolkien's first translator Zinaida Bobyr 'had to find a way to make it resemble the literature that was acceptable in the USSR, which meant that she had to reduce Tolkien's text either to a fairy tale or to science fiction.'[6]

The resulting text – it would be stretching things to call it a 'translation' – abridged and amended *The Hobbit* and *The Lord of the Rings* under the title *The Lay of the Ring* [Повесть о Кольце]. A bizarre frame narrative features a character called Tolkien who claims to have received the text from a scientist friend working at 'the Institute of Difficult Studies in Derbyshire', alongside numerous characters drawn from a Polish science fiction novel Bobyr had also translated.[7] Despite Bobyr's efforts to emasculate Tolkien's work for the Russian censors, they refused publication, but the text was typed and copied and circulated among literati in Russia. Bobyr eventually published more faithful translations of both *The Hobbit* and *LotR* in 1991, but her earliest attempts are now considered to be 'Soviet propaganda' by some readers.[8] As Mark Hooker has chronicled in his *Tolkien through Russian Eyes*, Bobyr's bastardisation was just the first of 'many exemplars [of Tolkien's work which] began as *samizdat*, illegal, oft-copied typescript versions passed around during the Soviet era'.[9]

Tolkien's work remained in a similar vein of distortion until the publication of authorised translations by Vladimir Muravyev and Andrej Kistyakovskiy in 1992, after the fall of the Soviet Union. Tolkien was considered a reactionary Western writer by the Soviet authorities, who tended to view his work with the sort of

4. The title refers to the last of the Nazgûl which features prominently in Yeskov's tale; but the ambiguity of also referring to Frodo which occurs in Russian is lost in Tolkien's English term 'ringwraith'.

5. See Maria Komenkovich, 'The Secret War and the End of the First Age: Tolkien in the (former) USSR', *Mallorn* 29 (1992), 33–38; and Olga Markova, 'When Philology Becomes Ideology: The Russian Perspective of J.R.R. Tolkien', trans. Mark T. Hooker, *Tolkien Studies* 1 (2004), 163–70.

6. Markova, op. cit., p. 163.

7. This was Stanislaw Lem's *Eden*.

8. 'I won't now tell of such a famous example as the scandal around the *LoTR* translation made by Zinaida Bobyr in early 1980s. The book was totally violated, new characters were added, all the motivations were changed and as a result Tolkien's book appeared to be a Soviet propaganda.' Excerpted from the Ukrainian blog *Catching the Arrow*, 10 October 2009 entry <http://sister-martha.livejournal.com/1619.html?thread=10067> [accessed 10 August 2012].

9. Timothy Wickham-Crowley, 'Tolkien through Russian Eyes (review)', *Tolkien Studies* 2 (2005), 285–87, p. 285.

suspicion that Markova discovered was still circulating long after the collapse of Communism. Markova cites a 1997 Russian literary journal which stated baldly that *LotR* was 'an encoded description of the conflict of the political darkness of the East and the freedom of the West, and a prediction of the inevitable fall of Mordor and its analog on the real earth, the Soviet Union'.[10]

Inspired to sneak Tolkien past the Soviet censors, who objected to this supposed Cold War subtext to *LotR*, translators like Bobyr felt free to add, delete, amend or distort as they saw fit. The critic Timothy Wickham-Crowley notes that 'The sheer level of textual bastardisation, bowdlerisation, and unnecessary and mind-boggling deletions and insertions is impressive ... To see those alterations for even a few selected passages shows us that many Russian translators clearly felt authorised to (a) do Tolkien better than he did himself, (b) alter him to fit with their perceptions of a Russian cultural audience, (c) remove elements that might attract the attention of censors or censurers, or (d) some combination of those elements.'[11]

After 1991, Tolkien proved influential over a generation of Russians, some of whom adopted the War of the Ring as an analog of the fall of Communism. Others adapted the mythos for live action roleplaying. But Russian copyright laws, which lack Western stringency, contributed to a fast and loose treatment of Tolkien and other writers, despite the existence of authorised translations. As early as 1985, Nick Perumov was writing fan fiction based on the world Tolkien had created. Set in the Fourth Age, some three centuries after the War of the Ring, his two novels about 'hack-and-slash' hobbits - Эльфийский Клинок (Elven Blade) and Черное Копье (Black Lance) proved popular with the friends among whom he circulated them, and were eventually re-edited and published as a single volume entitled Кольцо Тьмы (Ring of Darkness), which sold enormously in Russia and established Perumov as a professional writer.

Perumov's trilogy – a third book entitled Адамант Хенны (The Adamant of Henna) was published in 1995 – features the adventures of Folko Brandybuck, the heir of Merry, as he leads his hobbit and dwarf comrades against a new threat rising from the East, where Olmer seeks to gather the remaining rings of the Nazgûl. Perumov's texts are notable for two innovations; warlike hobbits and a humanised, sympathetic depiction of Uruk-hai.

Inspired by these inversions, and by Perumov's popularity, other Russian writers began to look at inverting Tolkien's mythos. In 1992, Natalia Vassilyeva (known by her pen-name Nienna) and her co-writer Illet (N. Nekrasova) wrote Черная Книга Арды, or *The Black Book of Arda*, which was a retelling of

10. Markova, op. cit. [5], p. 165.
11. Op. cit. [9], p. 286.

'The Ainulindalë' and *Quenta Silmarillion* sections of *The Silmarillion* from Melkor's perspective. In the Black Book, Eru Ilúvatar and his Valar are depicted as cruel tyrants demanding total obeisance, and Melkor by contrast becomes a misunderstood and wise teacher and martyr who simply wishes to go his own way. By 1995, after an expanded version was published in two volumes, *The Black Book of Arda* was so popular in Russia it had spawned its own subculture, a mash-up of Goth, Middle-earth and live action roleplaying known as Niennism.

One can hence speak of a burgeoning tradition in Russian fantasy literature of subverting Tolkien's *oeuvre*, entirely outside of Western copyright law, to erode his binary good versus evil paradigm. This is the context in which we should consider Kyrill Yeskov's *The Last Ringbearer*. Yeskov attained prominence as a scientist and is best known for his discovery of a number of new genera of arachnids, but he is also an accomplished fiction writer with a track record of reworking existing texts from new perspectives, specifically to accommodate contemporary science. Prior to *The Last Ringbearer*, Yeskov wrote *The Gospel of Aphranius*, a recalibration of the Gospel narrative from the perspective of Pilate's head of secret police, a character whom he borrowed from Mikhail Bulgakov's *The Master and Margarita*. While Yeskov's fiction is available for purchase in Russia, the Tolkien estate has understandably prevented its publication in the West. However, the emergence of an English translation online in 2010 attracted the attention of publications like *The Guardian* and *Salon* magazine, as well as thousands of readers.

The alternative title of Nienna's *Black Book of Arda – Chronicles of the Defeated* – illuminates the starting point for Kyrill Yeskov when he came to write *The Last Ringbearer*. Indeed, the opening section of Yeskov's novel is entitled Vae Victis, or *The Path of the Vanquished*. Both texts illustrate their intentions in these subtitles – to subvert Tolkien's good versus evil paradigm by offering the perspective of the losers. This is not a uniquely Russian phenomenon, of course. The first organised Tolkien society, the Fellowship of the Ring, published in 1960 a brief four-page story chronicling the First to Fourth Ages from Sauron's perspective, written by George Heap, in the first edition of their short-lived fanzine *I Palantir*.[12]

There is an estimable tradition of inverted narratives in literature, from Voltaire's *The White Bull*,[13] which retells the Biblical tale of Nebuchadnezzar from the villain's point of view, up to more contemporary texts like Margaret Atwood's *Penelopiad*, the *Odyssey* from the wife's perspective, or *Jack Maggs*,

12. George Heap, 'Departure in Peace', *I Palantir* 1, (1960), 4–7.

13. Yeskov has claimed to have been educated amid a 'nest of Voltaireans.' Kirill Yeskov, *The Last Ringbearer* (1999), trans. Yisroel Markov, 2010, updated trans., 2011, unpublished edition, p. 247 <http://ymarkov.livejournal.com/280578.html> [accessed14 February 2012].

Peter Carey's reconstruction of *Great Expectations* from Magwitch' point of view. Yeskov himself dates the origin of the tradition back to the First Century Greek writer *Dio Chrysostom*.[14] Such inverted texts are especially prevalent in fantasy literature.[15] Marion Zimmer Bradley's renowned *Mists of Avalon* series reworked the Arthurian legends from the perspective of female protagonists, while Fred Saberhagen's nine *Dracula File* novels told the story from Vlad Dracul's perspective. More recently, Gregory Maguire's *Wicked* series follows in a tradition initiated by Philip Jose Farmer's *A Barnstormer in Oz*, by inverting Frank L. Baum's classic series. The Inklings themselves were not immune to this method of fiction writing. C.S. Lewis's final work, the 1956 novel *Till We Have Faces* is an retelling of the Cupid and Psyche myth that haunted him his entire life, from the perspective of Psyche's 'evil' older sister Orual. Even Tolkien flirted with the methodology in the fragment 'Tal-Elmar' (from *The Peoples of Middle Earth*) wherein Tal-Elmar witnesses Númenórean colonisation of Middle Earth, and relates it from the perspective of one of those colonised.

So much for Yeskov's bona fides. 'The World is Text', characters tell us throughout *The Last Ringbearer*, a phrase the author tells us in his notes is 'a reference to Umberto Eco's "open text" philology.'[16] Eco's 1962 work *Opera Aperta* explored the notion of closed and open texts. A closed text is, for Eco, one that is narrowly focused, potentially didactic, shorn of nuance and ambiguity, whereas an open text which permits and luxuriates in the nuances of language and meaning is deemed the more rewarding. If we consider Tolkien's paradigm of good versus evil to be somewhat 'closed', then Yeskov seems intent on opening it up to nuance and ambiguity. If *LotR* is a tale told in black and white, Yeskov's novel comes in fifty shades of grey.

Some readers have considered *The Last Ringbearer* to be closer in tone to the work of John Le Carré than J.R.R. Tolkien, but despite the plots within plots and

---

14. 'The founder of this literary tradition of playing with others' masks and backdrops was one Dio Chrysostomos, a Greek who lived under the Roman Empire; dissecting Homer's text with the scalpel of irony, while strictly abiding by his "facts", he had rather convincingly proved that the Greek Achaeans had suffered a resounding defeat at the hands of the Greek Trojans and went home emptyhanded, and that the rest was all pure PR, to use a modern term.' Op. cit., p. 247.

15. Yeskov is not alone in reconstructing an alternative narrative out of *LotR*. Michael Aquino's 2003 novel *Morlindale* is presented as a series of scrolls written between Melkor, Sauron, the Witch-King of Angmar, and the Blue Wizard Pallando. Parts of *The Silmarillion* and *LotR* are retold in this epistolary form, recasting Tolkien's world as a rebellion of Melkor and his followers against the authoritarian and cruel Valar. Aquino's novel is significantly marred by the epistolary form and turgid style, as well as the ambiguous glosses and footnotes whose authorship (whether that of Aquino himself or his characters) is unexplained. As a text it is clearly much more 'fanfic' than Yeskov's work. It also emerged some four years after *The Last Ringbearer*. It, too, is not commercially available in English due to copyright constraints.

16. Op. cit. [13], p. 237.

spy-versus-spy narrative, Yeskov's primary purpose in reworking *LotR* appears to be based on an objection to Tolkien's science, perhaps unsurprising coming from a man best known professionally as a biologist.[17] Yeskov began by querying the practicalities of Middle-earth's geography, concluding as science journalist Henry Gee does that the arena of the War of the Ring must be only a small north-western fraction of the world of Arda. Gee suggests a non-submerged Rockall plateau as a possible contender for Middle-earth,[18] but acknowledges that few of its features are cognate. He is also not alone in noticing that 'the line of the continental shelf off north-west Europe looks startlingly like the northwest of Middle-earth, with The Bay of Biscay matching the Bay of Belfalas.'[19] Tolkien himself suggested that '[t]he action of the story takes place in the North-west of 'Middle-earth', equivalent in latitude to the coastlands of Europe and the north shores of the Mediterranean.[20] But this is not a purely 'Nordic' area in any sense. If Hobbiton and Rivendell are taken (as intended) to be about the latitude of Oxford, then Minas Tirith, 600 miles south, is at about the latitude of Florence. The Mouths of Anduin and the ancient city of Pelargir are at about the latitude of ancient Troy.' He expanded on this in a 1966 interview with Henry Resnick, in which he explained: 'Rhûn is the Elvish word for east. Asia, China, Japan, and all the things which people in the West regard as far away. And south of Harad is Africa, the hot countries.' He added that Mordor 'would be roughly in the Balkans'.[21]

So there is more to Arda than Middle-earth, and Yeskov intends to introduce those wider world perspectives to the War of the Ring. If we are encouraged by Tolkien to think of *LotR*, or indeed *The Hobbit*, from an in-world perspective, that is, to consider them as narratives extracted from the *Red Book* text initiated by Bilbo as *There and Back Again*, equally Yeskov offers us an in-world perspective of his own. His narrative is presented 'from the standpoint of an imaginary

17. Yeskov is employed at the Paleontological Institute of the Russian Academy of Sciences as a world-renowned expert on arachnids, and is responsible for discovering several new genera of spiders.

18. Doggerland, the contiguous territory of Britain, Ireland and northwest Europe encompassing what is now beneath the North and Irish Seas, which slowly submerged as ice melted after the last ice age between 18,000 BC and 5,500 BC, comes closest to Middle-earth of any historical geological territory that has actually existed on Earth. It was described by Dr Richard Bates of St Andrews University in July 2012 as 'the real heartland of Europe until sea levels rose to give us the UK coastline of today.' See 'Hidden Doggerland underworld uncovered in North Sea', *BBC News*, 4 July 2012, <http://www.bbc.co.uk/news/uk-scotland-edinburgh-east-fife-18687504> [accessed 4 July 2012].

19. Henry Gee, *The Science of Middle Earth*, Souvenir Press, London, 2004, p. 61.

20. Op. cit. [1], Letter 294, p. 376.

21. Henry Resnick, 'The Hobbit-forming World of J.R.R. Tolkien', *The Saturday Evening Post*, 2 July 1966, vol. 239, issue 14, 90–94.

modern Gondorian revisionist historian,' and 'is intended to cast the entire work as an alternative history written in the real Arda, where The Lord of the Rings is the accepted "mainstream" version of actual historical events.'[22]

What is that 'mainstream' version? We can summarise it as a war of aggression launched by a coalition of Isengard and Mordor, with additional mercenary allies from the South and East, upon the free peoples of the West, primarily Rohan and Gondor. The aim of the war is total domination, and the methods used are overwhelming military force and seeking to obtain the Ring of Power. Only through a series of almost implausible heroics does the defensive coalition manage to destroy the One Ring, thereby weakening the opposition and bringing the war to a conclusion. But what happens to Mordor after the War? We are told in a single line that, before wedding Arwen, Aragorn pardons the Haradrim and Easterlings who surrendered, 'and the slaves of Mordor he released and gave to them all the lands about Lake Núrnen to be their own' (*RotK*, 'The Steward and the King', 1005).[23]

So the slaves inherit Mordor. Unless we concur with Peter Jackson's non-canonical cinematic approach, in which Sauron's hordes appear to be mere puppets whose strings are cut and who perish when the Ring is destroyed, then we are left with the conundrum of what happened to those armies in the aftermath of the War. Are they the slaves referred to by Tolkien, or does this term merely relate to the backline forces stationed behind the lines who produced the food and equipment needed by the armies?

Yeskov provides an answer, predicated on his approach of rewriting the history from the perspective of the losers: they were massacred in an Elvish-led genocide. This can obviously be read in keeping with the old Soviet understanding of *LotR* as a text which expresses Western hegemony, in which case the notion of a genocide in the East has obvious parallels with the obscenity of Russian losses during World War II. But Yeskov is more subtle than this, and his actual motivation again is to resolve what he perceives as science-based gaps in Tolkien's mythography. If the Orcs are mere automatons, driven only by pure evil as Tolkien would have it, then there is little to regret in their eradication. As Dimitra Fimi notes, '[i]n all of Tolkien's "legendarium" the Orcs are hardly ever described in detail – they are only identified as evil'.[24] But Yeskov re-opens the suggestion of racism in Tolkien, which has been debated extensively by critics like Michael Drout, Tom Shippey, Stephen Shapiro and Anderson Rearick, in a wholly new way by presenting the Orcs and Trolls as humans of a different

22. Op. cit. [14], p. 247.
23. J.R.R. Tolkien, *The Lord of the Rings*, Unwin Paperbacks, London, 1978. All quotations from *LotR* are taken from this edition.
24. Op. cit. [2], p. 155.

race to the Westerners. This is partly justified by Tolkien's own writings on the matter, since he described the Orcs in a letter as 'squat, broad, flat-nosed, sallow-skinned, with wide mouths and slant eyes: in fact degraded and repulsive versions of the (to Europeans) least lovely Mongol-types.'[25] One of the heroes of Yeskov's story, Tzerlag, is introduced as 'a typical Orocuen by his looks, short and wide-faced – in other words, the very 'Orc' that mothers of Westernesse use to scare unruly children'.[26]

This amendment of Tolkien's fantasy architecture both resolves the ongoing problem of the origin of the Orcs,[27] and adapts the *LotR* narrative to Yeskov's more politically nuanced version of Middle-earth. As Linda Hutcheon once wrote, 'a theory of fantasy literature must … draw upon a concept of fictive referents ... because surely vampires, devils, unicorns, and hobbits exist only in words. Only language can allow us to conceive of the absent, the unreal, the supernatural.'[28] A similar point was made by Tzvetan Todorov in his *Introduction to Fantastic Literature* in 1970. *The Last Ringbearer* does retain some elements of the Supernatural, especially in relation to the existence of magic in Middle-earth, though its remit is significantly reduced. In this subversion, Yeskov takes literally Tolkien's own statement, in *On Fairy-Stories*, that we cannot apply the term 'supernatural' to entities such as fairies (or, by extension, Elves, hobbits, trolls or Orcs), because 'they are natural, far more natural than' mankind. Note that Yeskov is not laying an accusation of racism upon Tolkien, but upon the peoples of the West within Middle-earth; as *LotR* is the narrative of the victors, it is they who have demonised and dehumanised their vanquished enemies. As Henry Gee astutely noticed, as early as *The Hobbit* one can identify different races of Orcs, and the racial schema underpinning Tolkien's Middle-earth implies 'a parade of forms starting with Moria Orcs and proceeding in sequence through Mordor Orcs, Uruks, Squint-Eyed Southerners, Dunlendings, Bree-Men, Rohirrim, Men of Gondor and finally High Númenóreans aspiring to transcendent Elfhood.'[29] Patrick Curry describes any reconstruction of the races of Middle-earth as analogues to races of humanity as 'a crude simplification',[30] and it is highly likely

25. Op. cit. [1], Letter 210, p. 274.
26. Op. cit. [13], p. 4.
27. Tolkien struggled endlessly with constructing a coherent origin for Orcs. Late in his writing career, he considered the idea of Orcs as corrupted Men rather than Elves, or corrupted fallen Maia, and even the possibility of Orcs as automata created by Sauron. See J.R.R. Tolkien, *Morgoth's Ring*, ed. Christopher Tolkien, Houghton Mifflin Harcourt, Boston, 1993, pp. 408–24.
28. Linda Hutcheon, *Narcissistic Narrative: the metafictional paradox*, Routledge, London, 1984, p. 98.
29. Op. cit. [19], p. 80.
30. Patrick Curry, *Defending Middle-Earth: Tolkien, Myth and Modernity*, Floris Books, Edinburgh, 1997, p. 52.

that Tolkien would have agreed. Nevertheless, this is Yeskov's first principle in his recasting of the War of the Ring from the perspective of the losers. His first task is to demonsterise the forces of Sauron by making them as human as the Men of the West.

This spectrum of being is paralleled by a sliding scale of relative industrialisation. From the earthly paradises of the Elven arboreal havens, via the bucolic Shire, agrarian Rohan and Romanesque Gondor to the dark Satanic Mills of Isengard and Mordor, we encounter a spectrum of relative industrialisation that is as much moral as it is infrastructural. The clear moral delineation between Sauron and his allies and the combined forces of the West is evoked repeatedly by contrasting their relative responses to industrialisation and scientific experimentation. We can surmise why Tolkien envisaged such a spectrum. As Henry Gee suggests, 'Tolkien objected to the kinds of heavy industry and urbanisation that destroys rural landscapes and wilderness.'[31] More expansively, Patrick Curry describes how 'Tolkien himself, of course, was deeply hostile to modernity, root and branch – capitalism (especially industrialism), unrestrained science, and state power alike.'[32]

It follows, then, that moral authority rests relatively with those who impact least upon nature in Tolkien. While the Elves clearly possess advanced technology in *LotR*, it is based on what we might call 'magic' rather than industrial science. The Elves may not agree with that description, and indeed they seem puzzled on the two occasions that the hobbits ask them to demonstrate their magic in Lothlórien (*FotR*, 'The Mirror of Galadriel', 381; 'Farewell to Lorien', 390).[33] Henry Gee's conclusion 'that there is no such thing as magic in Middle-earth' seems disingenuous given his own valiant failure to scientifically explain so many Elvish phenomena in terms that are compatible with our own laws of physics and chemistry; from the mysterious Elven rope that apparently responds to the morality of those who touch it, to the astonishingly nutritious Lembas bread and ultra-light yet impermeable Mithril, what seems magical to us is, we must conclude, the product of Elvish technology that is far more sophisticated and mature than our own. As Arthur C. Clarke once wrote, 'any sufficiently advanced technology is indistinguishable from magic'.[34]

It is important to recognise that, as Gee states, 'the Elves had an "industrial"

31. Op. cit. [19], p. 187.
32. Op. cit. [30], p. 25.
33. Galadriel tells Sam she does 'not understand clearly' what the term magic means, and Pippin receives the same answer from an Elf as the Fellowship prepare to leave Lothlórien. See op. cit. [23].
34. Arthur C. Clarke, 'Foreword to Millennial edition,' in his *Profiles of the Future: An Enquiry into the Limits of the Possible*, Indigo, London, 1999, p. 2.

phase that started with Fëanor in the First Age and culminated with the Elven-smiths of Eregion in the Second, but partly as a result of the disastrous wars with Morgoth and Sauron consequent on such industrialisation, Elvish technology became far more organic and less obvious'.[35] Hence Yeskov's novel describes a war predicated on a clash of competing technologies: Elvish magic versus Mordorian *magia*, or the 'machine' as Tolkien put it in a 1951 letter to his editor. Yeskov's hypothesis depends on pursuing Tolkien's physiological and topographical descriptions of Middle Earth to a logical conclusion. If Mordor is the scorched earth wasteland described by Tolkien, how could the innumerable hordes of Sauron's army be fed and maintained? Yeskov's answer is by technological advancement and trade. Yeskov's Mordor is a parliamentary monarchy led by the 'nominal power' of 'King Sauron the VIII' which is suffering from desertification as a result of climate change,[36] a hypothesis Yeskov based on a geological analysis of Tolkien's Middle Earth topography, and Mordor has as a result reduced its professional armies to balance an ever-decreasing budget. However, it is known in Arda as 'the World's Smithy', a designation for England at the height of the Industrial revolution according to Yeskov,[37] 'and it could trade its manufactured goods for any amounts of food from Khand and Umbar', which explains the Mordorian threat to Elven hegemony in the West.

This inversion of Tolkien's Mordor presents us with a depiction of Barad-dûr as the Enlightenment capital of Arda, a sort of ancient Rome or early medieval Baghdad, or as Yeskov describes it, 'that amazing city of alchemists and poets, mechanics and astronomers, philosophers and physicians, the heart of the only civilisation in Middle Earth to bet on rational knowledge and bravely pitch its barely adolescent technology against ancient magic.'[38]

This burgeoning advancement is an obvious threat to Elven domination in the West, and via the mediation of vested proxies like Gandalf (who stands to claim domination of the White Council) and Aragorn (who seeks to usurp the House of Húrin), they provoke a war designed to eradicate the Mordorian threat and restrict the spread of industrialisation. In *The Last Ringbearer*, Yeskov offers the defeated Mordorians some cold comfort, however. Though 'the mysterious Mordorian civilisation' may be only a footnote of history in his imaginary Gondorian historian's text, nevertheless the final reflexive act of defiance by Mordor's remnants against Elven magic proves definitive. In the distant future of Arda, the destruction of Elven power forces Aragorn to renounce his plans for global domination based on Elven support and instead open up Gondor to global

35. Op. cit. [19], p. 183.
36. Op. cit. [13], p. 14.
37. Op. cit. [13], p. 9.
38. Op. cit. [13], p. 7.

trade, ushering in the modern age. The political institutions Aragorn introduces to counterbalance the power of a resentful Gondorian nobility become the bedrock of early democracy in Middle-earth, and his success is largely based on stolen Mordorian technology.

Yeskov's novel demonstrates the positive elements of industrialisation that Tolkien's narrative refuses to countenance. Tolkien's binary good versus evil, pastoral versus industrial paradigm is questioned cleverly by Yeskov in what amounts to an imaginative and enlightening recreation of Tolkien's universe that sets his novel far above the many other bastardisations of Tolkien that have emanated from Russia or elsewhere. We do not need to accept Yeskov's Middle-earth as in any way canonical or legitimate to acknowledge his core point: Tolkien's admirable attachment to rural England blinded him to the possibility that industrialisation can sometimes be positive and progressive, and that few if any conflicts are ever entirely black and white.

'Legal bother: Law and related matters in The Hobbit'

Murray Smith

This essay considers the importance of law in The Hobbit concerning three legal matters. First, Bilbo Baggin's contract with Thorin and Company; second, the Lake-men's claim for reparations; and third, Bilbo being 'Presumed Dead'. They take place against a background of morality and business. First, the legitimacy of Thorin's claim to be king, the dwarves' claim to the treasure, and their hiring of Bilbo. Second, the fact that they and others are business peoples, influencing their attitudes towards law. I believe that this law was used by Tolkien to give The Hobbit an important legal framework, fundamental to the story, with a very modern air. The law was based on concepts that emerged in the nineteenth century, and on the post-WWI claims for reparations from Germany, making the book a sophisticated one.

INTRODUCTION

The essay is an overview and analysis of what I believe is the importance of law in *The Hobbit*, and related matters of morality and business. By 'law' I do not just mean specific legal documents, acts and institutions, but also attitudes towards law, and its relationship with morality and business. This importance becomes particularly clear in three incidents in the book: first, Bilbo's contract with Thorin and Company; second, the Lake-men's case for reparations for the death and destruction caused by Smaug's attack; and third, Bilbo being presumed dead by the laws in his country. These three incidents take place against a background of morality and business. First, the legitimacy of Thorin's claim as King Under the Mountain, the dwarves' claim to the treasure stolen by Smaug, and the legitimacy of their hiring Bilbo Baggins for the job. Second, the fact that not just the dwarves, but also hobbits, Elves and Lake-men are business peoples, to a greater and lesser degree, influencing their attitudes towards law. It is no shock that the dwarves hire Bilbo under a contract, a very important document, whose rights he stands over. Also, the Lake-men insist on the importance of reparations, as well as payment for the help given. It is my belief that this law was used by Tolkien to give *The Hobbit* an important legal background, fundamental to the story, associated with morality and business. This legal background has a very modern air, the law Tolkien uses being based on concepts that emerged in the nineteenth century and in the post-WWI legal claims for reparations, adding to the book's sophistication.

THREE LEGAL MATTERS

1. Bilbo's contract with Thorin and Company:

This is divided into three parts: first, the agreement between Bilbo and Thorin and Company; second, comparing it with the English law of contract; third, arguing that Bilbo is an independent contractor.

a. The agreement:

Gandalf scratched 'a queer sign' on Bilbo's front-door (*TH*, 'An Unexpected Party', 18),[1] 'the usual one in the trade, or used to be. *Burglar wants a good job, plenty of Excitement and reasonable Reward*' (*TH*, 'An Unexpected Party', 28). Bilbo received a letter, signed by 'Thorin & Co.', containing the agreement, in particular:

> Terms: cash on delivery, up to and not exceeding one fourteenth of total profits (if any); all travelling expenses guaranteed in any event; funeral expenses to be defrayed by us or our representatives, if occasion arises and the matter is not otherwise arranged for.

To accept, Bilbo had to turn up at 'the Green Dragon Inn, Bywater, at 11 a.m. sharp. Trusting that you will be *punctual*'. This Bilbo did (*TH*, 'Roast Mutton', 38–39).

When the Mountain's secret entrance was found, Thorin pointed out that now was Bilbo's time 'to perform the service for which he was included in our Company', the time for him 'to earn his Reward.' Bilbo was a little indignant, because 'I have got you out of two messes [the spiders and the Elvenking's cells] already, which were *hardly in the original bargain*, so that I am, I think, already owed some reward' (*TH*, 'Inside Information', 203, my italics). After they hid from Smaug, and the dwarves 'began to grumble' at him, he angrily pointed out: 'I was *not engaged to kill dragons*, that is warrior's work, *but to steal treasure*.'(*TH*, 'Inside Information', 210, my italics)

After surviving going down a second time, Bilbo was promised by Thorin: 'you shall choose your own fourteenth [share]' (*TH*, 'Inside Information', 219); and he later took the Arkenstone on those grounds. But he had an uncomfortable

1. J.R.R. Tolkien, *The Hobbit*, HarperCollins, 1991. All quotations from *TH* are taken from this edition.

feeling that this 'had not been really meant' to include it (*TH*, 'Not at Home', 225). Later, he gave away his share, to resolve the conflict with the Lake-men and Elves. When some Elves called him 'that queer little creature that is said to be their servant', Bilbo snorted 'Servant, indeed!' calling himself Thorin's 'companion'.

Talking with Bard and the Elvenking in 'his best business manner', Bilbo pointed out his interest in the matter, taking out the letter, 'crumpled and much folded'. It was a fourteenth share 'in the *profits*, mind you', he being 'only too ready to consider all your claims carefully, and deduct what is right from the total before putting in my own claim'. Bilbo was 'willing to let it [the Arkenstone] stand against all my claim … I may be a burglar – or so they say: personally I never really felt like one – but I am an honest one, I hope, more or less' (*TH*, 'A Thief in the Night', 253–56). He later explained to the enraged Thorin: 'Take it that I have disposed of my share as I wished'. To redeem the Arkenstone, Thorin promised one fourteenth of the hoard 'in silver and gold'. This would be 'the promised share of this traitor [Bilbo] ... and you can divide it as you will' (*TH*, 'The Clouds Burst', 259–60).

Thorin did not keep this agreement; but his successor Dain did. Bard said the treasure was 'as much yours [Bilbo's] as it is mine, though old agreements cannot stand'. Though Bilbo was willing to 'lay aside' his claim, Bard wished that Thorin's repented words 'that we should give you little' should not prove true. He 'would reward you [Bilbo] most richly of all'. Bilbo accepted only 'two small chests, one filled with silver, and the other with gold, such as one strong pony could carry' (*TH*, 'The Return Journey', 259–60). Might he also consider them payment for his help in rescuing the dwarves twice?

b. The English law of contract:

In English law, a 'contract' is a voluntary agreement between two parties, with six elements. First, an offer made by one party to the other; second, the other party accepting this offer; third, an intention by the parties to be legally bound; fourth, the agreement is supported by consideration. Fifth, the parties have the legal capacity to enter into a contract. Sixth, the contract must not be illegal.[2] This general outline of what is in a contract emerged in the nineteenth century, due to the actions of judges and writers.[3]

2. J. Beatson, A. Burrows, and J. Cartwright, *Anson's Law of Contract*, 29th edn, Oxford University Press, Oxford, 2010, pp. 1–2; Ewan McKendrick, *Contract Law: Text, Cases, and Materials*, 4th edn, Oxford University Press, Oxford, 2010, pp. 3–5.

3. A. H. Manchester, *A Modern Legal History of England and Wales 1750–1950*, Butterworths, London, 1980, pp. 67–74; *Anson*, op. cit., pp. 16–17; McKendrick, op., cit. p. 6.

i. Offer:

This is a statement by a party of a willingness to be legally bound by its terms. The relevant contract here is a 'bilateral' one, each party making a promise or promises to each other. There is a difference between an offer and an intention to treat (or negotiate). Advertisements, in bilateral contracts, are generally seen as intentions to negotiate.[4]

ii. Acceptance:

The acceptance by the other party must correspond with the offer made, called the 'mirror image' rule, or else the acceptance is a counter offer. An offeror, the person making the offer, may state that the offer's acceptance must be made in a particular manner.[5]

iii. Intention to be legally bound:

The parties intend to be legally bound by the terms of the agreement reached between them.[6]

iv. Consideration:

To enforce a promise, the person to whom that promise was made has to have given something in return. The law makes a distinction between a legally enforceable bargain and a promise to make a gift. While the consideration has to be something of value, it need not be adequate.[7]

v. Capacity to contract:

The law limits the capacity of certain persons to bind themselves by contract. 'Thorin and Company' is, I believe, not a limited company with a legal personality separate from its individual members, but a 'partnership', a form of contract which can be entered into by two or more people combining their money, goods or labour with a view to profit.[8]

vi. A contract must not be illegal:

English law will not enforce illegal contracts.[9] A partnership agreement can be illegal if the purpose for which it is formed is illegal, and also, though the

---

4. *Anson*, op. cit. [2], pp. 30–31, 33–34; McKendrick, op. cit. [2], pp. 45, 56–63.
5. *Anson*, op. cit. [2], pp. 42–43, 51–52; McKendrick, op. cit. [2], pp. 82, 103–104.
6. McKendrick, op. cit. [2], pp. 273–77.
7. *Anson*, op. cit. [2], pp. 91, 93, 99–101; McKendrick, op. cit. [2], pp. 149–51.
8. Geoffrey Morse, *Partnership Law*, 7th edn, Oxford University Press, Oxford, 2010, pp. 84–85.
9. *Anson*, op. cit. [2], pp. 379, 384–85. See also Mindy Chen-Wishart, *Contract Law*, 3rd edn, Oxford University Press, Oxford, 2010, p. 459.

purpose can be attained by legal means, it is carried out in an illegal way.[10]

All six elements met:

The agreement between Bilbo and Thorin and Company meets all these elements of a valid contract, particularly the sixth. Bilbo, an 'honest' burglar, is helping some people take back their property. He survived in the Elvenking's caves by stealing food and drink, but paid compensation, explaining, 'some little return should be made for your, er, hospitality. I mean even a burglar has his feelings' (*TH*, 'The Return Journey', 275). This compensation presumably includes his theft of food and drink from a village by the Forest River (*TH*, 'Barrels Out of Bond', 179–80). I therefore agree with Tom Shippey's description of him as a 'bourgeois burglar',[11] with, in my opinion, a 'bourgeois' attitude about the importance of law.

c. Servant, indeed!

The legal basis for employment in English law is the contract of employment between the 'employer' and the 'employee',[12] the older terminology being 'master' and 'servant'. A person in business on his own is an 'independent contractor' or a 'self employed person', working under a 'contract for services'.[13] Due to legal intervention in favour of employees, employers have tried to classify many as independent contractors, resulting in courts looking behind the written agreement.

In English law when John Rateliff estimated *The Hobbit* was written (1930-33),[14] the main test the courts used was the 'control' test.[15] If one party exercised sufficient control over a second, the relationship of employer and employee existed. In Walker v. The Crystal Palace Football Club Ltd. [1910] 1 KB 87, this test determined that a professional football player was an employee.

I believe that Bilbo Baggins was an independent contractor. Using the control test, the dwarves do not treat him as an employee. Indeed, he on two occasions *led* them. Thorin calls Bilbo their 'companion'; and he confronted Smaug alone, using his own equipment. He rejected the Elves calling him a 'servant', and is therefore free to give away his reward.

He also has the financial and social freedom to do so. In financial terms, he

10. See op cit [8] p. 87.
11. Tom Shippey, *The Road to Middle-earth,* rev. edn. HarperCollins, London, 2005, pp. 82–83.
12. *Halsbury's Laws of England*, 5th edn, vol. 39, Lexis Nexis, London, 2009, p. 17, para. 1.
13. See op. cit., n. 1.
14. John D. Rateliff, *The History of the Hobbit*, vol. 1: *Mr. Baggins*, HarperCollins, London, 2007, pp. xi–xx.
15. Malcolm Sargeant and David Lewis, *Employment Law*, 5th edn, Pearson Education, Harlow, 2010, pp. 20–21.

can do without the treasure. In a letter to *The Observer* of 20th February 1938, Tolkien said that Bilbo had 'independent means'.[16] In social terms, the Baggins family were 'very respectable', because of wealth and 'also because they never had any adventures or did anything unexpected'. By contrast, Bilbo's Took relatives were richer but 'not as respectable', because members would 'have adventures' (*TH*, 'An Unexpected Party', 13–14)

While my view is that the Baggins family are 'gentry', landowners who live off the rents of their lands, Bilbo is 'aggressively *middle* middle-class' in his behaviour, including, I feel, in his attitude towards law.[17]

2. Reparations:

In the original manuscript of *The Hobbit*, the Lake-men's attitude to the dwarves after Smaug's attack is particularly vengeful:

> The anguish of the Lake-men & <wrath> of the Master. They now hate the dwarves as source of the <trouble>: some even suggest the <?driving forth> of the dragon against them was deliberate.

The Elvenking and his army join with Bard and the Lake-men; and 'They go north to capture <the> dwarves and the gold'.

Rateliff pointed out that while the anger of the Lake-men was 'understandable enough', their 'eagerness to fix blame and demand reparations smacks more of post-Great War politics than *wergild*'.[18] I agree with this view, and believe that Tolkien may have been influenced by immediate post-WWI sentiments in the UK towards Germany, which affected the attitudes of political leaders in their dealings with the latter, along with their more vengeful French allies, who with Belgium occupied the Ruhr in 1923.

a. Aftermath of Smaug's attack:

To distract attention from criticism, the Master blamed Smaug's attack on the dwarves:

> 'Who played on our soft hearts and our pleasant fancies? What sort of gold have they sent down the river to reward us? Dragon-fire and

16. Humphrey Carpenter, ed., *The Letters of J.R.R. Tolkien*, with the assistance of Christopher Tolkien, HarperCollins, London, 1995, Letter 25, p. 25.
17. Op. cit. [11], p. 82.
18. John D. Rateliff, *The History of the Hobbit*, vol. 2: *Return to Bag-End*, HarperCollins, London, 2007, pp. 569, 572.

> ruin! From whom should we claim the recompense of our damage, and aid for our widows and orphans?' (*TH*, 'Fire and Water', 238)

Some people then claimed that the dwarves had stirred Smaug up against them deliberately!

While Bard rebuked such behaviour, all thought of the treasure. After being helped by the Elvenking, all the Lake-men still able, and most of his array marched to the Mountain (*TH*, 'Fire and Water', 238–41). Challenged by Thorin, now 'King under the Mountain', Bard identified himself as Smaug's slayer and Girion's heir, the treasure containing 'much of the wealth of his halls and towns'. He also spoke of 'the sorrow and misery' of the people of Lake-town, who had 'aided you in your distress'.

Thorin's reply, influenced by 'the power that gold has upon which a dragon has long brooded' and by his dwarvish heart, was that the Lake-men had no significant legal claim on the treasure:

> *The treasure was not his [Smaug's] that his evil deeds should be amended with a share of it*. The price of the goods and the assistance that we received of the Lake-men we will fairly pay – in due time. *But* ***nothing*** *will we give, not even a loaf's worth, under threat of force*. (*TH*, 'The Gathering of the Clouds', 246; 248–49; my italics)

Bard again appealed for charity, and mentioned again his own claims. Thorin again pointed out the presence of soldiers, including the Elvenking's. Bard refused to dismiss the Elves, due to the Elvenking's help. Later, an ultimatum was delivered to Thorin, '*calling himself* the King under the Mountain' (*TH*, 'The Gathering of the Clouds', 249, my italics), for at least a twelfth of the treasure be given to Bard 'as the dragon-slayer and heir of Girion'. From that he will aid the Lake-men; but, 'if Thorin would have the friendship and honour of the lands about, as his sires had of old, then he will give also somewhat of his own for the comfort of the men of the Lake.'

Thorin shot an arrow at the speaker, leading to a declaration that the mountain was besieged. They would not fight; 'but we leave you to your gold. You may eat that, if you will!' Thorin was 'so grim' that 'the others would not have dared to find fault with him; but indeed most of them seemed to share his mind', except for Bombur, Fili, Kili and Bilbo (*TH*, 'The Gathering of the Clouds', 250–51).

b. Making Germany pay:

Due to World War I's devastation, many in the UK had a great deal of anti-

German feelings, and wanted Germany to pay for that war,[19] encouraged by sections of the press and many politicians.[20]

A general election took place on 14th December 1918, the electorate being three times what it was at the last election in 1910.[21] When Prime Minister David Lloyd George began his election campaign on 24th November, the audience wanted to hear about his plans to punish the Germans. On 29th November, he said that Germany must pay 'up to the limit of her capacity to do so'. Also, jurists had concluded that the Kaiser was guilty of 'an indictable offence'. He issued a Statement of Policy on 5th December, which stated, 'The Kaiser must be prosecuted'. On 11th December, he gave an estimate of war damage of £24 million.

Some coalition colleagues went further. George Barnes said, 'I am for hanging the Kaiser'. Sir Eric Geddes said that the Germans 'are going to pay every penny, they are going to be squeezed as a lemon is squeezed – until the pips squeak'. The Coalition parties won 525 out of 707 seats; but Lloyd George knew that he remained Prime Minister by the grace of the majority Conservative Party, led by Andrew Bonar Law.[22]

When the Paris Peace Conference began in January 1919, Lloyd George and French Prime Minister Georges Clemenceau were aware of their political dependence on taking a hard line with Germany.[23]

On 8th April, two hundred and thirty-three Conservative MPs pointed out to Lloyd George that their constituents 'always expected' him 'to present the bill in full' to Germany. Bonar Law went to Paris and discussed the matter with Lloyd George, who returned to confront his critics.

Public opinion in the UK began to change. When the Treaty of Versailles was presented to the Germans, signed by them on 28th June, surprise was expressed at the harshness of the terms.[24]Particularly harsh was Article 231, where Germany and her allies had to accept the responsibility 'for causing all the loss and damage' to the Allied and Associated Governments and peoples 'as a consequence of the

---

19. Ruth Henig, *Versailles and After: 1919–1933*, 2nd edn, Routledge, London and New York, 1997, pp. 1–3.
20. Peter Rowland, *Lloyd George*, Barrie and Jenkins, London, 1975, p. 466; Erik Goldstein, 'Great Britain: The Home Front', in *The Treaty of Versailles: A Reassessment after 75 Years*, Cambridge University Press, Cambridge, 1998, 147–48, pp. 152–53.
21. Rowland, op. cit., p. 466; Charles Loch Mowat, *Britain Between the Wars 1918–1940*, Methuen, London, 1983, pp. 2–3; Goldstein, op. cit., pp. 153–54; Roy Hattersley, *David Lloyd George: The Great Outsider*, Abacus, London, 2012, pp. 481–45.
22. Rowland, op. cit. [20], pp. 467–75; Mowat, op. cit. [21], pp. 4–7; Goldstein, op. cit. [21], pp. 155–56; Hattersley, op. cit. [21], pp. 487–88, 495.
23. See op. cit. [19], pp. 3–4.
24. Goldstein, op. cit. [21], pp. 162–64; Hattersley, op. cit. [21], pp. 504–507.

war imposed upon them by the aggression of Germany and her allies'. Article 232 required Germany to make 'complete reparation' for this. Article 233 said that the amount would be determined by a Reparations Commission, which decided on 132 billion gold marks.[25] The 'war guilt' clause and the level of reparations caused lasting resentment among Germans. Widespread evasions concerning the terms, including reparations, were one result.[26]

c. 1923: Occupation of the Ruhr and hyperinflation:

After the Reparations Commission declared Germany to be in default, France invaded and occupied the Ruhr on 11th January 1923, along with Belgium. The German government, under Chancellor Wilhelm Cuno, ordered a campaign of passive resistance.

To pay for this, the government printed more money, exacerbating the already significant level of inflation such that, by November, the German mark had collapsed, 1 US dollar equalling 630 marks. Wages and salaries were revised with prices on a daily basis.

Gustav Stresemann, who replaced Cuno on 12th August, abandoned passive resistance and introduced a new currency in November. The intended psychological effect worked; and inflation began to reduce.[27]

The hyperinflation and the danger of a German collapse led to intervention by the UK and the USA. Under the Dawes Plan of April 1924, the Ruhr would be evacuated, reparations rescheduled, the Reichsbank reorganised, and a loan of 800 million marks made. This resolved the crisis, but left a lasting legacy of bitterness in Germany.[28]

d. Worthless money:

The demand of the Lake-men for reparations may have been influenced by this demand for reparations from Germany and the occupation of the Ruhr. We

---

25. Marc Trachtenberg, *Reparation in World Politics: France and European Economic Diplomacy, 1916–1923*, Colombia University Press, New York, 1980, pp. 84, 133–34; F.L. Carsten, *Britain and the Weimar Republic*, Batsford Academic and Educational Ltd, London, 1984, pp. 123–43; op. cit. [21], pp. 20–22, 37; A.J. Nicholls, *Weimar and the Rise of Hitler*, 4th edn, Macmillan, London, 2000, pp. 58–62; Conan Fischer, *The Ruhr Crisis, 1923–1924*, Oxford University Press, Oxford, 2003, pp. 12–13; Hattersley, op. cit. [21], pp. 506–507.

26. See op cit [19], p. 20.

27. See op. cit. [19], pp. 37-39; Nicholls, op. cit. [25], pp. 99–105; Fischer, op. cit. [25], pp. 26–232, and *passim*.

28. See op. cit., [19], p. 39; Nicholls, op. cit. [25], pp. 113–14; Patrick O. Cohrs, *The Unfinished Peace After World War I: America, Britain and the Stabilisation of Europe, 1919-1932*, Cambridge University Press, Cambridge, 2006, chapter 7 and *passim*.

have demands for compensation, backed by force, encouraged by a politician to ensure his political survival. The dwarves being told that they could 'eat' their now worthless gold has echoes of the hyperinflation of 1923.

3. Presumption of death:

a. Bilbo's return and its consequences:

Bilbo returned home at nearly lunchtime on 22nd June, finding an auction in Bag End, with 'Messers Grubb, Grubb, and Burrowes', selling 'the effects of the late Bilbo Baggins Esquire'. The sale had begun at 10 a.m., with most things already sold. His cousins the Sackville-Bagginses were 'busy measuring his rooms to see if their own furniture would fit'. He was "Presumed Dead', and not everybody that said so was sorry to find the presumption wrong'.

Bilbo's return was more than 'a nine days' wonder'. In fact, 'The legal bother, indeed, lasted for years. It was quite a long time before Mr Baggins was in fact admitted to be alive again'. To save time, he had to buy back 'quite a lot of his own furniture'. Many of his silver spoons 'were never accounted for. Personally he suspected the Sackville-Bagginses'. Never admitting that he was 'genuine', they were 'not on friendly terms with Bilbo ever after. They really had wanted to live in his nice hobbit-hole so very much' (*TH*, 'The Last Stage', 282.).

b. Some more law:

In English law, there is a 'presumption', a supposition the law requires or allows. Almost every presumption is 'rebuttable', one that holds good in the absence of evidence to the contrary.[29] Included is the 'presumption of death', a presumption that someone has died.[30]

This presumption emerged over the nineteenth century, from decisions of the courts. It allows the courts to grant a declaration of presumed death of the relevant person, allowing that person's estate to be administered.

The presumption is in three parts: (i) no acceptable affirmative evidence that a person was alive during a continuous period of seven or more years; (ii) persons likely to have heard from him during that period have not done so; and (iii) all due inquiries have been made appropriate to the circumstances. If all three are satisfied, there is a rebuttable presumption of law that the person died sometime within that period.[31]

29. *Oxford Dictionary of Law*, 6th edn, Oxford University Press, Oxford, 2006, pp. 407–408; op. cit. [12], vol. 11, p. 834, para. 1097.

30. *Oxford Dictionary of Law*, op. cit., p. 408.

31. See op. cit. [12], vol. 11, p. 836, para. 1100; Gregory Durston, *Evidence: Text and Materials*, Oxford University Press, Oxford, 2008, pp. 157–59; Peter Murphy, *Murphy on Evidence*, 11th

i. Absence of seven or more years:

This evolved from the use by analogy of two statutes. The first was the Bigamy Act 1604,[32] which exempted from its penalties anyone who married while already married to another 'continually remaining beyond the Seas' for seven years, or whose spouse was absent from the other for seven years 'in any Parts within his Majesty's Domains', one not knowing the other to be living within that time.

This was replaced by the Offences Against the Person Act 1861,[33] which exempted from its penalties anyone marrying a second time, whose spouse was 'continually absent' for seven years, and not known by that person to be living within that time.

The second statute was the Cestui Qui Vie Act 1666,[34] about estates in land granted by lease for a life or for lives. If those for whose life or lives the estates were granted remained 'beyond the Seas, or elsewhere absent themselves in this Realm' for seven years, 'and no sufficient and evident Proof be made' that they were alive, in a case the judges shall direct the jury to give their verdict as if such person or persons were dead.

These statutes were used in related cases to form the first part of the presumption. An early case was Doe d. George v. Jesson (1805) 6 East. 80 at 85. Lord Chief Justice Ellenborough looked at these statutes, and held:

> the presumption of the duration of life, with respect to persons of whom no account can be given, ends at the expiration of seven years from the time when they were last known to be living. Therefore in the absence of all other evidence to shew that he was living at a later period there was fair ground for the jury to presume that he was dead at the end of seven years from the time he went to sea on his second voyage.

In Hopewell v. De Pinna (1809) 2 Camp. 111, the judge, again Ellenborough, ruled that it was for the defendant to prove that her husband was 'alive within seven years'.

This presumption of life until the end of seven years, by way of analogy to these statutes, began to be put into textbooks, then this cessation of presumption of life asserted itself in the form of an affirmative presumption of death, both in

edn, Oxford University Press, Oxford, 2009, pp. 684–86; Adrian Keane and Paul McKeown, *The Modern Law of Evidence*, 9th edn, Oxford University Press, Oxford, 2012, pp. 662–65.

32. 1 James I, c. 11.

33. 24 & 25 Victoria, c. 100.

34. 19 Charles II, c. 6.

judgements and in textbooks.[35]

ii. Persons likely to have heard from him have not done so:

They tend to be relatives and friends of the absent person; but courts have decided otherwise, depending on the evidence. In Doe d. France v Andrews (1850) 16 QB 756, the attempt to presume the death of a person failed, a person claimed as likely to have heard of him being a remote cousin, who had not known of his existence.

In Dunn v. Snowden (1862) 2 Dr. & Sm. 201 at 202-3, a testator, who made a will in favour of two nephews, died in 1851; and one nephew went missing in 1848. Since then, 'none of his family or friends had heard of him, or could, though they endeavoured to do so by proper means, obtain any tidings of him'. It was decided that the property be distributed on the presumption that the nephew died after the testator.

iii. All due inquiries been made:

This will depend on the evidence. In the case of In re Creed (1852) 1. Drewry. 235 at 237, the court ruled that there was 'no sufficient inquiry to justify any order'. A testator gave property in trust to his sister for life, the remainder equally between his nephews and nieces living at the time of her death. One nephew went missing before the sister's death in 1838; and the petitioners did 'nothing in the way of effectual inquiry'.

In the case of In the Goods of Matthews [1898] P. 17 at 18, a person disappeared from his home on 24th November 1894. The inquiries made were such that the judge held: 'The time since the disappearance is, no doubt, short, but the inquiries made seem to have been very ample'. Leave was granted on 22nd November 1897 to depose that his death had occurred on or since 24th November 1894.

iv. Issue of life or death at a particular time:

If someone is trying to assert that a person was alive or dead *on a given date*, the person has to prove that fact by sufficient evidence.[36] This was decided in the case of In re Phené's Trusts (1870) LR 5 Ch. 139 at 152. The testator left the residue of his estate to be divided equally among his nephews and nieces. One nephew had been missing before his uncle's death on 5th January 1861. The judge held that the presumption of when the nephew died was 'a matter of fact to be proved by evidence, and that the *onus* of proof rests on his representative',

35. James Bradley Thayer, *A Preliminary Treatise on Evidence at the Common Law*, Sweet and Maxwell, London, 1898, pp. 323–24.

36. See op. cit. [12], vol. 11, p. 837, para. 1101.

something not done. The estate of the uncle was divided among the nephews and nieces found to have survived him.

Arising from this case was the question of the date when death can be presumed. Two arguments have been made. The first is that death can be presumed at the date of the proceedings, assuming a continuous period of absence for seven years runs back from that date. This is supported by the Privy Council decision of Lal Chand Marwari v. Mahant Ramrup Gir and Another (1926) 42 TLR, 159 at 160-1, which pointed out that the only presumption was that when the suits were instituted the relevant person was no longer alive.

A second argument, preferred by some,[37] is that death can be presumed at the end of a continuous period of absence for seven years. In the case of In re Westbrook's Trusts [1873] WN 167, the court ruled that a person died seven years after he was last heard of.

v. Can be shorter than seven years:

A court, even if the primary facts required to ground the presumption are not proved, can infer death or life from the available evidence. A person absent for *less* than seven years can have death so presumed by a court in two main circumstances. First, if that person was, when last heard of, aged, infirm, or ill; and second, if, when last heard of, the person had been exposed to extraordinary peril.

A. Aged, infirm or ill:

In Webster v. Birchmore (1807) 13 Ves. Jun. 362, it was held that a person 'must be taken to have died', after being absent 5-6 years, having been in a very bad state of health. In In re Beasney's Trusts (1869) LR 7 Eq 498 at 500, the missing person made no application for his October 1860 dividends of a sum of money. Advertisements were placed in newspapers, requesting information, but none was received.

The judge ruled that the person died before 14th November 1860, when his half-sister died, therefore she survived him and became entitled to the trust fund. That person was 'of drunken habits, and when last seen was in so emaciated a state that his death might have been expected at any time'.

In the case of In the Goods of Matthews, the decision was perhaps also due to the fact that the person was seventy-three years of age when he disappeared.

B. Extraordinary peril:

This term includes a storm, an earthquake, and a possible or actual shipwreck.

37. See Murphy, op. cit. [31], p. 685; Keane and McKeown, op. cit. [31], p. 664.

The case of In re Hutton (1837) 1 Curt. 595, was where a person boarded a ship in July 1835. That ship, and everyone on board, were not heard of; and on 16th February 1837, the court granted administration of his estate, presuming that he was dead.

The case of In the Goods of Hurlston [1898] 1 P 27 at 28, concerned a person aboard a steamer shipwrecked on 9th June 1897, not among the survivors. The judge ruled on 17th January 1898 that his death occurred 'on or after the alleged date'.

Where does Bilbo fit in here?

Bilbo's leaving as he did, with the dwarves, could have led to a finding that he was suffering from a mental infirmity; and his death could therefore be presumed within the almost fourteen months he was absent. Those likely to have heard from him had not done so; and due to the nature of the Shire 'due inquiries' would not have been made outside its borders.

BACKGROUND: MORALITY AND BUSINESS

1. Legitimacy:

a. So-called king:

The legitimacy of Thorin's claim to the kingship, and his people's right to (most of) the treasure is almost unquestioned. At Lake-town, he proclaimed himself Thror's heir, only challenged publicly by the raft-elves. While the Master privately believed that Thorin and his people were frauds, 'He was wrong. Thorin, of course, *was really* the grandson of the King under the Mountain, and there is no knowing what a dwarf will not dare and do for revenge or the recovery of *his own*' (*TH*, 'A Warm Welcome', 188–89; 192–93; my italics).

Thorin's title was unquestioned by Bard and the Elvenking, except when the ultimatum was given to Thorin, 'calling himself' King under the Mountain (*TH*, 'The Gathering of the Clouds', 250). This public and insulting refusal to recognise Thorin's royal title might be an effect of the dragon-sickness on Bard. Paul Kocher commented correctly that Bard was 'a little too eager to resort to arms' for this reason, being rebuked by the Elvenking.[38] I would add to this that insult to Thorin and his people.

Such a refusal to recognise a royal title took place in the Hundred Years' War (1337-1453) between the Kingdoms of England and France.

38. Paul Kocher, *Master of Middle-earth: The achievement of J. R. R. Tolkien*, Penguin Books, Harmondsworth, Middlesex, 1974, p. 26.

King Edward III of England was permitted by a great council in 1337 to revive a claim to the French throne, rejected in 1328 in favour of Philip, Count of Valois, crowned Philip VI, whose kingship he had previously accepted. He began to refer in correspondence to Philip as *de facto* King of France, including 'Philip, calling himself King of France'. He did not formally proclaim himself rightful King of France until 26th January 1340, publically calling Philip an illegitimate monarch, including 'Philip of Valois who calls himself King of France'. The claim was a bargaining counter, and a legitimate excuse to those who wanted to join with Edward against Philip.[39]

b. A partnership, not a company:

Despite the dwarves calling themselves 'Thorin and Company', my view is that they are, under English law, a 'partnership', governed by the Partnership Act 1890.[40]

It is, under section 1(1), 'the relation which subsists between persons carrying on a business in common with a view of profit.' Section 1(2) says a partnership is not a 'company'. Unlike a limited liability company, a partnership has no separate legal personality from the partners. Section 4(1) says, 'Persons who have entered into partnership with one another are for the purposes of this Act called collectively a firm, and the name under which their business is carried on is called the firm-name'. Being called 'and Company' means nothing legally.[41]

Important is section 6. Any act intended to bind the firm by anyone authorised, 'whether a partner or not, is binding on the firm and all the partners'. The contract offered to Bilbo was therefore legally binding on all the dwarves.

Most important is section 9. Every partner is 'liable jointly' with the others 'for all debts and obligations of the firm incurred' while a partner. After death, 'his estate is also severally liable' for 'such debts and obligations'. The estates of any dwarves who died would be legally bound to pay Bilbo's funeral expenses, hence 'us or our representatives'.

Partnership, the preferred medium for the professions, is widely used in other areas of business.[42] The firm of Grubb, Grubb, and Burrowes holding the auction would tend to be viewed in English law as a partnership.

Tolkien may have deliberately blurred the distinctions in English law between

39. A.R. Myers, ed., *English Historical Documents, 1327–1485*, Eyre and Spottiswoode, London, 1969, pp. 66–68; Clifford J. Rogers, *War Cruel and Sharp: English Strategy Under Edward III, 1327-1360*, The Boydell Press, Woodbridge, 2000, pp. 174–78, 183–85; W. Mark Omrod, *Edward III,* Yale University Press, New Haven and London, 2011, pp. 190–96, 212–14.
40. 53 & 54 Victoria, c. 39.
41. Op. cit. [8], p. 2.
42. Op. cit. [8], p. 4.

'company' and 'partnership'. First, using the word 'company' in its older meaning, dating from 1389, of 'A body of persons combined or incorporated for some common object, or for the joint execution or performance of anything'. The more modern definition of 'company', 'An association formed to carry on some commercial or industrial undertaking', dates from 1553, and tended to be used for larger associations.[43] Second, Thorin is a legitimate king, who heads the partnership and gives it his name.

2. Business peoples:

Tolkien portrayed four peoples as 'business peoples', with a good ability for business, including a use of law: dwarves, hobbits, Wood-elves and Lake-men. These portrayals, particularly of the dwarves, may have been influenced by his background and upbringing as part of the 'prosperous bourgeoisie' of Birmingham, another business people.

a. Dwarves:

Thorin described to Bilbo the close and very profitable commercial relationship between the dwarves and Dale before Smaug. They made 'the most marvellous and magical toys'; and 'the toy market of Dale was the wonder of the North' (*TH*, 'An Unexpected Party', 32). Their contract with Bilbo was compatible with Shire law, illustrating a familiarity in drawing up such documents.

The dwarves began the journey with no weapons, and in the encounter with the trolls were nearly as incompetent as Bilbo, excepting Thorin, the only dwarf to arm himself from the trolls' cave (*TH*, 'Roast Mutton', 45–47; 50–51).

Later, it was explained that the dwarves intended to pay Bilbo 'really handsomely' for his services: 'they had brought him to do a nasty job for them, and they did not mind the poor little fellow doing it if he would; but they would have done all their best to get him out of trouble'. They were then summed up as a business people: 'dwarves are not heroes, *but calculating folk with a great idea of the value of money*'. Some are tricky, treacherous and 'pretty bad lots'; some are 'decent people like Thorin and Company, if you don't expect too much' (*TH*, 'Inside Information', 203–204, my italics).

Only after the dwarves later armed themselves did they emerge as fighters, and Thorin as a king (*TH*, 'Not at Home', 227). His refusal to consider how his restored realm can survive as an economically viable state, without the goodwill of its neighbours, showed how he had abandoned his business principles, due to the dragon-sickness.

43. *The Oxford English Dictionary*, 2nd edn, vol. 3, Oxford University Press, Oxford, 1989, p. 589.

When Thorin found out what Bilbo did with the Arkenstone, he ignored any contractual issues (*TH*, 'The Clouds Burst', 259) while promising to pay one fourteenth of the treasure for the Arkenstone, he had no intention of keeping his word, failing as both a ruler and a businessman.

The dwarves finally showed that they were ferocious fighters during the Battle of Five Armies. This battle, plus Dain keeping Thorin's agreement, led to a restoration of the older commercial relationship between the Mountain, Dale and Lake-town.

b. Hobbits:

Bilbo insisted on properly knowing the details of the burglary, 'putting on his business manner (usually reserved for people who tried to borrow money off him), and doing his best to appear wise and prudent and professional'. He also asked about 'risks, out-of-pocket expenses, time required and remuneration, and so forth' (*TH*, 'An Unexpected Party', 31–32). His questions were answered by the contract. As mentioned, he used his 'best business manner' when talking with Bard and the Elvenking. Bilbo was therefore one of a people who are involved in business, including having a law of contract. Grubb, Grubb, and Burrowes were possibly a partnership.

c. Wood-elves:

They being fond of wine, it and other goods were brought from the South, or from distant vineyards. These goods came upriver, or over land, to the Long Lake. From Lake-town, barrels of goods were brought up the Forest River. When empty, the Elves cast them into the river, where they were carried to a place near the eastern edge of Mirkwood, then collected and floated to Lake-town (*TH*, 'Barrels Out of Bond', 171; 175–86). The Wood-Elves are, therefore, also a business people, the Elvenking understanding Bilbo's contract.

d. Lake-men:

After the dwarves, they are most referred to as a business people. 'They still throve on the trade that came up the great river from the South and was carted past the falls to their town [Lake-town]'. Singing songs about the return of Thror and Thrain, 'this pleasant legend did not much affect their daily business'. Some trade was carried on with the Wood-elves, with whom they were friends, despite 'occasional squabbles about river-tolls' (*TH*, 'A Warm Welcome', 185–86; 188–93). Uniquely, they are a republic with an elected leader, the Master, who owes his position partly to having 'a good head for business' (*TH*, 'Fire and Water', 237–38). Bard therefore understood Bilbo's contract.

e. Prosperous Bourgeoisie of Birmingham:

Tolkien said in 1956 that 'as an Englishman brought up in an 'almost rural' village of Warwickshire on the edge of the prosperous bourgeoisie of Birmingham ... I take my models like anyone else – from such 'life' as I know'.[44] This is a reference to himself and his brother Hilary living with their mother Mabel in 1896-1900 in Sarehole, outside Birmingham.[45]

He was overwhelmingly part of that 'prosperous bourgeoisie': Birmingham's commercial middle class.[46] That city was a centre of the United Kingdom's Industrial Revolution, where both his parents came from, and in or near to which he spent sixteen of his early years.[47] His father's family had been piano manufacturers and music dealers; and his maternal grandfather once owned a drapery business.[48] Throughout his life, he was close to relatives with strong business connections, either themselves, or by birth or marriage.[49]

Tolkien might have gained some knowledge of the law discussed due to his background and upbringing; and his portrayal of the dwarves as 'calculating folk' might owe something to businessmen he knew, including relatives, as could his portrayals of the hobbits and Lake-men.

Maggie Burns suggested that the dwarf-made 'toys' might also include an older definition meaning small goods in any material. An 1800 poem called Birmingham the 'Toy Shop of the World', due to that city's great reputation for such objects. She also suggested that hobbits were 'based to a large degree' on people Tolkien knew in Birmingham when young, as well as individuals he knew; and that the Master of Lake-town 'bears a close resemblance' to Joseph Chamberlain (1836-1914), a Mayor of Birmingham who rebuilt that city before his involvement in national government.[50]

3. The importance of law and its limitations:

---

44. Op. cit. [16], Letter 181, p. 235.

45. Humphrey Carpenter, *J.R.R. Tolkien: A Biography*, George Allen & Unwin, London, 1977, pp. 19–24; Christina Scull and Wayne G. Hammond, *The J.R.R. Tolkien Companion and Guide*, vol. 2: *Reader's Guide*, HarperCollins, London, 2006, p. 115.

46. Carpenter, op. cit., p. 19.

47. Scull and Hammond, op. cit. [45], p. 115.

48. Carpenter, op. cit. [45], pp. 9–10, 18–19; Scull and Hammond, op. cit. [45], pp. 1008–1009, 984.

49. Carpenter, op. cit. [45], p. 14; Scull and Hammond, op. cit. [45], pp. 424–25; Maggie Burns, 'Prosperous Bourgeoisie of Birmingham: Relatives of J. R. R. Tolkien', *Amon Hen* 216 (2009), pp. 22–23; Christina Scull and Wayne G. Hammond, *The J.R.R. Tolkien Companion and Guide*, vol. 1: *Chronology*, HarperCollins, London, 2006, pp. 3, 772; Christine Ahmed, 'William Charles Mountain J.P. and Grace Bindley Tolkien', *Amon Hen* 236 (2012), pp. 11–13.

50. Maggie Burns, '...A local habitation and a name...', *Mallorn* 50 (2010), pp. 28–30; Scull and Hammond, op. cit. [49], p. 329.

Three things can be obtained from looking at Tolkien's portrayal of law in these three matters. First, the importance of having societies governed by the rule of law, including laws of contract sharing the same principles. Bilbo's contract is written by a partnership of dwarves, set up or sanctioned by a legitimate king, its terms acceptable to the laws in his country, understandable by Bard and the Elvenking. Also, the Shire has a legal procedure for presuming dead a hobbit gone missing, based like the contract and the dwarf partnership on English law.

Second, law, while important, is not sufficient to resolve matters where personal and other factors come into play, first seen when the Elvenking imprisons the dwarves, because it was 'a crime to wander in my realm without leave.' After their 'disturbance', he had 'a right to know what brings you here', and would keep them in prison until they 'learned sense and manners!' (*TH*, 'Barrels Out of Bond', 168)

The king is within his legal rights; but the narrator does not think him morally justified, pointing out his weakness for treasure, and an 'old quarrel' with dwarves (*TH*, Flies and Spiders, 163) The reader has, therefore, no problem with Bilbo helping the dwarves escape. That king redeems himself by helping the Lake-men, being 'lord of a good and kindly people' (*TH*, 'Fire and Water', 240). Also, he was a restraining influence on Bard, successfully fighting the greed that had so influenced the latter and Thorin, hoping for 'something that will bring reconciliation' (*TH*, 'The Clouds Burst', 262) He is, unlike those two, an experienced monarch.

Concerning reparations, Kocher rightly said, 'A Solomon might well pick his way gingerly among these claims and counterclaims'.[51] Like the Germans who resented the fact that they had, under threat of force, to take the blame for World War I and pay for it, the dwarves resented being blamed for Smaug in similar circumstances, this muting their criticisms of Thorin. Bard, even while compromising, allowed his gold-influenced anger to show by referring to Thorin as 'calling himself' king, an explanation for his firing the arrow. Bilbo tried to resolve this impasse, being an independent contractor, owing no allegiance to Thorin, being independently wealthy, and having a significant social standing in his own country.

Third, we look at the moral issues; because Bilbo made a moral decision to try and resolve the conflict by giving away the Arkenstone, despite his misgivings. Particularly brave of him was his decision, another moral one, to return to the dwarves, saying they 'can do what they like to me'. He refused an offer to stay, not wanting to 'leave my friends like this, after all we have gone through together'. Also, he had promised to wake Bombur at midnight! (*TH*, 'A Thief in

51. Op. cit. [38], p. 25.

the Night', 256)

CONCLUSION

Tolkien gave *The Hobbit* an important legal framework, fundamental to the story, with a background of morality and business. Particularly important is Bilbo Baggins' contract. Being an independent contractor allowed him to make the moral decision to give away the Arkenstone. Because the dwarves, hobbits, Wood-elves and Lake-men are business peoples, the contract is understandable and recognised as lawful by all.

This use of law gives the framework a very modern air, the law used based on concepts that emerged in English law in the nineteenth century, also the post-WWI claims for reparations against Germany. In addition, the dwarves act more like businessmen than warriors for most of the story, perhaps influenced by businessmen known to Tolkien, including relatives. This might have also influenced his portrayals of the hobbits and the Lake-men.

But this law has limitations. Even legitimate claims are ignored when personal and other factors come into play. The Elvenking's right to imprison the dwarves is ignored by Bilbo; Thorin refused Bard's legitimate claim. Bilbo tried to resolve the conflict by making a moral decision, making a second to return to the dwarves. This use of law as fundamental, but having limitations, any resolution coming from people acting in a moral manner, makes *The Hobbit* a sophisticated book.

'Tolkien's Faërian Drama: Origins and Valedictions'

Janet Brennan Croft

In On Fairy-Stories, Tolkien introduces the concept of Faërian drama. Faërian drama is a form of Elvish art one can almost but not quite grasp and understand, something the witness/participant will ponder and work through for the rest of his life. I will suggest that Tolkien may have been influenced in his development of the concept by Sir Gawain and the Green Knight and the dream-like events that Gawain experiences and what he learns from them. I will examine some examples of Faërian drama in Tolkien's fiction and poetry, concentrating especially on his final story, Smith of Wootton Major, and the experiences Smith has in Faery.

In his essay *On Fairy-Stories*, Tolkien introduces the concept of Faërian Drama: plays which the Elves present to men, with a 'realism and immediacy beyond the compass of any human mechanism', where the viewer feels he is 'bodily inside its Secondary World' but instead is 'in a dream that some other mind is weaving' (*OFS*, 63–64).[1] The viewer/participant gives it primary belief' while it is happening. Faërian drama is a form of Elvish art a human can almost but not quite grasp and understand, something the witness/participant may ponder and work through for the rest of his or her life. While Tolkien describes Faerie in ambivalent terms at different points in drafts of *On Fairy-Stories*, both suggesting its actual reality and treating it as a conceit (one version includes the phrase '[t]he marvels of Faerie are true, if at all, only on a different plane',[2] the concept of faërian drama is a useful tool for thinking about the profound work the subconscious does, in cases where the mind is deeply conflicted or in need of major change or growth and thus receptive when presented with an opportunity for a transformative experience.

I will quote most of the relevant passage here from the published *On Fairy-Stories* so we will all have it fresh in our minds:

> Now 'Faërian Drama' – those plays which according to abundant records the elves have often presented to men - can produce Fantasy

1. Verlyn Flieger and Douglas A. Anderson, eds, *Tolkien On Fairy-Stories*, HarperCollins, New York, 2008, pp. 63–64. Subsequent citations to *OFS* refer to this edition.
2. 'Manuscript B', in op. cit., 206–96, p. 265.

> with a realism and immediacy beyond the compass of any human mechanism. As a result their usual effect (upon a man) is to go beyond Secondary Belief. If you are present at a Faërian drama you yourself are, or think that you are, bodily inside its Secondary World. The experience may be very similar to Dreaming and has (it would seem) sometimes (by men) been confounded with it. But in Faërian drama you are in a dream that some other mind is weaving, and the knowledge of that alarming fact may slip from your grasp. To experience directly a Secondary World: the potion is too strong, and you give to it Primary Belief, however marvellous the events. You are deluded - whether that is the intention of the elves (always or at any time) is another question. They at any rate are not themselves deluded. This is for them a form of Art, and distinct from Wizardry or Magic, properly so called. They do not live in it, though they can, perhaps, afford to spend more time at it than human artists can. The Primary World, Reality, of elves and men is the same, if differently valued and perceived.
>
> We need a word for this elvish craft, but all the words that have been applied to it have been blurred and confused with other things. Magic is ready to hand, and I have used it above, but I should not have done so: Magic should be reserved for the operations of the Magician. Art is the human process that produces by the way (it is not its only or ultimate object) Secondary Belief. Art of the same sort, if more skilled and effortless, the elves can also use, or so the reports seem to show; but the more potent and specially elvish craft I will, for lack of a less debatable word, call Enchantment. Enchantment produces a Secondary World into which both designer and spectator can enter, to the satisfaction of their senses while they are inside; but in its purity it is artistic in desire and purpose.[3]

This is all well and good, but as Verlyn Flieger and Douglas Anderson point out in their commentary on *On Fairy-Stories*, 'no definition of what the faërian [drama] consists of is given [and] no examples of such 'plays' or 'abundant records' are given'; Tolkien's description actually 'does little to clarify the concept'.[4] So how can we arrive at a good definition of what Faërian Drama actually is? Perhaps the best way is to work backwards, by investigating several

3. Op. cit. [1], pp. 63–64.

4. 'Editors' Commentary', in op. cit. [1], 85–121, p. 112.

examples of what we might classify as faërian drama because they appear to produce the effects which Tolkien describes.

EXAMPLES

Christopher Garbowski has done just this in his article on the Christmas film *It's a Wonderful Life*, which he considers a classic example of the faërian drama at work. Here the viewer of the film can clearly see that the intent of the drama – the film-within-a-film of the Pottersville sequence – is not the mere *manipulation* of magic, but enchantment and *recovery*. George Bailey is intended, through participating in this drama, to recover his proper perspective on life and his will to live.[5] Garbowski suggests that the 'primary goal' of faërian drama is 'a meeting of the aesthetic and the ethical',[6] which is clearly what angel-in-training Clarence intends in presenting George with a palpable vision of a Georgeless alternate reality.

Another scholar who has recently tried to define faërian drama is Péter Kristóf Makai, who makes the claim that immersive computer games are the closest approach to faërian drama we currently have, and that they have the potential to go even further. What his model lacks is the sense of an outside, non-human agency (e.g., Elves) creating these immersive experiences for an ethical as well as aesthetic purpose - though there is no reason ethical purpose could *not* be part of the future development of such games, particularly if game designers consciously choose to use Tolkien's 'theoretical foundation' as a basis.[7] One might even say, to carry this metaphor further, that the truly evolved faërian cyber-drama would be a therapeutic game that upgrades or reboots or installs new 'software' in the player's mind. But as Makai points out, 'Describing [the fairies] is not needed for a theory of Fantasy because only the *actions* of the fairies matter.' So, as he goes on to say, 'even if we do not have Tolkien's definition of the matter … of Faërian Drama, we do know its effects on the spectators witnessing it'.[8] Makai says 'We know precious little about what roles the fairies play in their other-worldly dramas after they have weaved their enchantment on its spect/actor', and goes on to quote Flieger: fairies 'are [not] the chief actors in fairy-stories; they are there simply to interact with … the human being who … wanders into

5. Christopher Garbowski, '*It's A Wonderful Life* as Faërian Drama', *Mythlore* 90 (2002), 38–48, p. 39. Frank Capra, director, *It's A Wonderful Life*, RKO Radio Pictures, Los Angeles, 1946.
6. Garbowski, op. cit., p. 45.
7. Péter Kristóf Makai, 'Faërian Cyberdrama: When Fantasy Becomes Virtual Reality', *Tolkien Studies* 7 (2010), 35–53, p. 35.
8. Op. cit., pp. 41–42.

the enchanted world'.[9] Thus perhaps how and by whom the effects were created is not nearly as important as the receptivity of the mind of the participant.

What other examples might come to mind? I would suggest that one of the purest examples possible is the Ur-story from which *It's a Wonderful Life* descended: Charles Dickens's *A Christmas Carol*.[10] There are several important elements to consider here. There is the preparatory softening of Scrooge's mind so he is more receptive: the reminders of the anniversary of Marley's death, the inescapability of the Christmas season, several ghostly occurrences on his trip home that evening, even his head cold and indigestion. There is the dramaturge of the event, Marley's Ghost, setting the scene and stating unequivocally the ethical purpose of the visitations: the 'chance and hope' of Scrooge escaping a fate like his own.[11] There is the 'satisfaction' of Scrooge's senses at each change of scene, in Dickens's loving piling-on of sensual detail after detail, and Scrooge's dreamlike feeling of being part witness, part participant in each stave – in some cases able to physically affect his environment, in others not. And then there are the undeniable ethical results, exactly as intended by the spirits, of the aesthetic experience: Scrooge's reclamation as a man of generosity and moral purpose, 'as good a friend, as good a master, and as good a man, as the good old city knew'.[12]

Bottom's Dream, in *A Midsummer Night's Dream*, might serve as an example as well – though it might better be termed Titania's Dream, for its purpose was the recovery of Titania's proper love for Oberon, rather than providing any ethical lesson for the poor foolish mortal caught up in it. It seems the Elves do practice faërian drama on each other, after all. Whether Bottom remains lastingly 'transported' by his accidental experience is up to the intent of each production's director; in the Michael Hoffman-directed movie starring Kevin Kline, a trace of faerie remains with bully Bottom, for though he remains a buffoon and a fey grace touches Flute's acting, not his own, he has been given the gift of catching glimpses of Faerie all around him.[13] But generally, Bottom feels not 'the slightest pain of humiliation'; he 'seems to have learned nothing about himself' and is

9. Verlyn Flieger, *Splintered Light: Logos and Language in Tolkien's World*, Kent University Press, Kent OH, 2002, p. 23.

10. Paul Davis, *The Lives and Times of Ebenezer Scrooge*, Yale University Press, New Haven, 1990, pp. 146–70.

11. Charles Dickens, *The Annotated Christmas Carol*, ed. Michael Patrick Hearn, Avenel, New York, 1976, p. 80.

12. Op. cit., p. 172.

13. For how this production sets up Bottom to be receptive to the Faërian drama in which he is about to participate, see Frank P. Riga, '"Where is that Worthless Dreamer?" Bottom's Fantastic Redemption in Hoffman's *A Midsummer Night's Dream*', *Mythlore* 95/96 (2006), 197–212. Michael Hoffmann, director, *A Midsummer Night's Dream*, Fox Searchlight Pictures, Los Angeles, 1999.

'entirely content with who he is.[14] However, there are other, more straightforward examples of faërian drama at work in the play: consider the young lovers lost in the woods and led 'up and down, up and down' by Puck. In line with the classic effects of faërian drama, they 'awaken to a better understanding of their own human weaknesses and need for charitable forbearance'.[15]

The movie *Groundhog Day* is another excellent example to consider. Here, Bill Murray's character Phil Connors never sees the mechanism behind the faërian drama or knowingly meets a dramaturge or other denizen of Faerie; he never knows why or how he repeats the same day over and over, and the viewer has no indication as to how long he does this (one viewer suggests it may be about thirty-four years, but there are many other estimates, from three months to a thousand years). The contradictions inherent in the way the repetition works (like knowledge and muscle memory from learning piano or ice carving being retained the next 'morning', but not hangovers or injuries) can be explained if this is a deliberate example of faërian drama at work. And here again there is a clear ethical goal: the rehabilitation of the Scrooge-like Phil as a man capable of emotional self-control and unselfish love, though we never learn whose goal it is.

We can also see Faerian drama translated into science fictional terms in technologies like *Star Trek: The Next Generation*'s holodeck or the virtual reality simulator of *The Thirteenth Floor*. In (the American version of) *Life on Mars*, a Faërian drama state – a 'neural stimulation program' – is sought out willingly, with technical assistance, as a way to while away the time in suspended animation as the crew sleeps its way to Mars. The meteor shower they encounter alters Sam Tyler's program, which was originally designed to insert him in a police drama in 2008; instead, he is pushed further back, to 1973, with memories of the 2008 program memories intact; and while he lacks his 2035 memories, his crewmates play roles in the program, enabling him to work through his serious father issues and come to a realisation about his attraction to his commanding officer, Colonel Annie Norris. The illusion that we are witnessing Sam Tyler's personal faërian drama is not as perfectly maintained as it is in *A Christmas Carol* or *Groundhog Day*, for we as the audience are privy to scenes that he does not see – Gene Hunt burning his bribe money in 'Have You Seen Your Mother, Baby, Standing in the Shadows', or Annie's interactions with her roommates in 'Coffee, Tea, or Annie', for example. But for the audience, one level removed from Sam, these serve the

---

14. David Bevington, 'Dream and Vision in Shakespeare's Plays', in Nancy van Deusen, ed., *Presenting the Past, Volume 2: Dreams and Visions: An Interdisciplinary Enquiry*, Brill Academic Publishers, Boston, 2010, 259–79, pp. 261–62.
15. Op. cit.

function of cut-scene (non-play narrative) segments in computer games.[16]

DEFINITIONS

So given these examples, how might we define the elements of a proper Faërian drama? First, as a participant, one is in some way or another clearly not in the realm of one's every-day life; however, the vision feels real and as if one is immersed in it (that is, it 'satisfies the senses' in Tolkien's terms). In part this is because one can act, think, and move within the vision, though perhaps with certain limitations, and one's actions have consequences that either are as expected or that follow the logic of the secondary world – that is, events do not occur in the illogical or random fashion they might in a mere dream. Applying this to computer games, Makai says '*we* have to move and act, to which actions the faërian machine responds by displaying the results of our actions'.[17] Also unlike a dream experience, as Garbowski points out, the participant is (more or less) free to refuse to enter the play, though 'the consequence of such a rejection is being robbed of the opportunity of *recovery* that has been proffered'.[18]

And there is often (though not always) a feeling of joining a world already in progress, that will continue after one leaves; in modern terms, one might compare the faërian drama to an interactive MMORPG (massively multi-player online role-playing game), but entered into not at one's own instigation but at the near-irresistible invitation of something outside oneself. There is also often a sense of the fragility of the vision – that it may end unexpectedly or one may be ejected from it unceremoniously for bad behavior: as Tolkien describes it, 'while he is there it is dangerous for him to ask too many questions, lest the gates be shut and the keys be lost' (*OFS, 27*).[19] One may, while there, experience 'appalling perils as well as profound pleasures'.[20] Additionally, the participant must be ready for

16. Simon Gallagher, 'Just How Many Days Does Bill Murray REALLY Spend Stuck Reliving 'Groundhog Day'?', *What Culture*, 2 February 2011 <http://whatculture.com/film/just-how-many-days-does-bill-murray-really-spend-stuck-reliving-groundhog-day.php> [accessed 25 June 2012]. Harold Ramis, director, *Groundhog Day*, Columbia Pictures, Los Angeles, 1993. by Michael Katleman et al, *Life on Mars: The Complete Series*, ABC Studios, Los Angeles, 2009. One could go on – elements of Faërian drama can readily be found in sources as diverse as *The Wizard of Oz* (the movie version), *Alice in Wonderland*, the Dagobah swamp episode in *Star Wars*, *Back to the Future* (with Marty McFly serving as the instrument of Faërian drama for other characters!), George MacDonald's short story 'The Shadows,' Kurt Vonnegut's *The Sirens of Titan*, and so on.

17. Op. cit. [7], p. 45.

18. Op. cit. [5], p. 46.

19. Op. cit. [1], p. 27.

20. Gregory G. Pepetone, 'Another Side of the Inklings: *Smith of Wootton Major*', in his *Hogwarts and All: Gothic Perspectives on Children's Literature*, Peter Lang, New York, 2012,

the experience, his or her mind in a liminal state ready to be overturned and re-aligned by the vision, like Scrooge on the anniversary of his partner's death or Phil Connors after a day of ego-fuelled rage when he just cannot escape the frustrations of Punxatawney, PA.

Perhaps most importantly, the moral purpose of the drama or vision may or may not be announced at its inception, but is entirely clear in retrospect: recovery, with its implications of redemption, reclamation, and personal (spiritual, emotional, or psychological) growth. Remember, as Garbowski put it, that Faërian drama is an act of sub-creation at the highest level of art, and its 'primary goal' is 'a meeting of the aesthetic and the ethical.' Rather than providing closure in the traditional sense, the Faërian drama experience leaves the character 'at a juncture after which nothing can remain the same'.[21] The participant is privy to 'otherworldly revelations, reserved for those who are temporarily privileged as well as burdened'.[22] The 'spect/actor,' to use Makai's term, 'enact[s] a story in some shape or form that is reminiscent of narrative progress towards a desired goal: the (happy) end, Tolkien's *eucatastrophe*'.[23] The faërian drama is a clear dividing line in the participant's life; there is before, and there is after.

SOURCES

Where else, besides a probable familiarity with *A Christmas Carol* and *A Midsummer Night's Dream*, might Tolkien have encountered a foundation on which to base his theory or conceit of Faërian Drama? In particular, where might we find those 'abundant records' of which he so assuredly speaks? I would suggest that he was referring to sources he was familiar with as a scholar: medieval dream visions, such as *Pearl*, and tales of encounters with the fantastic that read like dream visions without an explicit dream frame, like *Sir Gawain and the Green Knight*.

'At the simplest level,' according to J. Stephen Russell, 'a dream vision is the first person account of a dream; the dream report is usually preceded by a prologue introducing the dreamer as a character and often followed by an epilogue describing the dreamer's reawakening.' Within the prologue, 'the reader often learns that the dreamer was distressed or concerned about some unnamed problem or worry.' The dream may record events that seem 'superficially naturalistic' or 'self-consciously allegorical'; common elements may include an enclosed garden, 'preternatural light, talking animals, or a personified figure of authority,'

143–56, p. 155.
21. Op. cit. [5], pp. 44–45.
22. Op. cit. [20], p. 151.
23. Op. cit. [7], p. 50.

and 'the dreamer is *always* a character in his dream narrative'. The reawakening, the return to the real world, provides closure for the narrator and the narrative.[24] *Pearl* is what we might think of as the *locus classicus* of the dream vision, but the genre goes back to Gilgamesh's dream of the coming of Enkidu to tame his wildness, and stretches to include Dante's *Divine Comedy*, with its narrator starting out wandering in a dark wood rather than conventionally dreaming._I would suggest that for a dream vision or tale of the fantastic to fit the definition of Faërian Drama we are developing, the dreamer or narrator must be somewhat troubled in mind or else, as we might say now, in need of an intervention, and he must find in the vision some sort of response to what troubled him in the prologue. Finally, the epilogue must show the ethical and aesthetic purpose of the vision having some effect. Without some purpose or effect, a dream of the fantastic is just Enchantment and nothing more.

While Tolkien was familiar with an extremely wide range of medieval literature, I will concentrate on *Pearl* and *Gawain* for this paper since we have his translations and notes.[25] *Pearl* is perhaps the easiest to understand as a Faërian drama, though it is couched in entirely Christian terms. Here is a dreamer who is aware, both before and after, that he dreams. It is a dream in which he feels that he physically acts and learns something that eases his soul's unrest, and in which his senses are satisfied that the fantastic and allegorical landscape is real. The river is truly a river – though the pebbles on its bed are jewels, it is a physical river too fast and deep to wade.[26] The character of the pearl-maiden herself, elf-like in appearance and as reserved and detached from the dreamer as an elf, speaks and acts in a manner that is a quite obviously didactic melding of the aesthetic and ethical. The Jeweler is 'educated' by his 'visionary experiences',[27] yet a central question of the poem is 'how a human being can properly interpret, and convey to others, a superhuman experience'.[28] In Tolkien's notes on *Pearl*,

24. J. Stephen Russell, *The English Dream Vision: Anatomy of a Form*, Ohio State University Press, Columbus, 1988, pp. 5–6.

25. The manuscripts of Tolkien's translations of *Sir Gawain and the Green Knight*, *Pearl*, and *Sir Orfeo* were left unpublished at his death in 1973. He was first thought to have worked on his translation of *Pearl* in the mid-1950s and *Gawain* around 1950, but Christopher Tolkien provides no date for *Orfeo* (Christopher Tolkien, *Sir Gawain and the Green Knight, Pearl, and Sir Orfeo*, Del Rey, New York, 1975, 'Preface', pp. vii–x, vii). However, we know he first worked professionally on *Gawain* very early in his career, when he collaborated with Professor E.V. Gordon on his 1925 edition ('Preface', p. ix).

26. J.R.R. Tolkien, *Sir Gawain and the Green Knight, Pearl, and Sir Orfeo*, Del Rey, New York, 1975, *Pearl*, lines 127–28.

27. Kathryn L. Lynch, *The High Medieval Dream Vision: Poetry, Philosophy, and Literary Form*, Stanford University Press, Stanford, 1988, p. 193.

28. Steven F. Kruger, *Dreaming in the Middle Ages*, Cambridge University Press, Cambridge,

he writes of its medieval author that 'men, aware of the vagaries of dreams, still thought that amid their japes came visions of truth'.[29] While he does not use the term Faërian Drama here, it's clear he is thinking along the same lines as he does in *On Fairy-Stories*:

> [T]he narrated vision in the more serious medieval writing represented, if not an actual dream, at least a real process of thought culminating in some resolution or turning-point of the interior life – as with Dante, and in *Pearl*. And in all forms, lighter or more grave, the 'I' of the dreamer remained the eyewitness, the author, and the facts that he referred to outside the dream (especially those concerning himself) were on a different plane, meant to be taken as literally true.[30]

The pearl-maiden treats the dreamer with 'the hardness of truth … all is revealed to him, and he has eyes, yet he cannot see.' The dreamer had to be in the right frame of mind to receive the vision and profit from it; if he had instead 'received it incredulously or rebelliously … he would have awakened by the mound again' in the same state of woe and fear of mortality as before.[31] And remember, mounds are both graves and entrances into Faërie.

The events of *Sir Gawain and the Green Knight* can be read, though they are presented as 'superficially naturalistic' occurrences, as a dream-vision much like that in *Pearl*. The frame is Arthur's court; the initial challenge – our growing suspicion of Gawain's tendency to hubris, and the nightmarish beheaded-yet-speaking 'fay-man' with his deadly challenge represent the prologue.[32] Gawain's *adventures* in seeking the Green Chapel provide the softening; 'at whiles with worms he wars, and with wolves also, / at whiles with wood-trolls that wandered in the crags'.[33] By the time he reaches Bertilak's castle, exhausted by hunger and cold, he is ripe for the dreamlike threefold-testing of his courtesy devised by the fairy queen Morgan le Fay.[34] On his return to the real world of Arthur's court we see him chastened and newly ashamed of his weaknesses. In Tolkien's opinion, through Gawain's temptations and reactions 'he becomes a real man',[35] rather

---

1992, p. 135.

29. Op. cit. [26], 'Introduction', 1–22, p. 14.
30. Op. cit., p. 15.
31. Op. cit., p. 18.
32. Op. cit. [26], *Gawain*, line 28.
33. Op. cit. [26], p. 51.
34. Op. cit. [26], p. 118
35. Op. cit. [26], 'Introduction', p. 7.

than a prig who is a little too proud of his own perfect courtesy and piety; he is 'peculiarly fitted to suffer acutely in the adventure to which he is destined'.[36] And this is the central point of the practice of Faërian Drama – this experience was designed to lead Gawain, specifically and exclusively, through a series of trials and temptations uniquely suited to expose his peculiar weaknesses and frailties, and chasten, strengthen, and mature him.[37]

FRUITION

Let us move on to representations of Faërian Drama in Tolkien's fictional works – what he winds up doing with this concept and these examples in his own art. *The Lord of the Rings* is full of dreams and visions, some of which might qualify as Faërian Drama or at least medieval dream visions, though they are not clearly designated as such. Frodo in particular seems susceptible; his visions in Galadriel's mirror and on Amon Hen and his dreams in the House of Tom Bombadil seem more guided and purposeful than would be the case if his subconscious were merely working through the materials in his own mind. One might find more examples elsewhere in the legendarium (not so much in *The Hobbit* perhaps, although Bilbo does dream, of home and dancing bears and dinner). True Faërian Drama, however, seems to play more of a part in the shorter fiction and poems: *Leaf by Niggle*, the poems 'The Sea-Bell' and 'The Last Ship', and especially *Smith of Wootton Major*.

I want to examine *Smith of Wootton Major*, which Shippey has called Tolkien's 'Valedictory Address',[38] as the key and final statement about Faërian Drama in Tolkien's work. Verlyn Flieger warns us when embarking on study of *Smith* that 'the more you try to define it the less you see',[39] so we must tread warily. *Smith* is capable of many readings – as an autobiographical allegory of professor/writer's life,[40] as Tolkien's farewell to art,[41] as his anxiety and grief at facing the end of

36. Op. cit., p. 6.

37. *Sir Orfeo*, the third item in this collection, does not really work as a dream-vision – until you count the dream in which the King of Elfland appears to Heurodis with his demand that she come with him to his kingdom (op. cit. [26], *Orfeo*, lines 173–75). But we have too little of that dream to really work with here, and it is Orfeo's adventures which are the focus of the poem, not any Faërian drama Heroudis may experience.

38. Tom Shippey, *J.R.R. Tolkien: Author of the Century*, Houghton Mifflin, Boston, 2001, p. 303.

39. Verlyn Flieger, 'Pitfalls in Faerie', *Saga: Best New Writings on Mythology* 1 (1996), 157–71, p. 160.

40. Op. cit. [38].

41. Paul Kocher, *Master of Middle-earth: The Achievement of J. R. R. Tolkien*, Penguin Books, Harmondsworth, 1974. This is supported by Tolkien's own notes: J.R.R. Tolkien, 'Suggestions for the ending of the story', in Verlyn Flieger, ed., *Smith of Wootton Major*, HarperCollins,

life,[42] as proof of the concept of *On Fairy-Stories*[43] as a lesson in stewardship,[44] as a text about mysticism and religion.[45] What I want to look at, using faërian drama as my approach, is the mechanism of *how* and just a glimpse of *why* the story manages to bounce.

Tolkien says himself that *Smith* 'is a 'Fairy Story', of the kind in which beings that may be called 'fairies' or 'elves' play a part and are associates in action with human people, and are regarded as having a 'real' existence, that is one in their own right and independent of human imagination and invention'.[46] As Flieger insists in her debate with Tom Shippey on allegory in *Smith*, 'Its subject is the experience of a human in the Faery world' and '[t]he purpose of fairy tales is not to make sense but to give the reader a glimpse of the perilous realm'.[47]

But is that all there is? While Flieger at the time of this debate was against any allegorical reading of *Smith*, she admitted that 'the opacity of the story invites interpretation.' She insisted that 'the actual experience of enchantment by *Smith* ... is at the center of Smith' but he has 'a total lack of any key to the meaning of the phenomena to which he is witness'.[48] I think Smith finds that the meaning of his adventures 'increases with re-reading',[49] as it were; with Shippey, he might say, in later life, 'I do not know, but am still thinking about it'.[50]

As with anything else he touches, Tolkien is by no means simplistic here in *Smith*. Smith's experiences do not perfectly fit the definition of Faërian drama we have developed at all points – and yet the sum of his adventures incontrovertibly *is* an example of the mechanisms and effects of Faërian drama. Perhaps the first difference we must deal with is the fact that young Smith is not troubled in mind or in need of an intervention when he receives the star at the age of nine. What Smith experiences in Faery does not impact him with the straightforward didacticism of what the ghosts showed Scrooge. This is, in fact, because it is not Smith who is in need of intervention, but his village and society. As Tolkien's

---

London, 2005, 81–83, p. 81.

42. Humphry Carpenter, *J.R.R. Tolkien: A Biography*, HarperCollins, London, 2002, p. 323; these cited by name only in Verlyn Flieger, 'Afterword', in Flieger, op. cit. [41], 59–68, p. 65.

43. Flieger, 'Afterword', op. cit., p. 60.

44. Matthew Dickerson and Jonathan Evans, *Ents, Elves, and Eriador*, University of Kentucky Press, Lexington, 2006, p. 181.

45. Martin Sternberg, '*Smith of Wootton Major* Considered as a Religious Text', in Margaret Hiley and Frank Weinreich, eds, *Tolkien's Shorter Works: Essays of the Jena Conference 2007*, Walking Tree, Zurich, 2008, 293–323.

46. J.R.R. Tolkien, 'Smith of Wootton Major [essay]', in Flieger, op. cit. [41], 84–101, p. 84.

47. Verlyn Flieger and Thomas A. Shippey, 'Allegory Versus Bounce: Tolkien's *Smith of Wootton Major*', *Journal of the Fantastic in the Arts* 46 (2001), 186–200, p. 187.

48. Op. cit., pp. 188–89.

49. Op. cit., p. 192.

50. Op. cit., p. 198.

essay on *Smith* reveals, the village of Wootton Major had become 'comfortable and self-satisfied', even vulgarised, losing its long connection with Faery.[51] The rulers of Faery, out of love for Man or the obligations of kinship, or even a mutual necessary interdependence of which Men are unaware, devise a plan for the 'enlightenment and vivification'[52] of Wootton Major, in which certain humans will be chosen as a type of 'Apprentice'[53] to visit Faery and bring back a whiff of the air of that perilous country to their families and society. In this way, the 'actual experience of enchantment', as Flieger insists, *is* at the center of the story – but there is also a clear ethical purpose behind the simple aesthetic one.[54]

So how does the story fit and mis-fit the definition of Faërian Drama we developed earlier? While we have established that it is society, not Smith, that requires intervention, young Smith does acquire the star when he is in a liminal state. The Feast of Good Children is a once-in-a-lifetime ceremonial experience, to which not all children are invited, and his kindness in giving the coin from his slice to Nell sets him apart from the other children. It is on his tenth birthday, another liminal date, when the star makes itself known and Smith begins to develop his beautiful voice, his skill in craftsmanship, and the ability to visit Faery. As Tolkien says of Gawain, Smith is already 'peculiarly fitted to … the adventure to which he is destined'.

The faery world is entirely outside of the reality of the mundane world, yet Smith clearly is fully satisfied in his senses while there – he tastes the bitter tears of the birch, and he experiences the swiftness and joy of dancing with the Queen and her ladies. There are physical results of his travel; the star shines brightly when he returns, and he may be tired after a particularly long journey. He is able to carry artifacts home from Faery, like the Queen's Living Flower or the lily bell toy for young Tomling. He encounters reminders, such as the elven mariners returning from war, that Faery is a vast world with concerns of its own that extends physically and temporally far beyond the understanding of the human participant.

51. Op. cit. [46], pp. 92–93.
52. Op. cit., p. 99.
53. Op. cit., p. 96.
54. Why would Faerie care what goes on in the primary world and minds of men? 'Faery is a vast world in its own right, that does not depend for its existence upon Men, and which is not primarily nor indeed principally concerned with Men. The relationship must therefore be one of love: the Elven folk, the chief and ruling inhabitants of Faery, have an ultimate kinship with Men and have a permanent love for them in general. Though they are not bound by any moral obligation to assist Men, and do not need their help (except in human affairs), they do from time to time try to assist them, avert evil from them and have relations with them […]. [T]he Elvenfolk are thus 'beneficent' with regard to Men […] It is of course possible that they have a 'moral' obligation (the sanctions of which we do not know).' Op. cit. [46], pp. 93–94.

Another departure from what we might consider the typical Faërian drama is that Smith experiences not just one dramatic incident but forty-eight years of adventures. Instead of just 'before and after,' there is before, during, and after. Yet this is not so unusual, after all; while the Jeweler may have but one dream of his Pearl and George Bailey only need an hour or so in Pottersville to learn his lesson, Gawain's encounter with Faery stretches over several days, Scrooge experiences three distinct episodes punctuated by mundane sleep, and Phil Connors may relive the same day, but does so an uncountable number of times. The 'lesson' Smith must 'learn' for the sake of his society is in fact best served by – and perhaps it simply *is* – his prolonged exposure to Faery.

And what lesson is this, in the end? What precisely is the moral and ethical purpose of this particular long drawn-out episodic Faërian drama? Smith is 'a learner and explorer;[55] he learns many things in his travels, 'some of which gave him joy, and others filled him with grief',[56] and some which 'he could not clearly remember nor report to his friends'.[57] This joy and grief becomes a grace that shows through in his craft, both in the shapeliness and delight of what he forges and his singing while he works.

Martha Sammons suggests that Recovery is the lesson Smith learns, in the sense Tolkien uses the term in *On Fairy-Stories*. Not for his own sake, for he was young enough when selected never to have lost the clear sight of childhood, but in that he was chosen to experience and pass on the revitalising perspective of Recovery to those in his community capable of seeing. Smith's lasting grace is that even though he gives up the star, initially crying out that he can no longer see clearly, yet his, shall we say, baptised imagination and clear sight returns almost immediately.[58]

And yet Smith *does* also take a personal lesson away at the end. David Doughan proposes that the ultimate theme of *Smith* is renunciation, and that the story shares a philosophical theme with the Book of Job: 'The Lord gave, and the Lord hath taken away; blessed be the name of the Lord'.[59] This is supported by Tolkien's own statement that one of the points of the tale is sacrifice, and the handing on, with trust and without keeping a hand on things, of power and vision to the next generation'.[60] It is, as Tolkien writes, 'An old man's book ... weighted

55. Flieger, op. cit. [41], p. 24.
56. Op. cit., p. 37.
57. Op. cit., p. 26.
58. Martha Sammons, 'Tolkien On Fantasy in *Smith of Wootton Major*.' *Mythlore* 43, (1985), 3–7, p. 6. See also Flieger, op. cit [41], p. 47.
59. David Doughan, 'In Search of the Bounce: Tolkien Seen through Smith', in Trevor Reynolds, ed., *Leaves from the Tree: J.R.R. Tolkien's Shorter Fiction*, Tolkien Society, London, 1991, 17–22, p. 20.
60. Tolkien, 'Suggestions for the ending of the story', op. cit. [41], p. 81.

with the presage of 'bereavement".[61] Like Bilbo and Frodo giving up the Ring in their vastly different ways, like Galadriel resisting the temptation of power and like the Elves leaving Middle-earth at the conclusion of *The Lord of the Rings*, like Arwen dying alone and bereaved in the autumn leaves on Cerin Amroth, Smith's hard lesson at the end of his visions and adventures is that of letting go, giving up, and passing on the gift. As Doughan puts it, 'a voluntary acceptance of renunciation is preferable to any attempt to hold on to the perceived good when the time has come to let it go'.[62] And like the grace in art which Smith brings back from Faery, this renunciation of his gift is a moral *exemplum* to all who are privy to it.

Nokes's short exposure to an episode of didactic and straightforward Faërian Drama – the revelation of Alf as the King of Faery and the granting of his wish – may seem simply a comic afterthought at the end of the story, but here we are meant to contrast Smith, in his humility and openness to experience, with a mind not prepared to receive evidence of Faery, thinking it was just a dream 'which (like Ebenezer Scrooge) he attributes to bad eating habits'.[63] Nokes is of course affected anyway as he becomes thinner and thinner – and yet he denies Faery to the end, showing there is indeed more work for young Tim to do in returning Faery to Wootton Major.

CONCLUSION

The episode of Nokes and the Fairy King underscores that one purpose of the story *Smith of Wootton Major* is to remind us that Faery is all around and may be trying to get our attention for our own sakes – for our individual and societal reclamation and recovery. In fact all stories of Faërian Drama and dream vision share this deep theme in one way or another. 'For while in *Smith* Tolkien concedes that Faery is perilous to the traveler, he also wants to show it as necessary to humankind. Where the Fairy-story essay spoke of the dangers, the Smith essay concentrates almost entirely on its beauty, on its spiritual value, and its beneficent and necessary influence on the human world'.[64] It may behoove us, whether we believe in fairies or not, to look on the experiences of characters who have participated in Faërian drama in subcreated works as a template for how we can best benefit from such experiences in our own lives. In examining these abundant fictional records for clues of faërian intervention, we find a reminder to

61. Humphrey Carpenter, ed., *The Letters of J.R.R. Tolkien*, with the assistance of Christopher Tolkien, Houghton Mifflin, Boston, 2000, Letter 299, pp. 389–90.
62. Op. cit. [59], p. 21.
63. Op. cit. [20], p. 155.
64. Op. cit. [39], p. 165.

be aware of our own liminal states and psychological needs, and to be prepared to ponder and pore over our experiences in the twin faery lights of ethic and aesthetic. To be Scrooge, not Bottom; Smith, not Nokes.

'Tolkien's women of Middle-earth'

Chris Barclay

This paper is an exploration of the feminine in Tolkien's works, looking particularly at the female archetypes of the Madonna, the Lover, the Remarkable Woman and the Mother. The themes explored include orphan- and sibling-hood as well as Tolkien's biography.

INTRODUCTION

A few years ago I decided to combine my enjoyment of the works of Tolkien with my 'professional' interest in women; I trained in gynaecology, and then as a GP, and I have a particular interest in women's health. So why not study the women in Tolkien's Middle-earth legendarium? I thought. And to that end I bought a new edition of *The Hobbit*, some marker pens and a notebook. I re-entered Middle-earth at 'The Unexpected Party', the first chapter of *The Hobbit*, with a purpose. At first all went well. By page two I had discovered my first woman, Mrs Bungo Baggins (a.k.a. Belladonna Took). I planned to list and categorised all the female characters.

Discovering Belladonna was a good start. It was a shame that her husband had predeceased her by eight years, and that she had died at a ripe old age some years prior to the action. In fact I realised quite quickly that she was not truly a character in her own right. She was a literary device. A way of saying to the reader that soft domesticated old Bilbo had a wild side – something 'Tookish' inherited from his mother. I recorded Belladonna's entry and continued, and continued. In fact I got through to the end of the book and failed to find another woman. There were some female creatures (Beorn's sheep, and a deer with her fawn for example), there were acknowledgements to the existence of women as wives, widows and maidens – but not one was named or involved in the sweep of the narrative. In fact, that is not quite true. There was one other woman but she was alluded to, rather than mentioned, and that was Gollum's grandmother, the matriarchal river-hobbit who taught young Sméagol to suck 'Eggses' (*TH*, 'Riddles in the Dark', 87).[1]

By the time I had finished *The Hobbit*, my curiosity had been well and truly

1.J.R.R. Tolkien, *The Hobbit*, 3rd edn, George Allen & Unwin, London, 1966. All quotations from *TH* are taken from this edition.

aroused. To investigate further I resolved to identify all the female characters in *The Lord of the Rings*, and *The Silmarillion* as well. I also decided to look at the life of the author to see if his biography and personal life journey might illuminate my study. If Tolkien had set out to reveal 'A mythology for England', where were all the women; why were they absent? What was there about Tolkien that it did not seem right, or perhaps (I was beginning to think) that it never even occurred to him to populate his stories with women and the feminine? The Scientific Method is ingrained in me and a hypothesis emerged during my enquiries: Tolkien's women of Middle-earth are not normal women, maybe unusual or atypical might be better words, but not representative of women in real life. To investigate further I began to tabulate, categorise and analyse Tolkien's women of England and Arda.

I will begin firstly by looking at Tolkien's life and the women he had significant encounters with, then with this in mind I will go on to look at the principal female characters in *The Lord of the Rings*, and *The Silmarillion*, Tolkien's Women of Arda, and see if there are correlations to the Women of England he actually knew. I shall conclude with a brief physicianly impression of the story of Erendis, mother of Númenor's first ruling Queen, and ask if in her story Tolkien might have employed that literary style he famously 'cordially disliked in all of its manifestations', allegory. (*LotR*, 'Foreword to the Second Edition', xvii).[2]

TOLKIEN'S WOMEN OF MIDDLE-EARTH

In the early summer of 1912 Ronald Tolkien was nineteen. He had just completed his first year as an undergraduate. In a few weeks he would be walking, and sketching, through the countryside of Berkshire. In 1912, the first shots of the Great War were still two years away. In five years Ronald would be a married man and seeing action in the battle of the Somme. In 1912 Ronald was a sociable young man. He found fulfillment in sport, scholarship and the fraternal company of likeminded peers; a mode that had characterised his school years and which would continue to characterise him for the rest of his professional life.

Alongside this sociable masculine life was romance. He was in love. Ronald's romance with Edith ran parallel with, though totally separated from, compartmentalised if you will, from his otherwise predominantly masculine existence. When his guardian, Father Morgan had discovered the liaison he insisted it end immediately. Ronald dutifully complied. But if duty was one of Ronald's virtues so was tenacity. In the summer of 1912 Ronald's twenty-first

2. J.R.R. Tolkien, *The Fellowship of the Ring*, HarperCollins, London, 1993. All quotations from *FotR* are taken from this edition.

birthday, and passionate reunion with Edith was seventeen months in the future. And only when their engagement was announced did his close friends hear (for the very first time!) of Edith.

By the end of the Great War, Ronald had the outlined his three great epic tales, of Húrin, of Gondolin and most importantly the magical love story of Lúthien and Beren. In the late spring of 1917, with his war behind him, and in a Yorkshire copse, Edith danced and sang for Ronald, life and legend touched; and for a moment in time, Edith was Lúthien and Lúthien was Edith.

After the war Ronald rapidly ascended academia's slippery pole and aged just thirty-three returned to Oxford as Professor, a remarkable achievement. His boyhood habits persisted; he re-joined a (mostly) male world, and co-founded more all-male clubs, dedicated to scholarship - beer and rambling having replaced the sport of his youth. But Ronald continued to inhabit two separate lives, one at home as a husband and father, and another in the almost totally masculine worlds of academia and pubs with his cronies. Ronald was a sister-less orphan, but devoted brother, husband, father and nephew, a soldier, a gifted scholar, a devout Roman Catholic and a respected academic. The significant women in his first forty years appear to have been few, and will be discussed later.

LotR is about six times as long as *The Hobbit* and includes more female characters in the story, but not many more. A few female hobbits get mentioned, mostly in the first couple of chapters and mainly as amusing asides, for example Dora, Frodo's elderly aunt. She was given a waste paper basket in recognition of her extensive handwritten correspondence. The apparently beautiful (at least in her own opinion) Angelica received a convex mirror. In addition there were of course Lobelia Sackville-Baggins and Mrs. Maggot.

Fleeing the Shire, Frodo, Sam, Merry and Pippin meet with Bombadil in the Old Forest, who leads them to the wonderful and curious river-woman's daughter, Goldberry. They found no women in Bree. No Mrs. Butterbur, no chambermaids or bar maids; no serving wenches. They found no women in the wilderness. Just one woman was encountered in Rivendell, Aragorn's paramour and very distant cousin, Arwen. The newly formed fellowship found no women in Hollin and none in Moria. One woman is mentioned in Lothlórien, Galadriel, accompanied by her maidens. After the breaking of the fellowship Merry and Pippin find an openly acknowledged and pitiable absence of females in Fangorn. No women inhabited Isengard. Would Saruman have strayed from the path of wisdom had he fallen in love with a good woman, instead of lusting for the Necromancer's ring? Aragorn, Gimli and Legolas, the Three Hunters, encounter Rohan's only named woman, Éowyn, in Edoras. The only female creature Frodo and Sam met on the remainder of their quest was that last unhappy child of Ungoliant, Shelob the evil female spider, Sauron's 'cat', guarding the back door into the Realm of

Mordor.

Only one female inhabitant of Minas Tirith is named, Ioreth the garrulous herb mistress. We are told that she had professional sisters. The three previously mentioned principal female characters eventually join Ioreth in Minis Tirith: Éowyn for healing, Arwen for marriage and Galadriel as a wedding-guest. So, in *LotR* there are just four principal female characters: Goldberry, Arwen, Galadriel and Éowyn.

Of course the elder days intrude frequently into the narrative and the observant will have noticed Elbereth sung to by Noldor Elves in Woodhall, and her name invoked during the struggles with Shelob and the Silent Watchers. A brief rendition of the Lúthien story is given by Aragorn on Weathertop; Elwing is remembered in Imladris by her son Elrond. Queen Berúthiel (or at least her cats) is mentioned by Aragorn in Moria. And the enchanting but tragic story of Nimrodel is recalled by Legolas in the woods of Lothlórien. Galadriel was one of just three characters whose biographies stretch back from the end of the Third Age of Middle-earth to the days of bliss in Aman even before the dawn of the Fist Age of the sun. And allusions to her 'back-story' can be discerned through the text. Rosie Cotton enters the narrative during the Scouring of the Shire, when the bashful Sam at last (almost) declares his romantic interest. Why so few women? Why were there more named men of Rohan (and even named horses) than principal women in *LotR*?

Turning to the Elder Days many more female characters are found populating *The Silmarillion.* Tolkien included divine, firstborn (elf) and mortal women (human, dwarf and hobbit). There is but One God, but many of those of divine or angelic order were considered female. There are seven feminine Valier including most notably Varda (Elbereth) and Yavanna. There are numerous parallels between Tolkien's Valier and female gods in other mythologies. In Yavanna we can see many of the qualities of Demeter of the Greeks and Ceres of the Romans. In Varda one can see parallels with the Juno of the Romans, and Hera the wife of Zeus of the Greeks. Strikingly however there are no parallel equivalents in Tolkien's Arda with Venus or Aphrodite, goddesses of love. The Valier may have been female (or more accurately angelic beings inhabiting or clothed with a female physical presence – not essentially 'women' if you will), and indeed several were described as being the spouse of one or other of the male Vala, but none appeared to be a truly sexual being. There was no Eros and certainly no Venus. The joys of the carnal were unknown to Tolkien's goddesses and (in Christopher Tolkien's rendition of *The Silmarillion* at least) they did not appear to be fertile in a reproductive biological sense. This is a curious omission because without sexual love the whole point of God's creation of Arda, that is the Elves, humans, dwarves and even hobbits, would never have come into existence, and nor would they have propagated their kind within a stable society. The second rank of the divine, the Maiar, included Melian, Arien and Uinen, one of whom did conceive and have a daughter.

The first woman, if one excludes Melian the Maia, to enter the narrative was Míriel, mother of Fëanor. Of the first-born Lúthien, Aredhel, Idril and Elwing are the other major characters, and of the mortal (or human) women Morwen, Nienor/Níniel, Aerin, the unfortunate wife of Brodda, Haleth, and ultimately Tar-Míriel (later re-named Ar-Zimraphel), wife of Pharazôn whose hubris finally destroyed Númenor.

Tolkien did not relish intrusion into his personal life. Still less did he like theories constructed, and conclusions being drawn, suggesting that his work was informed by events from his own personal history.[3] With this in mind I trod cautiously. My sources were all published and in the public domain. This was secondary research. To be brief, in my reading of both Tolkien's personal life and in his *legendarium*, women seem to fall quite neatly into four archetypal groups.

Firstly and not surprisingly I would suggest The Mother figure as an important archetype. The tragedy of Tolkien's orphaning is well known; his widowed mother died after a short devastating illness, just eight years after her husband's untimely death. Mabel was just thirty-four years old and left the Tolkien brothers, twelve-year-old Ronald and his younger brother Hilary to the guardianship of the family's priest. Being ostracised by her family when she had converted to Roman Catholicism appears, in Tolkien's mind, to have been a factor in his mother's premature death: '[she was] worn out with persecution, poverty and largely consequent, disease, in the effort to hand on to us small boys the Faith.'[4] 'My dear mother was a martyr indeed.'[5] He cherished the memory of his remarkable and devoted mother ever after.

Considering how many famous sons populate the pages of Tolkien's writings, there are few mothers of significance in the annals of Arda:

- Míriel, the mother of Fëanor, wife of Finwë
- Melian, the mother of Lúthien, wife of Thingol
- Morwen, the mother of Túrin, wife of Húrin
- Aredhel, mother of Maeglin and wife of Ëol
- Idril (daughter of Elenwë), mother of Eärendel, wife of Tuor
- Elwing, mother of Elrond and Elros, wife of Eärendel
- Erendis, mother of Ancalimë, wife of Aldarion, the Mariner King of Númenor

3. Humphrey Carpenter, ed., *The Letters of J.R.R. Tolkien*, with the assistance of Christopher Tolkien, George Allen & Unwin, London 1981, Letter 213, p. 288.
4. Op. cit., Letter 266, p. 354.
5. Humphrey Carpenter, *J.R.R. Tolkien, A Biography*, Unwin Paperbacks, 1978, p. 39.

- Mrs Maggot, mother of several children, wife of Farmer Maggot of Bamfurlong.

The obverse of the 'The Mother' coin is of course The Absence of Mother – the orphan – and, as can be seen from the list below, the orphan is a common characteristic of a surprising number of Tolkien's characters, not just of Middle-earth, but also of Númenor and even Aman. Consider some of the motherless characters in these stories, of whom there are many:

- Fëanor
- Beren
- Idril, and her husband Tuor
- The brothers Elrond and Elros whose transformed mother left them
- Arwen (whose mother left Middle-earth for Aman) and Aragorn
- Frodo Baggins (and in a way Bilbo too)
- Gollum perhaps (his grandmotherly matriarch is mentioned, but no parents)
- Sam perhaps (son of Hamfast 'the Gaffer' and Bel Goodchild, who is conspicuous by her absence)
- Boromir and Faramir (whose stories movingly parallel Ronald and Hilary's experience of bereavement)
- Éowyn and Éomer (children of Théodwyn).

My second archetype is that of the Madonna, Our Lady, Mary the Blessed Virgin and Mother of God. Tolkien had every reason to be a devoted Roman Catholic. There was of course his revered mother's example, and the great kindness shown him and his brother by Father Morgan, who went considerably further than the extra mile for the boys. Tolkien acknowledged that his Catholic sensibilities unconsciously inspired characters and objects in his imaginative world. In a 1952 letter to Rev. Robert Murray (grandson of the founder of the Oxford English Dictionary and a family friend), he readily admitted that the Virgin Mary forms the basis for all of his 'small perception of beauty both in majesty and simplicity'.[6]

'It is not surprising, he admits, that the character of Galadriel – a created being endowed with radiant beauty, impeccable virtue, and powers of healing – resonates with the character of our Blessed Mother'.[7] The woman who preeminently fills the role of a Madonna in Arda is of course Galadriel. Her Royal ancestry, beauty,

6. Op. cit. [3], Letter 142, p. 172.

7. J. Boffetti, 'Tolkien's Catholic Imagination', *Crisis*, 1 November 2001 <http://www.crisismagazine.com/2001/tolkiens-catholic-imagination-2> [accessed 12 November 2015].

resistance against evil and refusal to succumb to temptation has led some to see in her some reflections of the Virgin Mary. True, she was tempted by Frodo's offer of The Ring and confessed that she had pondered what she might do if she possessed it. She was tempted, but resisted these sinful promptings; she passed the test (*FotR*, 'The Mirror of Galadriel', 357).

Mary was by marriage distantly of a Royal Household. She too was wise and obedient, she may not have sinned and through her the world was blessed. Mary is said to have left this world and its sorrows and was admitted bodily to heaven, the Assumption. Tolkien may well have had Mary in mind as he developed the character and biography of Galadriel. Like Mary, Galadriel was known as The Lady of Light. In Catholic tradition Mary is said to judge with gentleness and mercy, as did Galadriel when visited by the fellowship of the Ring. Mary was sinless and resisted temptation as did Galadriel; Aragorn described Galadriel as having no evil in her (*FotR*, 'The Mirror of Galadriel', 349). Mary's son was murdered on the cross. Galadriel's only child, Celebrían, also suffered, and in a way died to the world, leaving it for the heavenly realm of Valinor for the healing of her hurts. Galadriel, like Mary, was the object not only of love but mystical devotion, in her case by Gimli. It was this that prompted him to boldly beg a few strands of her hair to preserve and cherish as an heirloom. In Catholicism such heirlooms, or relics, are venerated, perceived as being imbued with divine virtue. And like Mary, Galadriel did not die but was transported to the heavenly realm.

Tolkien's devotion to the Mary mirrored, I believe, in his creative devotion to the unfolding story of Galadriel. His revisionary work on her history, expunging story lines of her rebellion and disobedience to the Valar, was actively pursued throughout his life. Indeed Christopher Tolkien even states that his father's last writings on the legends of Middle-earth and Valinor, penned within a month of his death, probably concerned Galadriel and Celeborn. He was busy revising her biography in the months and weeks before his death.[8] In Tolkien's mythology the Valar, although God like in some senses, were in fact angelic beings created by the One God, Ilúvatar. It could be that Galadriel's 'disobedience' to the Valar may not have been contrary to a greater obedience to the one true God. Was this the direction Tolkien's revisionism was working? (*UT*, 'The History of Galadriel and Celeborn', 231–32).[9] His Church has for two thousand year been adding, embellishing and revising Mary's story, ultimately elevating her to her present intercessory status, just short of the Divine. And so if over the years Galadriel

8. Christina Scull and Wayne G. Hammond, *The J.R.R. Tolkien Companion and Guide*, vol. 1: *Chronology*, HarperCollins, London, 2006, pp. 773–74.

9. J.R.R. Tolkien, *The Unfinished Tales of Númenor and Middle-earth*, ed. Christopher Tolkien, George Allen & Unwin, London 1980, 'The History of Galadriel and Celeborn and of Amroth King of Lórien', 229–67.

became a Madonna-like figure for Tolkien, then it would not be a surprise to discover that, like his church, he would want her story to be expunged of even the merest hint of a dark side.

Other Madonna figures include quite obviously Varda (Queen of Heaven), but also Idril Celebrindal. Idril was the daughter of Turgon and Elenwë, who perished crossing the Helcaraxë, the northern icy waste bordering Middle-earth. Elenwë was the only Vanyar Elf to leave Valinor during the rebellion. And Turgon had a Vanyar grandmother, Indis. Idril was by blood therefore more than half Vanyar, which accounted for her golden hair. It might also explain or support her role in the story as a Madonna figure: a Royal child of Vanyar ancestry, and mother of her own Holy Family who, with her husband Tuor, fled into exile from a despotic ruler in order to protect their Christ-like son, Eärendel from death.

The third archetypical female I would suggest is The Lover. Tolkien's teenage romance, enforced separation and, when he turned twenty-one, his subsequent determined pursuit of Edith Bratt, is a dramatic love story. Why he compartmentalised it (and her) totally from his family, guardian and close friends is curious. Their marriage and the anxiety of being a soldier seeing action on the Somme was followed by a moment of high romance and passion. During the war years Tolkien had started composing the legends that eventually became the core of *The Silmarillion*. The Tale of Lúthien and Beren is perhaps the most powerful, influential and even magical story he ever wrote. The story of Beren and Lúthien was so important that he replayed it several times: Thingol and Melian, Idril and Tuor perhaps, and of course Aragorn and Arwen. Ronald's experience of Edith's fabulous singing and dancing in a woodland glade appears to have enlivened the Lúthien legend with real passion. Edith and Ronald were married for fifty-five years and biographies describe a marriage, which for the first half at least had its strains and conflicts. Yet, the cherished image of Edith dancing among the hemlock in 1917 remained vivid for the rest of his life. The Lúthien motif was used by the grieving Ronald in a letter just after Edith's death; 'But the story has gone crooked, and I am left, and I cannot plead before the inexorable Mandos'.[10]

My final archetype is what I have called 'The Remarkable Woman'. Tolkien had, it would appear, relatively few significant connections with women in his life. This was especially so during his younger adult years, at the time he was bringing Middle-earth and Arda into being. Of course there was his mother, his wife and later his daughter. But the only other significant real women that leap out of the pages of biography are his aunt Jane Neave and his illustrator Pauline Baynes. Aunt Jane was one of the Suffield sisters, on his mothers' side of the family. A child of the Victorian era, she was a graduate, car driver, seasoned

10. Op. cit. [3], Letter 340, p. 420.

traveller and a farmer at a time when this was unusual (remarkable?) for women. She was also widowed very early. There is no doubt that she was a close friend and confidant of Tolkien, who visited her regularly (her first farmhouse was called Bag End!). There have even been suggestions that she may have been an inspiration for the character of Gandalf.[11]

Pauline Baynes was also remarkable. She was born in India, the daughter of the Raj Commissioner of Agra and moved to England aged five years with her older sister. She later studied at The Slade School of Art, and worked as a cartographer during the Second World War. Famously, she illustrated C.S. Lewis's Narnia books. Greatly respected by Tolkien for her illustrations for several of his publications including *LotR* and *The Adventures of Tom Bombadil*, he later graciously commented that her illustrations 'reduce my text to a commentary on her drawings'.[12] Indeed her drawings were among the first to publicly portray Middle-earth visually. She died in 2008.

In his Middle-earth writings several remarkable women grace Tolkien's stories. Bilbo's mother, Belladonna Took was actually described as a remarkable daughter, (one of the three in fact) of the Old Took. Apart from her ancestry Belladonna is hardly mentioned as a character, and certainly does not to have any applicable maternal biography, other than the fact of her having borne Bilbo. We just have to accept without supporting evidence that she was 'remarkable'. Lobelia Sackville-Baggins (née Bracegirdle), Frodo's battle-axe distant aunt certainly deserves inclusion in this category too. She had flaws in her character: light-fingered, over-opinionated and jealous. But her stout, umbrella wielding, opposition to the occupation of the Shire (*RotK*, 'The Scouring of The Shire', 990),[13] and the popular reaction on her release from the Lockholes (*RotK*, 'The Scouring of The Shire', 998) suggests there was more to her too than met the eye. Other nominations I could suggest include Mrs. Maggot; the fertile farmer's wife with a sense of humour, and of course Ioreth, the previously mentioned herb mistress of Minas Tirith, of whom Robert Foster observed that 'Her folk wisdom was exceeded only by her loquacity'.[14]

And so let us turn to the one female who whose characterisation, I would argue, appears closest to that of a 'real woman', Erendis, the Mariner's Wife. She was probably the last woman Tolkien created to inhabit Arda. Good news (of an

11. A. H. Morton and J. Hayes, *Tolkien's Gedling, the birth of a legend*, Brewin Books, Studley, 2008, p. 72.
12. Op. cit. [3], Letter 120, p. 133.
13. J.R.R. Tolkien, *The Return of the King*, HarperCollins, London, 1993. All quotations from *RotK* are taken from this edition.
14. Robert Foster, *The Complete Guide to Middle-earth*, Unwin Paperbacks, London, 1986, p. 212.

easy and blissful life) doesn't make good copy, and Tolkien was no exception here. We do not read much about the glory of Valinor, though we do read about its darkening; we do not read much about the glory days of Gondolin, so no descriptions follow Tuor's arrival until Aredhel departs only to return some time later with a son in tow. And it is so too with Númenor. The only big story about Númenor in *The Silmarillion* relates to its destruction brought on by Ar-Pharazôn. But much earlier in the chronology of Númenor, is the tragedy described in the tale of The Mariner's Wife.[15]

In the story of the Mariner's wife Tolkien explores the course of a romance between two equally determined people. Aldarion, the man destined to be King, falls slowly in love but entirely on his own terms. He decides when he will pursue his chosen one, and when he will not. The woman's wants and needs are heard, but never really listened to. Her heart-felt requests carried little weight in his decision making. For Aldarion is the mariner of the story, a man in love with the high seas, exploring far-away lands, most comfortable in the company of sailors. His first and forever love affair was with the ocean. All other obligations came a distant second, whether it was obedience to and respect for his father, his duties as future monarch or to the woman he wooed and pursued, and for a time loved. Lines from Masefield's poem 'Sea Fever' could have been written for Aldarion:

> I must go down to the seas again, for the call of the running tide
> Is a wild and clear call that may not be denied.[16]

Erendis on the other hand was not of the royal line of Elros, though she was born into an aristocratic family. Her heritage was of the first House of Men, she was a distant relative of Morwen and Nienor. In fact Tolkien's description of her is reminiscent of Morwen in her prime, a raven-haired woman of remarkable beauty and possessed of a distinctly Elven air. Like Aldarion she was a person of strong character. Her mother described her as someone who would have 'all or nothing' and when she first encountered and secretly gave her heart to Aldarion it appeared that her lot would indeed be nothing. For six years she loved him from afar, six years during which Aldarion was unaware of her existence. During that time she had nothing of him, but hoped for all. It would be a full fifty-eight years from the day she first set eyes on Aldarion till their betrothal and a further twelve until their marriage.

---

15. Op. cit. [9], 'Aldarion and Erendis, the Mariner's Wife', 167–209.
16. John Masefield, 'Sea Fever' <http://www.poetryfoundation.org/poem/242552> [accessed 12 November 2015].

During this long courtship Aldarion had become an accomplished mariner and had been away from Númenor on several prolonged voyages, the longest of which lasted fourteen years. Small wonder then that the 'all or nothing' Erendis needed some serious wooing to commit to marriage. For in her heart Erendis knew all along that Aldarion's need to sail and explore would not be negotiable. She may have known it, but she never accepted it, and never willingly shared him with the sea. And Aldarion would never let Erendis, or anyone else for that matter, prevent him voyaging. If she was 'all or nothing', he was 'all and everything', and therein lay the seeds of destruction, which flowered to blight their union.

Erendis and Aldarion were betrothed for twelve years, six of which he was abroad, and married for twelve, five of which he was away. During their short marriage they had one child, a daughter, Ancalimë. After her birth Erendis grudgingly consented to Aldarion's request to sail again. He promised to be back within two years but in the event it was five before his ship returned to port. An embittered Erendis had by then long since abandoned her opulent Royal residence and returned to a remote sheep farming area of Númenor's interior.

Her glacial coolness to him on his eventual return provoked the ever-stubborn Aldarion to withdraw from her and their marriage, and pursue his own agendas. When his father handed to him the Sceptre and he became king, Erendis refused to attend the ceremony and would have prevented their daughter doing so if she could.

Aldarion continued to voyage for the rest of his life, something unheard of in any of his Númenorian predecessors who never left the 'Land of Gift'. Erendis on the other hand lived in virtual purdah, surrounding herself exclusively with female servants. In due course her headstrong, manipulative and selfish daughter deserted her.

Had Aldarion shown even a speck of remorse at breaking his word to Erendis by returning three years later than promised, Erendis may have forgiven him and their union may have been healed. And on the other hand had Erendis accepted her husband's seafaring obsession and learned to be content with his periods of absence, the marriage may have succeeded. But neither would bend, neither would compromise. In later life Aldarion would reflect that their years of betrothal and early-married years had been the happiest of his life.

Tolkien wrote 'The Mariner's Wife' in 1960 when he was in his late sixties, the year after his retirement as Professor of English at Merton College, Oxford. Erendis was probably the last significant female character he created, although he continued to refine the histories of others, particularly Galadriel, until his death in 1972. In this story, which he never finished, Tolkien chose two themes to weave through the narrative. The first relates to a play between warmth and coldness, and the other to the giving of blessings before embarking on a voyage.

Tolkien beautifully uses terms of warmth and coldness, chill and frost, to describe not only the meteorology but also the climate of relationships. "Cold is the life of a mariners wife" Aldarion tells his frustrated father (*UT*, 'Aldarion and Erendis', 172), and later giving Erendis a diamond, he rebukes his father saying he gave it in gratitude for "a warm heart amid the coolness of others" (*UT*, 'Aldarion and Erendis', 173). Aldarion went on to treat Erendis with coldness himself and later an emotionally wounded Erendis suggests their relationship "is not yet chilled to death" (*UT*, 'Aldarion and Erendis', 181). Erendis later finds her bed cold, and descends into the pain of cold anger. Their relationship was one of brief blissful highs and deep squally lows; for Erendis and Aldarion unsettled weather was never far away.

The second theme of blessing before voyaging superficially relates to the custom of the captain's wife to tie a leafy bough from the evergreen tree Oiolairë onto the prow of the ship before departure. Erendis first does this on behalf of her future mother-in-law, the Queen, when Aldarion embarks contrary to the King's wish. After her betrothal Erendis once more brought Oiolairë for Aldarion. After their wedding when he insisted on the two-year voyage (that became five) Erendis pragmatically consented to, but would not bless, his departure. It was left to the wife of one of the ship's officers to perform the Oiolairë ceremony.

It was however during the earlier six year voyage between betrothal and marriage that the themes of blessing and Oiolairë, and elemental coldness intersected. During his difficult voyage home to Númenor from Middle-earth the winds were unfavourable and Aldarion's ships were blown far into the icy north. There the Oiolairë was frosted and it wilted: something without precedent. Tolkien wound this ill omen into the tale after Aldarion's return when Erendis's resolve to marry was all but exhausted. Despite his neglect Erendis magnanimously forgave the for once contrite Aldarion, but as ever, the woman who wanted it all prayed that 'winter' by which she meant further voyages abroad 'not return'. Winter did however return, and just as the frost had killed the Oiolairë so some years later Aldarion's determination to keep his wife out in the metaphorical cold eventually killed their marriage.

Although Tolkien stated plainly that he disliked allegory and insisted that there was none in *LotR*, one cannot miss the possible parallels between aspects of his own life and that of Aldarion. Both were able and determined men and both voyaged frequently to Middle-earth; Aldarion aboard the great ships of Númenor and Tolkien in the unfolding of the world he spent his life creating and populating. Aldarion travelled widely across Middle-earth and was a frequent guest of Gil-galad. He even met Galadriel. Tolkien, it has to be said, was an even more frequent visitor to Middle-earth, travelling widely through its lands and down the thousands of years of its unfolding history. When writing 'The Mariner's Wife' was Tolkien alluding perhaps, and with some regret, to his earlier life as a creative writer? Always a sociable man he found great pleasure and delight in the company of similarly minded men who also enjoyed smoking and drinking and indulging in lively conversation. He spent many an evening in the company of these friends and colleagues. This perhaps may have been to the detriment of some of his duties as a spouse and companion. When his children were young Tolkien was at his creative peak and his friendship with C.S. Lewis was at its height. Lewis, then a confirmed bachelor, would frequently keep his friends talking into the wee hours as if they did not have homes, children and wives to attend to. In his letters, and in Humphrey Carpenter's biography, there are suggestions that Edith Tolkien found those years as the wife of a successful and exceptionally busy, though perhaps relatively absent, academic a trial. Was Tolkien's Middle-earth work unblessed and viewed coolly at home? Ronald may have looked back with some regret at opportunities missed between them. But there the allegorical parallels stop. Tolkien was a devoted husband and father and certainly in the latter years of his career and into retirement ensured that Edith's desire for the sort of society and company she enjoyed, especially with her husband, was granted.

Tolkien never did finish the story of 'The Mariner's Wife' although he wrote the bulk of the tale and left outline notes concerning the remainder. Quite why he wrote it is not clear. He was a busy man and had pressing academic writings to complete as well as a desire to bring *The Silmarillion* to a conclusion. I suspect he wanted to document the first intrusion of the venal into the bliss of Númenor, one more marring of paradise. The tragic unfolding of the consequences of small sins is a theme that runs through much of Tolkien's writings. Was Aldarion's behaviour and treatment of Erendis the first pebble, as it were, which over the years and generations gathered force and later became the landslide that destroyed Númenor? How much greater a King could Aldarion have become had Erendis not turned her back on him so decisively? And how blessed would Erendis's life have been had Aldarion not treated her so cruelly? Certainly the child of this unhappy marriage matured into a mildly tyrannical Queen; as you sow, so shall you reap.

Poor Erendis lived out the remainder of her life, after her brief marriage, as a recluse behaving as if she were a widow. When old age came upon her she desired once more to see her husband and travelled incognito to his home in the coastal port of Rómenna. But when she arrived he was abroad and in the year 985 of the Second Age of Middle-earth Erendis, alone and unmourned, died. All Tolkien recorded was that she 'perished in the water' (*UT*, 'Aldarion and Erendis', 204).

Tolkien wrote several mortal women into his narratives: Morwen, Nienor, Haleth, Éowyn and Erendis for example. But women are few and far between in the unfolding history of Arda. They appear mainly as wives, sisters and daughters. They bear their tragedies and endure their fates, but such characterisation as there is is usually sketchy; a wife may have been dour and unapproachable, and her daughter doomed to unhappiness, but they populated someone else's biography; an orphaned young woman, spurned in love (though later healed of her death wish), flowers briefly, but is destined only to be a wife of another major male character. Even the immortal Galadriel has an otherworldly air; one senses a dreamlike separation, an ethereal distance, from the hard world of Middle-earth at the end of Third Age. Did anyone truly see Galadriel, or were they but visions, a holy apparition? Tolkien never created an Elizabeth Bennett, nor a Cathy nor a Tess, let alone a Laura Belaqua, a Lisbet Salander or a Sara Lund. Most of his women are, I contend, drawn rather thin, two dimensionally archetypal. The four main archetypes of The Madonna, The Mother, The Lover and the Remarkable Woman seem to me to chime with both the real and imaginary women in Tolkien's life and writings. There are around one hundred female characters in *The Hobbit*, *LotR*, and *The Silmarillion*, from Adamanta Chubb to Zimraphel, and yet for me only his last-born woman Erendis seems real.

'Colours in Tolkien'

Christopher Kreuzer

This paper examines the use of colours and colour symbolism in the works of J.R.R. Tolkien, looking at his role as both writer and artist, and drawing on the views expressed in On Fairy-Stories and A Secret Vice. Some thoughts on the topic of colour and light are followed by a survey and discussion of examples of colour symbolism in Tolkien's written works. The paper touches on colour names in his languages, and considers examples of 'many colours', concluding that Tolkien's use of colours in his writings demonstrates that he was a master of his craft.

> "White!" he sneered. "It serves as a beginning. White cloth may be dyed. The white page can be overwritten; and the white light can be broken."
>
> (*FotR*, 'The Council of Elrond', 252)[1]

INTRODUCTION

Earlier writings on the topic of colour symbolism and the use of colours in Tolkien's works have mostly focused on the 'colours' associated with light and dark, white and black, with other colours generally neglected. Much has been written on the symbolism of white and black, in particular their association with good and evil. This paper will concentrate more on the other colours used by Tolkien in his writings.

The *J.R.R. Tolkien Encyclopedia: Scholarship and Critical Assessment* includes the entry 'Colors' by Victor L. Parker.[2] Parker singles out white and black as the most obviously symbolic colours, while pointing out that the white/good and black/evil symbolism is not absolute, and that Tolkien's use of white 'grows complicated'. Examples include the white light of the Arkenstone and Silmarils, and Saruman turning from White to Many Colours. Parker states that Tolkien's use of black and darkness (an absence of light) 'harmonises with the

1. J.R.R Tolkien, *The Fellowship of the Ring*, Collins Modern Classics, London, 2001. All quotations from *FotR* are taken from this edition.

2. Victor L. Parker, 'Colors', in Michael D.C. Drout, ed., *J.R.R. Tolkien Encyclopedia: Scholarship and Critical Assessment*, Routledge, New York, 2007, 106–107.

Boethian view of evil as merely the absence of good'. Parker also singles out green as a colour of significance, and gives the colours of the wizards and the Three Rings as examples of a 'simple distinguishing device'. While stating that 'much remains for investigation, Parker does warn that we should not always expect to find symbolic value in colours.

This paper aims to show that a closer examination and survey of the topic makes possible a keener appreciation of the role of colours in language, and the evocative use of colours in a passage of writing, or a body of work as a whole.

TOLKIEN AS WRITER AND ARTIST

As a philologist and inventor of languages, Tolkien was keenly aware of the power of words to shape language and meaning. He talks about the use of colours as adjectives in his 1939 lecture (later published as an essay) titled *On Fairy-Stories*:

> The human mind, endowed with the powers of generalisation and abstraction, sees not only *green-grass*, discriminating it from other things (and finding it fair to look upon), but sees that it is *green* as well as being *grass*. But how powerful, how stimulating to the very faculty that produced it, was the invention of the adjective; no spell or incantation in Faerie is more potent.... When we can take green from grass, blue from heaven, and red from blood, we have already an enchanter's power.... We may put a deadly green upon a man's face and produce a horror; we may make the rare and terrible blue moon to shine; or we may cause woods to spring with silver leaves and rams to wear fleeces of gold, and put hot fire into the belly of the cold worm. But in such "fantasy", as it is called, new form is made; Faerie begins; Man becomes a sub-creator. (*OFS*, 122)[3]

These thoughts were not new. Tolkien had addressed the subject of the adjective and its role in language in an earlier address to a philological society in 1931. This address was published posthumously in 1983 under the title 'A Secret Vice' in the collection *The Monsters and the Critics and Other Essays*. Towards the end of that address, he declared that the invention of the free adjective allowed writers and poets to construct phrases such as 'green sun' and 'dead life' that 'set the imagination leaping', concluding:

3. J.R.R. Tolkien, 'On Fairy-stories', in Christopher Tolkien, ed., *The Monsters and the Critics and Other Essays*, HarperCollins, London, 1997, 109–61.

> Language has both strengthened imagination and been freed by it. Who shall say whether the free adjective has created images bizarre and beautiful, or the adjective been freed by strange and beautiful pictures in the mind? ('A Secret Vice', 219)[4]

The above passages give an insight into Tolkien as a writer and poet. However, when considering the use of colours in Tolkien's writings, it is important to remember that Tolkien was an artist as well as an author. His use of colours in his artworks and illustrations is described in Hammond and Scull's 1995 work *J.R.R. Tolkien Artist & Illustrator*. In the introduction to Chapter Two 'Visions, Myths and Legends', they describe Tolkien as a visionary who was 'like other men of genius with intense powers of visualisation' and was able to make his visions 'vivid to others'.[5] William Blake, who was also both poet and artist, is mentioned as an example of such a visionary. As well as his own art, Tolkien's writings have inspired a profusion of visual art that is rich in colour and varied in styles, contrast and media.

Tolkien's writing includes powerful and vibrant imagery of the landscapes that his characters travel through. When done well, the effect fires the imagination and 'paints' a picture of the landscape in the mind's eye of the reader. A good example of this is the explicit description of Galadriel appearing in Frodo's mind:

> Far off, as in a little picture drawn by elven-fingers he saw the Lady Galadriel standing on the grass in Lórien, and gifts were in her hands. (*TT*, 'Shelob's Lair', 704)[6]

Colour, and the varied language used to communicate tone and hues, is central to such depictions, with language used to shape and colour the picture in the reader's mind.

COLOUR AND LIGHT

The issue of colour, though, is intimately bound up with that of light. Verlyn Flieger's work *Splintered Light* (first published in 1983 and revised in 2002) examines how Tolkien's use of light and the splintering of that light can be seen

4. J.R.R. Tolkien, 'A Secret Vice', in Christopher Tolkien, ed., *The Monsters and the Critics and Other Essays*, HarperCollins, London, 2006, 198–223.
5. Wayne G. Hammond, and Christina Scull, *J.R.R. Tolkien: Artist and Illustrator*, HarperCollins, London, 2004, p. 35.
6. J.R.R. Tolkien, *The Two Towers*, Collins Modern Classics, London, 2001. All quotations from *TT* are taken from this edition.

as a metaphor, particularly for the evolution of his languages. Flieger notes that:

> The concept "to shine" breaks into many kinds of shinings, into "gleam", "sparkle", "radiant". Colour words appear – gold, silver, green, grey. Darker words come into being, words for dusk, dimness, twilight shadow.[7]

This evolution from light to colour (from an initial darkness) is seen in the lines directly preceding the just-cited passage where Frodo (in Shelob's Lair) sees Galadriel in his mind's eye:

> Then as he stood, darkness about him and a blackness of despair and anger in his heart, it seemed to him that he saw a light: a light in his mind, almost unbearably bright at first, as a sun-ray to the eyes of one long hidden in a windowless pit. Then the light became colour: green, gold, silver, white. (*TT*, 'Shelob's Lair', 703–704)

A similar process of evolution in language can be seen in the passage where Frodo enters Lothlórien:

> It seemed to him that he had stepped through a high window that looked on a vanished world. A light was upon it for which his language had no name.... He saw no colour but those he knew, gold and white and blue and green, but they were fresh and poignant, as if he had at that moment first perceived them and made for them names new and wonderful. (*FotR*, 'Lothlórien', 341)

This passage may describe what it would be like, in the dawn of the world, to be naming colours for the first time. Or it may describe what it is like to see 'unbroken light' and the colours associated with that primeval time.

As well as naming several colour words, Flieger, in the previously quoted passage, states that many kinds of 'shining' arose as Tolkien's languages evolved. This is seen also in the English words used for such descriptions in *The Lord of the Rings*, with the words glimmer, gleam and glitter used extensively. Used less often, but still to excellent effect, are words such as glow, glint, and glisten. These are not colours, but evoke a more subtle effect of quality and type of light, as well as adding poetic alliteration when used together or in close proximity in

7. Verlyn Flieger, *Splintered Light: Logos and Language in Tolkien's World*, 2nd edn, Kent State University Press, Kent OH, 2002, p. 86.

the text.

A third example of the progression from white light to colours can be seen in *The Silmarillion*, where the gems first made by Fëanor were 'white and colourless, but being set under starlight they would blaze with blue and silver fires brighter than Helluin' (*TSil*, 'Of Fëanor and the Unchaining of Melkor', 74).[8] This is followed by the Silmarils, 'as were they indeed living things, they rejoiced in light and received it and gave it back in hues more marvellous than before' (*TSil*, 'Of the Silmarils and the Unrest of the Noldor', 78), and culminates in the Nauglamír, which 'did reflect and cast abroad in marvellous hues the light of the Silmaril amidmost' (*TSil*, 'Of the Ruin of Doriath', 281).

Before turning to specific examples of Tolkien's uses of colours in his writings, the human perception of colours and landscapes should be considered in its historical context. Past societies and cultures (similar to those found in Middle-earth) viewed and named colours differently to how they are perceived by modern eyes and tongues. This topic, from the view of those that spoke Old English, was covered by Douglas Harper, author of the *Online Etymology Dictionary*. In a column from June 2002, he recounts the care needed when studying the etymology of the names of colours. Harper provides the famous example of the difficulties caused by Homer's 'wine-dark' sea from Ancient Greek, and goes on to describe how the colours perceived and named were different in Old English as well:

> Many surviving color words from Old English – dun, wan, sallow, bleak, dusky, swarthy, bright, murky, dark – refer to colors which are not hues. These words have more to do with chroma (reflectivity, brightness, quality of light) than with hue (wavelength).[9]

Harper makes the point that once you remove modern, bright artificial colours, the world (especially in the climate and vegetation of Northern Europe) becomes much duller, and this can explain why glitter and dark matter so much. Given that Tolkien would have been familiar with such arguments, it is possible that some of the 'visual palettes' of the landscapes of Middle-earth, and the heavy use of the language of light and shadows, arise as much from this consideration as from an evolution from an original unbroken light. In other words, Tolkien may

8. J.R.R. Tolkien, *The Silmarillion*, ed. Christopher Tolkien, Unwin Paperbacks, London, 1979. All quotations from *TSil* are taken from this edition.
9. Douglas Harper, 'Old English' *Online Etymology Dictionary*, 2002 <http://etymonline.com/columns/oldenglish.htm> [accessed 10 August 2012].

have deliberately created a pre-modern verbal palette of colour and 'quality of light' in which to set his stories.

HOW TOLKIEN USES COLOURS

The rest of this paper will look at some of the ways in which colours are used in Tolkien's writings. Colours are used extensively, and at times with poetic force, in his descriptions of landscapes. They are also used to produce associations and delineations within the story itself, between different places and times, and between different cultures and groupings of individuals and objects.

Well-known examples of simple groupings, mentioned previously, include the colour of the Istari (wizards), and the colours of the stones contained in the Three Rings made for the Elves. Other obvious examples are the heraldic colours used on the banners carried by the different armies that clash on the battlefields of Middle-earth.

The colours of the Istari (wizards) are: Gandalf the Grey, Radagast the Brown, Saruman the White, and the two Blue Wizards. The colours of the stones in the three Elven Rings are: Vilya (blue), Narya (red), and Nenya (white). Heraldic colours are used in banners, such as Rohan (White Horse on Green), Gondor (the White banner of the Stewards), Aragorn's banner (Silver Tree and Stars on Black), Dol Amroth (White Swan on Blue), Haradrim (Black Serpent on Red), the Orcs of Saruman and Mordor and Minas Ithil (White Hand and Red Eye and White Crescent Moon).

Colours are used extensively in the text when the reader is introduced to a new landscape or character or culture within Middle-earth. Examples include the Shire, Tom Bombadil, Rivendell, Lothlórien, Fangorn, Rohan, Gondor, Ithilien, Mordor. In each case, Tolkien's descriptions set up palettes of colours that help distinguish places and peoples from each other. Many of these colour palettes were used to great effect in the Peter Jackson films of *LotR*. One example is the Lórien palette, emphasised repeatedly in the text as silver, gold and green. Similar palettes can be constructed for other locations described in the text.

It is readily apparent that Tolkien uses a large colour vocabulary, i.e. his texts are rich in descriptions using colours and colour-related words, but the frequency of use of such words varies immensely. To take *LotR* as an example, black and white and grey dominate, along with related words such as dark and light and shadow, all appearing in the text numerous times in various forms. These colours and the symbolism associated with them are well documented; it is other colours, occurring less frequently, that will be examined in this survey.

Gold and silver are used extensively to describe objects made from those precious metals, but in addition to this they are used many times by Tolkien as colours. Green and red are common, with green used in large part to emphasise natural vegetation. Of the other colours yellow, blue and brown are rarer, while pink and orange appear to be absent, though saffron (yellow-orange) and dawn-rose (possibly pink) are used (both in the description of the Glittering Caves).

Purple is used to describe the high slopes of Mount Mindolluin and others of the White Mountains. This purple colour is likely heather, as seen on the hills and glens of Scotland. This is an example of colour being used to hint at the nature of the flora of Middle-earth, but doing so through poetic description.

Blue is used as a natural colour for sky and water. It is used in the clothing of Tom Bombadil and Goldberry, plus the banner of Dol Amroth, the cloaks of Lady Éowyn and Gandalf, and is the colour of the stone of Vilya. It is also used as a magical colour, such as the glow produced by Sting.

The red of the leather covers of the Red Book seems to be mundane and lacking symbolism, as are the uses of red to describe flowers and berries, firelight, the light of the rising and setting Sun, and of Borgil (Mars). The symbolic uses of red appear to be limited to the Red Eye, the stone of Narya, and the Red Arrow.

Yellow, though often supplanted by gold and golden in the more poetic passages, does feature, especially in bright clothing, as in the hobbits and Tom Bombadil's boots, or those with blond hair. The Sun is called the Yellow Face by Gollum.

Green is mostly used for describing trees and vegetated landscapes. This is not surprising, but what perhaps is of note is the sheer number of times the word green is added to such descriptions, and also when green vanishes or changes in the visual palette, such as when describing drearier landscapes or the desolation in or around Mordor. The tone shifts, with adjectives such as sickly, wan, pale, ghostly, haggard, used to describe the greens that survive in the stricken areas of the Marshes before the Black Gate of Mordor, with the stronger, darker greens returning when Ithilien is reached. The most symbolic green is that of the Elfstone given to Aragorn.

Green is not always wholesome. Sometimes it is used to denote evil:

> Then [Gollum's] eyes shone with a green-white light, reflecting the noisome Morgul-sheen perhaps, or kindled by some answering mood within. Of that deadly gleam and of the dark eyeholes Frodo and Sam were always conscious. (*TT*, 'The Stairs of Cirith Ungol', 689)

Verging on the nauseous is the green ooze that emerges from Shelob's wounded eye, and the trail of green-yellow slime from her belly wound. Frodo's face goes livid green after he is stung by Shelob.

Brown is rarely used. One notable use is when Treebeard's eyes are described as 'brown, shot with a green light' (*TT*, 'Treebeard', 452). Here, unlike in Gollum's eyes, the green is not overtly threatening. But brown, mostly a neutral wood or earth colour, can also have negative connotations, such as when describing the effects of the cloud that emerges from Mordor to cover Gondor:

> But no day came, only a dead brown twilight. (*TT*, 'Journey to the Cross-roads', 683)

> The world was darkling. The very air seemed brown, and all things about were black and grey and shadowless; there was a great stillness. (*RotK*, 'The Muster of Rohan,' 783).[10]

> The very air seems thick and brown.... The next day came with a morning like a brown dusk. (*RotK*, 'The Siege of Gondor', 790; 797)

Hair (where blond) is usually described as golden (Glorfindel and the Elves of Lórien and Galadriel). The guards of Meduseld are described as golden-haired, as is Éowyn. Flaxen is used and 'strawheads'. Golden is also used to describe hobbit hair following Sam's use of Galadriel's gift:

> All the children born or begotten in that year ... were fair to see and strong, and most of them had a rich golden hair that had before been rare among hobbits. (*RotK*, 'The Grey Havens', 1000)

Gold and golden is used more in Rivendell and Lórien (the Golden Wood), as opposed to mere yellow: 'eastwards there was a golden light on the land' (*FotR*, 'The Bridge of Khazad-dûm', 323). Indeed the very names of those woods contain Elvish words for gold.

Examples of silver as a colour appear more often than for gold/golden. Discounting the references purely to the metal, silver as a colour is used to describe the colour of starlight and moonlight, the torchlight of Gildor's Elves, and the lamps of the Elves of Lórien. Later, Galadriel's phial is said to burn with a silver flame.

Silver is also used to describe flowing water, or the sheen seen in mist and rains. The rain in Frodo's dream in Bombadil's house turns to 'glass and silver' (*FotR*, 'Fog on the Barrow-downs', 132), and the song of Lúthien refers to mists

10. J.R.R. Tolkien, *The Return of the King*, Collins Modern Classics, London, 2001. All quotations from *RotK* are taken from this edition.

of silver, while Frodo looking out from Hennuth Annûn across the valley of the Anduin sees “a wide gulf of silver fume” (*TT*, ‘The Forbidden Pool’, 669). Another example of a silver sheen is Shadowfax, who glistens like silver at night – many descriptions of him describe him as a flash of silver in the darkness. Similar uses of silver to describe water would be Goldberry’s clothes, as she is described first as clothed in silver-green, then later clothed all in silver. Particularly poignant are the silver tears of Anduin in the song of the Mounds of Mundburg after the great battle of the Pelennor Fields.

Symbolism (centred around the White Tree) is present in the use of silver to describe the Tree of Gondor, and in the livery and helms of the guards of the citadel of Minas Tirith, who wear the ‘black and silver’. Silver is also seen in heraldry, in the banner of the Swan of Dol Amroth. It may be that silver as a colour is especially associated with the Elves, as Elrohir and Elladan bear a banner of silver when escorting Arwen to Minas Tirith, and Elrond has a silver harp. Some of these examples may be related to silver as a metal, though some colour symbolism may also be present.

Silver is also associated with grey. The cloaks of Lórien are silver-grey and dusk-silver, and the description of them is particularly haunting:

> It was hard to say of what colour they were: grey with the hue of twilight under the trees they seemed to be; and yet if they were moved, or set in another light, they were green as shadowed leaves, or brown as fallow fields by night, dusk-silver as water under the stars. [One of the elves said]: “they have the hue and beauty of all these things under the twilight of Lórien that we love; for we put the thought of all that we love into all that we make.” (*FotR*, ‘Farewell to Lórien’, 361)

In this passage, the Elves make clear that their art involves putting hue (colour) into the things they make, and this relates to their perception of those colours. This recalls the comments Tolkien made on colours and subcreation in *On Fairy-Stories*.[11]

Less clear is what is meant by silver in Bilbo’s melancholic song in Rivendell, which contains a reference to a silver sun (*FotR*, ‘The Ring Goes South’, 271), or what the symbolism is of silver in the scene brought to mind in the Houses of Healing by the fragrance of athelas: ‘shores of silver far away washed by seas of foam’ (*RotK*, ‘The Houses of Healing’, 850). Maybe these examples are no more than poetic imagination, or maybe there is some inherent symbolism present.

11. Op. cit. [3].

The colour silver is also often associated with, and sometimes synonymous with, white and vice-versa. Some descriptions use multiple instances of silver and white, such as the following passage from Hennuth Annûn: 'the Curtain was now become a dazzling veil of silk and pearls and silver thread: melting icicles of moonlight' (*TT*, 'The Forbidden Pool', 668). Silk, pearls, ice and moonlight are all being used to reinforce the description of a silver-white colour. Another example of white being combined with silver is Minas Ithil, described as being silver-white in colour.

Silver has an additional symbolic use, to describe melodic sounds or voices. This is the same symbolism seen in descriptions of someone as 'silver-tongued', and in the quote from the September 1931 debate between Tolkien, Hugo Dyson and C.S. Lewis concerning myths as 'lies breathed through silver'.[12] Examples of melodic silver are: Nimrodel 'her voice as falling silver fell' (*FotR*, 'Lothlórien', 331), 'clear ringing as of silver trumpets' (*RotK*, 'Minas Tirith' 735), 'Three strokes it rang, like silver in the air' (*RotK*, 'Minas Tirith', 743).

Silver trumpets are mentioned by Tolkien in a letter from 1955 describing a visit to Italy:

> I am still staggered by the frescoes of Assisi. You must visit it. We came in for the great feast of Santa Chiara and the eve Aug. 11-12. High Mass sung by Cardinal Micara with silver trumpets at the elevation![13]

On the topic of silver and the sounds of words, Tolkien had the following to say about the heraldic colour 'argent' in a letter written in 1961:

> It is better, I think, at any rate to begin with, to hear "argent" as a sound only … in a poetic context, than to think "it only means silver". There is some chance then that you may like it for itself, and later learn to appreciate the heraldic overtones it has, in addition to its own peculiar sound, which "silver" has not.[14]

There is also extensive paired symbolism between gold and silver when the two are used together. Gold/silver symbolism is particularly evident in Lórien, where Celeborn's hair is silver compared to the gold of Galadriel, and the Mallorn

12. Humphrey Carpenter, *J.R.R. Tolkien: A Biography*, George Allen & Unwin, London, 1977, p. 147.
13. Humphrey Carpenter, ed., *The Letters of J.R.R. Tolkien*, with the assistance of Christopher Tolkien, HarperCollins, London, 1995, Letter 167, p. 223.
14. Op. cit., Letter 234, pp. 309–11.

bark of silver compared to its flowers of gold. Galadriel's song tells us that 'by the strand of Ilmarin there grew a golden Tree' (*FotR*, 'Farewell to Lórien', 363). Nearly all the silver and gold symbolism harks back to the Two Trees of Valinor (and before them, the Two Lamps), even that of the Sun and the Moon.

In both Rivendell and after the victory on the Field of Cormallen, gold and silver are used together to describe sounds: 'Then the enchantment became more and more dreamlike, until he felt that an endless river of swelling gold and silver was flowing over him' (*FotR*, 'Many Meetings', 227), and 'all the host laughed and wept, and in the midst of their merriment and tears the clear voice of the minstrel rose like silver and gold' (*RotK*, 'The Field of Cormallen', 933). These uses of gold and silver may symbolise the elevated 'colour' or 'tone' of poetry and song.

Sometimes the symbolism is more straightforward:

> The eyes were hollow and the carven beard was broken, but about the high stern forehead there was a coronal of silver and gold. (*TT*, 'Journey to the Cross-roads', 687)

Here, the silver and gold of the 'crown' adorning the head of the fallen statue in Ithilien uses natural colours (of flowers) to symbolise the metal of symbols of power.

In addition to such uses of individual colours, Tolkien paired colours together to create compound words to indicate mixing of colours along the spectrum. Examples are: black-grey, green-white, silver-white, blue-grey, grey-green, silver-grey, red-golden, golden-red, brown-green, green-white, green-yellow, silver-green. As well as combining colours in this way, he also modified colours with words indicating the quality of the light. Examples here include: green-shadowed, blue-gleaming. Finally, Tolkien also used compound words to evoke the colour or quality of an object or material, as in: flaxen-pale, huorn-dark, elven-grey, snow-white.

LANGUAGE AND NAMES

Turning to languages and names, the Quenya and Sindarin elements relating to the colours silver and gold are glossed in *The Silmarillion*:

> *laure* – "gold" (but of light and colour, not of the metal) in *Laurelin*; the Sindarin forms in *Glóredhel*, *Glorfindel*, *Loeg Ningloron*,

> *Lórindol*, *Rathlóriel*.[15]
>
> *celeb* – "silver" (Quenya *telep*, *telpë*, as in *Telperion*) in *Celeborn*, *Celebrant*, *Celebros*. *Celebrimbor* means "silver-fist", from the adjective *celebrin* "silver" (meaning not "made of silver" but "like silver, in hue or worth").[16]

Similar glossings cover other colours, such as red, blue, grey, black and white.

As well as the names in Quenya and Sindarin that contain colours, there are many in English as well, some of which are simply translations from the Elvish. Examples include: Silverlode, Silvertine, true-silver, Greyhame, Goldberry, Goldilocks. There are many more such examples, all illustrating the importance of colours. Of interest here are the comments Tolkien made relating to the translation of names that included colour or light-related elements.[17]

MANY COLOURS

A discussion of colours in Tolkien's writings would not be complete without considering the situation where many colours appear, most famously in the case of Saruman. The quote in the epigraph for this paper contains the words he spoke to Gandalf at Isengard, when Gandalf says he liked white better after Saruman reveals his new robes: 'woven of all colours [that] shimmered and changed hue so that the eye was bewildered' (*FotR*, 'The Council of Elrond', 252). The reply by Gandalf, responding to Saruman's claim that white can be overwritten and broken, is an oft-quoted one:

> In which case it is no longer white … And he that breaks a thing to find out what it is has left the path of wisdom. (*FotR*, 'The Council of Elrond', 252)

The closure to this scene comes much later, when Gandalf casts Saruman from the order of wizards:

> "Behold, I am not Gandalf the Grey, whom you betrayed. I am Gandalf the White, who has returned from death. You have no colour now, and I cast you from the order and from the Council." (*TT*, 'The

15. Op. cit. [8], p. 433.
16. Op. cit. [8], p. 429.
17. Wayne G. Hammond and Christina Scull, *The Lord of the Rings: A Reader's Companion*, HarperCollins, London, 2005, 'Nomenclature of The Lord of the Rings', pp. 750–82.

Voice of Saruman', 569)

This passage highlights the symbolic use of colour here. However, despite this warning about the breaking of light, it is clear that context is everything. Saruman's downfall arose from his attempt to engineer changes, and it is this active action that distinguishes this situation from others where light is broken into many colours. In the proper context, the natural breaking of light is seen as a thing of beauty, as in the description of the waterfall forming the Window of the Sunset:

> The level shafts of the setting sun behind beat upon it, and the red light was broken into many flickering beams of ever-changing colour. It was as if they stood at the window of some elven-tower, curtained with threaded jewels of silver and gold, and ruby, sapphire and amethyst, all kindled with an unconsuming fire. (*TT*, 'The Window on the West', 659)

The contrast with the ever-changing colours of Saruman could not be more marked.

CONCLUSIONS

The above examples are mostly from *LotR*. An examination of Tolkien's use of colours in his other works may give yet more insight into why his writings appeal to many on such a visual level. Even looking only at the use of colours in his best-known work, it is still possible to draw some conclusions.

The breadth and depth of the examples given here, and the thoughts articulated by Tolkien on languages and the use of adjectives, including colours as adjectives, show that he was a master of his craft, of fantasy and sub-creation, in both theory and practice, well aware of how to use colours to powerful effect in bringing his visions to life on the page. Though Tolkien did use colours for symbolic effect, some of the best examples of his writings are where he uses colours to describe natural landscapes and phenomena. I would like to close by quoting one such passage:

> Turning back they saw across the River the far hills kindled. Day leaped into the sky. The red rim of the sun rose over the shoulders of the dark land. Before them in the West the world lay still, formless and grey; but even as they looked, the shadows of night melted, the colours of the waking earth returned: green flowed over the wide

> meads of Rohan; the white mists shimmered in the watervales; and far off to the left, thirty leagues or more, blue and purple stood the White Mountains, rising into peaks of jet, tipped with glimmering snows, flushed with the rose of morning. (*TT*, 'The Riders of Rohan', 412)

As an example of the interplay of light and colour in his writings, such passages are without compare. Tolkien was truly a genius with 'intense powers of visualisation', able to make his visions 'vivid to others'.

'Thirty Years of Tolkien Fandom'

Nancy Martsch

I discovered Tolkien through *The Lord of the Rings* in the fall of 1966, when I was a student at UCLA, California. I went to the College Book Company to buy books, and saw a display of the Ballantine paperbacks (with their bright blue and pink covers) next to the checkout counter. I knew what they were, because I'd read a magazine article earlier that summer about '*The Lord of the Rings*, the newest craze sweeping the college campuses.'[1] You must understand that *I* was a senior and very full of myself: *I* did not go chasing after silly campus crazes. However, I bought a copy of *The Fellowship of the Ring* (just to keep informed), took it home and started reading it. And I was hooked. A few days later I am running back to the bookstore to buy the other two: '*Please let don't let them be sold out, please let them be there, please, please...*' The display is still there! OK, act casual, pretend you came here to get something else ... I didn't get much studying done that week.

Today, we tend to forget that, first of all, *LotR* is a rip-roaring adventure story. And second, thanks to the Peter Jackson films, the story has become well known. This last was not the case in 1966. I didn't even know if Frodo was going to make it! After I found out how the book ended I read the book again, this time more slowly, to enjoy the rest of the story. But for me Tolkien's work was a very private, very personal experience, not one which I could discuss with anyone. Later, in June of that year (or the perhaps it was year following), the student newspaper advertised a 'Tolkien Quest'. Participants would dress up as characters from *LotR* and raft down the Colorado River.[2] This made me very angry, because I felt that these people misunderstood the meaning of the story: a *quest* implies a goal, a purpose of deadly seriousness to which you dedicate your life. These people didn't have a *quest*, they had no reason to go down the river, they were just playing. This trivialised a solemn experience. I don't know if the Colorado River raft trip ever came off or not. But more than a decade would pass before I discovered fandom.

In the meantime I graduated with B.A. in Biological Illustration (which is illustrating scientific works), took a year's graduate work in Botany, worked

1. Henry Resnik, 'The Hobbit-Forming World of J.R.R. Tolkien', *Saturday Evening Post* Magazine, 2 July 1966.

2. The Colorado River forms the boundary between California and Arizona. It is popular with rafters.

for a while on campus as an illustrator, joined Mensa (of which more later), got married ... and eventually ended up in the family custom photo blow-up business. I read everything I could find about Tolkien: Lin Carter's *A Look Behind The Lord of the Rings, A Tolkien Reader, The Hobbit*. I discovered other fantasy writers: E.R. Eddison, Mervyn Peake, William Morris, Lord Dunsany. When I learned that Tolkien had a buddy called C.S. Lewis who had written a space trilogy, I read that, hoping to find another *LotR* – and was bitterly disappointed. (I didn't like Lewis's heavy-handed religious preaching, either.)

All this time I was a closet fan. When I read *LotR* for the third time, I realised that all of the names, both the Elvish and the English, had meaning. So I tried to find what the names meant, and started a dictionary of Elvish (and other languages). Then *The Silmarillion* came out, and oh, it was *wonderful*. The bible of the Elves! A sacred text. Even better than *LotR*. It greatly advanced my Elvish studies, too. In time I would discover Jim Allan's *An Introduction to Elvish*, buy books on language, and teach myself about linguistics. But for years I remained a closet fan.

I 'came out of the closet', so to speak, in 1979. My husband had gotten a job in Monterey, California (Monterey on the west coast, between Los Angeles and San Francisco). I had lived in the Los Angeles area all my life, and thought I was about to leave civilisation forever. So I went to the local science fiction and fantasy bookstore and bought everything they had on Tolkien (The name of the store was 'A Change of Hobbit': the Tolkien Estate and Saul Zaentz were less strict about copyright in those days. A lot of unauthorised stuff was published in the 1970s, too: miniatures, games, posters, etc.) The clerk saw what I was buying and said, "You know, there's a group that might interest you – it's called The Mythopoeic Society – there's their flyer on the bulletin board..." So I joined the Mythopoeic Society. And then the Tolkien Fellowships (which was based in Los Angeles). And I got their magazines.

That summer the Mythopoeic Society held its annual convention, Mythcon, in San Jose, California (just south of San Francisco). And the Guest of Honor was – Jim Allan!

We went – my first Mythcon! – and I brought my Elvish dictionary in a three-ring binder to show to Jim Allan. (As I recall, he wasn't impressed.) Through the Myth Soc I met some of the other contributors to Allan's book, and corresponded with them. They helped me with my Elvish studies, and shared some of their notes. (Tolkien fans are nice people.) Eventually – looking ahead here – the Elvish dictionary had progressed to the point where I wrote to the Tolkien Estate saying that I had written a dictionary of the languages of Middle-earth, and would they be interested? The reply was that a lot of material was still unpublished, so don't bother. A few months later Ruth Noel's book *The Languages of Tolkien's*

Middle-earth came out. That hurt. Ah, well ... During a period of unemployment I also designed a boardgame based on the Nirnaeth Arnoediad, though I didn't try to sell that one.

My husband's job didn't work out, so a year later we moved back to Los Angeles, where we became active in the local branch of the Tolkien Fellowships and attended their meetings. At this time everyone took personas from Middle-earth and dressed in costume (for special events), so I took the persona of the dwarf lady Dís Thrain's Daughter, because I was interested in jewelry and lapidary. I made a costume, a tunic and skirt with hand-wrought silver jewelry – at that time we didn't know that dwarf women wore beards.[3] In short, I became a full-fledged fan.

So what had been going on in fandom up to this time? This is just a broad general survey, taken from published material, because I had not been personally involved. Generally speaking, Tolkien fandom in the United States grew from two sources, student clubs and science fiction fandom. Science fiction fandom was already well-established by the time *LotR* was published, and science fiction fans were quick to recognise the importance of the work and to promote it among themselves. *LotR* was voted the International Fantasy Award by science fiction fans in 1957. Later SF fan Ed Meskeys would write about *LotR* in his magazine *Niekas*.

The first glimmerings of organised Tolkien fandom appeared around 1960. In February, 1965, Dick Plotz, a student at Columbia University in New York, started what would become the Tolkien Society of America. It might have been just another short-lived group, but for the fact that the paperbacks of *LotR* came out in that same year, and Tolkien readership (and with it TSA membership) exploded. Soon it became too much for Dick Plotz to handle, and Ed Meskeys helped him out. Then the Tolkien Society of America merged with the Mythopoeic Society in 1979. The Mythopoeic Society was founded in 1967 by Glen GoodKnight, a student at California State University at Los Angeles, because Glen felt that his favorite authors, C.S. Lewis, Charles Williams, and J.R.R. Tolkien ought to be studied as literature. Other groups were also founded in the 1960s and '70s, after the publication of the paperbacks: Richard West's The University of Wisconsin Tolkien and Fantasy Society (1966), The American Hobbit Association (Phil Helms, 1975), The American Tolkien Society (Reneé Alper) and the Tolkien Fellowships (Bernie Zuber), both in 1977, The New England Tolkien Society (Gary Hunnewell) in 1979, and others. England's Tolkien Society was founded

3. I wore the costume for my presentation: a long red plaid skirt, dark green tunic, with a silver belt and filet (headband), which I made myself – the belt of silver links set with garnet and quartz crystal; the filet, of silver wire with a carved aquamarine. Now that Peter Jackson's films have set the bar for costuming so high, this outfit would probably be unsuitable.

by Vera Chapman in 1969.

The 1960s and early '70s were a time of great social upheaval in the United States. There was the Civil Rights Movement, the Vietnam War, the Free Speech movement, riots, bombings, assassinations; Rock and Roll and the Beatles; Hippies and drugs. The press sensationalised everything: they depicted Tolkien fans as student radicals, costumed wackos, or hippies. (It's still being done today. In a recent interview with Christopher Tolkien in *Le Monde*, French Tolkien scholar Vincent Ferré noted that, for American Tolkien fans of the 1960s, *LotR* 'set the standard for the militants of the left, notably on the campus of Berkeley, in California'.[4]) While this was true to some degree – Tolkien fandom was largely a youth movement - this was a very distorted picture. *We were not all hippies!* I, for one, was very conservative. (No-one believes me, but it's true.)

So what did these Tolkien fans actually do? A noted before, science fiction fandom provided the template for Tolkien fandom. And what did Science Fiction fans do? They got together to discuss their favorite books, had parties, held local and regional conventions, and gathered for a big national convention called World Con. At which they discussed their favorite books, had parties, met their favorite authors, bought books, showed off their costumes and art, held a Banquet and gave out Awards – in short, the exact same things as Tolkien fans do today, except that science fiction fandom leans more toward hard science and Tolkien fandom is more literary. Tolkien fans also took personas from the stories, dressed in costume, and acted out scenes from the books. Bilbo's Birthday Party resembled a picnic, so picnic activities were adapted to Tolkien fandom. Once in the spring our Los Angeles group joined with the Orange County group (to the south of Los Angeles) to re-enact the Crowning of King Elessar. At other times we had picnics. At one of them we had a mushroom roll race – you pushed a mushroom along the ground with your nose. This has fallen out of use, fortunately.

In 1974 the role-playing game *Dungeons and Dragons*, heavily influenced

4. Raphaëlle Rérole, 'Tolkien, l'anneau de la discorde', *Le Monde*, 5 July 2012:
'La folie Tolkien était assez similaire à celle qui s'est développée autour d'Harry Potter', note Vincent Ferré, Professeur à Paris-XIII, qui dirige un Dictionnaire Tolkien à paraître a l'automne. Dès les années 1960, Le seigneur des anneaux devient un symbole de la contre-culture, notamment aux Etats-Unis. 'L'histoire, celle d'un groupe de personnes se révoltant contre l'oppression, dans un décor teinté de fantastique, sert d'étendard aux militants de gauche, notamment sur le campus de Berkeley, en Californie.'
('The Tolkien craze was rather similar to that which developed around Harry Potter', notes Vincent Ferré, Professor at Paris-XIII, who directs a Tolkien Dictionary which will appear in the fall. Since the years of the 1960s, The Lord of the Rings became a symbol of the counter-culture, notably in the United States. 'The story, that of a group of people revolting against oppression, in a setting tinted by the fantastic, set the standard for the militants of the left, notably on the campus of Berkeley, in California.' My translation.)

by Tolkien, was published. This, combined with historical reenactments, gave rise to the concept of live role playing. In the United States the medievalist impulse, especially in martial arts (such as sword fighting) and crafts (cooking, costuming, calligraphy, etc.) was absorbed into groups like the Society for Creative Anachronism and the Renaissance Pleasure Faire (both of which started in California in the mid 1960s) but in other counties these activities became associated with Tolkien fandom. *LotR* is so real that people don't want to just read it, they want to experience it, to know what it feels like to march across country with a pack on your back and a sword at your side and camp out and fight Orcs. That's what the Colorado River rafters were trying to do, although I didn't understand it at the time. After the fall of communism in Eastern Europe and Russia, entire armies of young people were camping out in the woods and fighting battles only loosely based on Tolkien's works. Tolkien fandom has influenced the lives of many people. It affects our choice of study, of careers: people have become scholars, artists, writers, game designers, film-makers, and in non-English-speaking countries, translators. All through their love of Tolkien.

But I've gotten ahead of myself. What was going on in Tolkien fandom in the 1960s and '70s? The one, salient difference between Tolkien fandom then and today is that Tolkien fandom then was on paper. People published paper newsletters. The Internet as we know it did not exist. Desktop publishing was in its infancy. Cell phones as we know them did not exist. People communicated in person, by telephone, or by mail. They wrote letters, by hand or typed. When *LotR* came out in paperback Tolkien was inundated with letters and packages from America. People wrote Letters to the Editor, expressed their opinions, carried on discussions, shared gossip and news. They shared their literary efforts, too. We still do the same thing today – but it's done on the Internet, in blogs, websites, twitter, Facebook, and so forth. Then, it was on paper.

Most fan groups could not afford professional printing, so they reproduced their magazines by xerox. You typed the text on the typewriter, cut out the blocks of text and art, pasted or glued them onto sheets of paper (that's why it's called 'cut and paste'), took the pasted-up sheets (called 'camera-ready copy', because it was ready to be photographed or copied) to the local copy center, ran off the requisite number of copies, addressed and mailed them. Newsletters were on paper.

And these early fan publications are still on paper. The majority have not yet been digitised. As a consequence, the early days of Tolkien fandom are not as well known. The situation is changing, however: the Mythopoeic Society has published an index to its journal *Mythlore*.[5] 'Beyond Bree' doesn't have an index

5. *Mythlore* Index, <www.mythsoc.org>. 'Beyond Bree' website, <www.cep.unt.edu/bree.html>.

but it does have a complete list of back issues posted on its website. An excellent fan magazine from the 1980s, 'Rómenna Meeting Report', has been digitised and is available on the Tolkien Guide website. Descriptions of the Tolkien Society's publications *Amon Hen* and *Mallorn* can be found on *tolkiengateway.net*. And Gary Hunnewell, who has probably the best collection of Tolkien magazines in the world, has donated his collection to the Tolkien archives of Marquette University, and is in the process of indexing them as the *Tolkien Fandom Review*. I strongly urge everyone to seek out these early fanzines: they contain a wealth of material.

So, what about 'Beyond Bree', the fan magazine which I edit? I mentioned that I became active in the Tolkien Fellowships. Its founder, Bernie Zuber, published the newsletter 'The Westmarch Chronicle'. I was greatly impressed by his magazine because (unlike most fan publications) it came out regularly and was professional looking. (Zuber was a professional artist.) And I thought to myself, I could do this.

I was a member of the American branch of Mensa, an organisation for people of high IQ, which was founded in 1946 in Oxford, England. Mensa officially 'takes no positions, has no opinions', it exists solely for people to meet each other. (Remember, this was before Facebook.) But within Mensa people with shared interests formed Special Interest Groups, or SIGs. Some are local (like the boardgames SIG, where I met my husband); others are national, which at this time meant newsletters. In the summer of 1980 I saw a Tolkien SIG listed in the national *Mensa Bulletin*. I wrote to the address given, received no reply, wrote to the SIGs Officer, explained what had happened and added that if the Tolkien SIG needed assistance, I would be willing to help. The reply came back to effect of, 'Congratulations, you're the new Tolkien SIG Co-ordinator!' So I posted some notices in the *Bulletin*, got a few inquiries, asked people what they wanted to do – no-one from the previous SIG ever got in touch with me, so we started from scratch. In March, 1981, I published the first 'Tolkien SIG News' – three pages. The lead article said that Ralph Bakshi would not make Part 2 of *The Lord of the Rings*. And I mailed it out, free, to everyone who had expressed interest. After the second newsletter, when I had some idea how much printing and postage were going to cost, I informed everyone that I would be willing to edit and publish the newsletter to provide a forum for the Tolkien SIG, but if they want to continue to receive it, they would have to reimburse me for their share of the printing and postage. At which point several of them promptly dropped out. So we started with six – count 'em, six! – paying members.

'Rómenna Meeting Report', <www.tolkienguide.com>. Descriptions of *Amon Hen* and *Mallorn*, <www.tolkiengateway.net>. *Tolkien Fandom Review*, <http://efanzines.com/TFR/index.htm>.

We held a 'Name the Newsletter' Contest, and the winner was 'Beyond Bree'. This was supposed to reflect the saying, 'Strange as news from Bree, not sure as Shire talk.' (The title 'News from Bree' belonged to another newsletter at the time, hence could not be used.) Bree is a crossroads: when you leave Bree you go on adventures, so Bree can represent both the world of Tolkien and Tolkien-related fantasy, Bree and beyond. At least that was the idea. It won with two votes.

I promoted the Tolkien SIG aggressively, to both Mensa and Tolkien groups. I quickly realised that the SIG needed Tolkien expertise, which was to be found outside of Mensa. So I contacted every Tolkien group I could find, and tried to arrange newsletter exchanges with them, as this both increased awareness of our group and was an excellent way to obtain news. (Remember, the Internet hadn't got started yet.) We also exchanged newsletters with Tolkien groups in Europe, which avoided the complications of currency exchange. (PayPal hadn't been invented yet.) And I sent 'Beyond Bree' to the three major Tolkien archives: Marquette University in Milwaukee, Wisconsin; Wheaton College in Wheaton, Illinois; and the Bodleian Library in Oxford, England. These three, plus the Tolkien Society in England, have complete sets of back issues of 'Beyond Bree'.

As a dedicated Tolkien enthusiast I also went to Tolkien events and gathered news myself. When Lester Simons of the Tolkien Society spoke to the Orange County group we drove miles to hear him; when Christopher Tolkien came to Mythcon at Marquette University my husband and I were there; we went to England for the Tolkien Centenary in 1992 and Tolkien 2005, and we would never have come to England otherwise. When the American Booksellers Association held its wholesale-to-the-trade convention in Los Angeles in June 1994, I wangled a pass through my connections at work, and was able to meet the representative for Tolkien's United States publisher, Houghton Mifflin. I gushed about 'Beyond Bree' and gave her a copy. As a result Houghton Mifflin sent me review copies of its books. This is a double-edged sword: the books are nice to have, but you are morally obligated to review the books, or else arrange to have someone else review them. For a while Ballantine Books sent science fiction paperbacks to 'Beyond Bree' for review, too.

I'm not going to go into the details of newsletter publishing, except for two pieces of advice: (1) Save early, save often, save off site and off line, and keep a copy of every newsletter you send out. And (2) bear in mind that each and every issue could be the reader's first issue, even his very first fanzine, and that person has just as much right to know what is going on as the old hands. So give full names and titles, spell out acronyms, and include references. Because if we do not aid and encourage new readers, then interest in Tolkien will die out.

After variations in size 'Beyond Bree' settled on 12 pages, because 6 sheets of standard paper weigh one ounce, the limit for postage in the USA. This limits us to news, reviews, letters, short articles, occasional art and poetry, and (very rarely) fiction.

So what did 'Beyond Bree' readers do? You can read more details on the 'Beyond Bree' website, but here are some highlights: We carry on lively discussions. We reviewed all the volumes of *The History of Middle-earth* as they came out, as well as other works. 'Beyond Bree' readers gathered information for Wayne Hammond's *J.R.R. Tolkien: A Descriptive Bibliography*. In 1985-6 we were publishing a series of articles on the differences between the American and English editions of *LotR* and *The Hobbit*. Rayner Unwin, who was a reader of 'Beyond Bree' (did I mention that I promoted the newsletter aggressively?) took note of some of these differences. In 1987 Houghton Mifflin published its one-volume corrected *The Lord of the Rings, Collector's Edition*, bringing the American edition in line with the English one. I like to think that 'Beyond Bree' played a small part in this.

'Beyond Bree' has published calendars and booklets. I was a founding member of the Elvish Linguistic Society, and attended their early meetings. I realised that there was a need for basic Elvish instruction, and wrote a series of Quenya language lessons which were printed in 'Beyond Bree' from August 1988 through June 1990, and later published in booklet form as *Basic Quenya* for the Tolkien Centenary in 1992. 'Beyond Bree' readers also gathered information about other Tolkien-related items: games, posters, calendars, music, which was published as *List of Tolkienalia*, again for the Centenary. Today there is so much Tolkien-related material that such a list in one book would be impossible. Now there are websites dedicated to specific Tolkien items: games, calendars, music, movie memorabilia, collectibles, and more. Again I urge everyone to seek out these websites, because they contain a great deal of information.

One of our readers, Ron Hyde, organised our first convention, Bree Moot, in October 1994 in Bettendorf, Iowa, at a former monastery converted into a hotel. We have had other Bree Moots since then, some in combination with other conferences. We sponsored events at international Tolkien conferences, Tolkien 2005 and 'The Return of the Ring' in 2012. And we instituted the 'Beyond Bree' Award, given 'In recognition of outstanding contribution to the study of J.R.R. Tolkien'. The recipients are chosen by the readers of 'Beyond Bree'. And of course I must mention our beautiful full-colour 'Beyond Bree' calendars, produced by Daniel Smith.

I certainly never thought I would still be doing this thirty years later. But 'Beyond Bree' has been the source of many friendships for me, and I hope that it has been and will continue to be a source of information, inspiration, and pleasure for its readers.

So, to sum up, what has happened in Tolkien fandom over the last 30 years?

- In literature: the publication of many works by and about Tolkien (including the twelve-volume *History of Middle-earth*), scholarly studies, and journals (such as *Tolkien Studies*). We old-timers had an advantage, because we could read each book as it came out, but today the scholar has to acquire all of this at once.
- In the non-literature department: games – Iron Crown Enterprises' Middle-earth Role Playing rose and fell – boardgames, collectible card games, video games, and now *LotR* Massively Multiplayer Online computer game, which is truly impressive. Music and theatre; all sorts of collectibles and movie memorabilia; and films – Ralph Bakshi's animated *LotR* made created quite a stir at the time, though that's largely forgotten now. And now we have Peter Jackson's films, to which I will return later.
- In non-electronic technology: the availability of xerox in the mid-1960s, which greatly enhanced the publication of fan newsletters.
- And in electronic technology: the personal computer, as opposed to the mainframe. With it you could produce professional-looking printing, crunch numbers, and play games, such as *Pong*.
- Digital technology: developed by NASA to send back data from space, its ability to encode sound and images gave rise to the CD, which eliminated the vinyl record; the digital camera, which put an end to traditional photography (and to my profession as a photo retoucher); video cinematography, which has replaced film; and now e-readers – the days of the paper book seem to be numbered.
- The Internet: started as a method used by scientists to send data in binary code over telephone lines, until people discovered that it could be used to send messages. When we returned to Los Angeles from Monterey, my husband got a job in a Research and Development company which sent its data (encoded in punched cards) over the phone lines to be run by a mainframe computer in San Francisco. The modem was called 'Gandalf', the receiving end, 'Morgoth'. Most of the employees didn't know what the names meant.
- Put these last three together and we have the Digital Revolution. We can now communicate with people all over the world in real time: our society has truly become global. We can search libraries from our home computers. With Amazon.com and PayPal, we can buy things from foreign countries without the hassle of currency exchange. Through e-Bay we can find all sorts of collectibles we could never find before (such as my first edition (thirteenth printing) of the Houghton Mifflin *LotR*).

And now let us turn to Peter Jackson's *Lord of the Rings* film trilogy. This has had an *enormous* influence. A whole new 'branch' of fandom has grown up around the films. (And their successors, *The Hobbit* trilogy.) I'm not going to get into the book versus film debate: suffice it to say that while the films differ greatly in detail from the books, they have managed to capture the spirit of the books, at least in part, in addition to introducing people to the rich world of Middle-earth. Ironically, the films seem to have gotten across the importance of Tolkien's work to the general public – even to some critics – in a way that the books never did. Like book fandom, film fandom has also had a profound influence on peoples' lives.

Book fandom began in the paper era. Film fandom is digital. Book fans make pilgrimages to England, film fans make pilgrimages to New Zealand. Although book and film fans share many of the same activities, film fans also have film-related interests, such as costuming, make-up, computer animation, and filmmaking. They make their own films, and some of them are very good, too.

Yet another branch of fandom which is largely ignored is game fandom, especially the online computer games. These are a world in themselves.

So now we have a generation gap between the paper era and the digital age and a gap between the book and other media. Most generations have a gap between the young and the old, as the young will often choose different ways to do things. But in our time this generation gap is exacerbated by the change in technology. We are not the first to experience major technological change: Tolkien lived through the change from horses to motor cars and airplanes. I confess that I am an old paper person and will probably remain so. I'm old enough to remember, when I was in junior high school, going to the library, copying out passages of text by hand, and then returning home to transcribe my notes on a manual typewriter, *because xerox wasn't available yet*. Today my neighbour's teenage daughter gives her book reports in Powerpoint with animation.

What will the future of fandom be like? It will probably be conducted digitally. Beyond this I don't know. But fandom will – should – continue.

We older fans need to remember that our way is not the only way, and welcome younger fans who may do things differently. And younger fans need to realise that they have not invented the wheel: a great history of fandom lies behind them. This history is rich and varied. I hope that you will learn more about it.

And, even though 'Beyond Bree' now has an electronic version, I will keep on publishing paper newsletters.

List of Contributors

Yoko Hemmi is a Professor of English at Keio University, Japan, where she teaches courses on English language, Tolkien and Medieval Irish and Welsh literature. Her research interests include Middle English romances, Celtic mythology and fairy legends. She is the author of an article on Tolkien's concept of 'native language' (in *Tolkien Studies*, 2010), and translated Tolkien's 'The Lay of Aotrou and Itroun' and 'Imram' into Japanese.

Jamie McGregor lectures in English at Rhodes University. Since 2009 he has taught an elective paper in Modern British Fantasy 1916-77, covering works by Tolkien, C.S. Lewis, T.H. White and Mervyn Peake. His article 'Two Rings to Rule them All: A Comparative Study of Tolkien and Wagner' appeared in *Mythlore* 29, 3/4, Spring/Summer 2011. A specialist in the relationship between Wagner and English literature, he celebrated the composer's bicentenary by impersonating him and recreating public readings of his opera libretti.

Nick Groom is Professor of English at the University of Exeter and has published widely on the Gothic and on Romanticism. This essay draws on research for his book for Oxford University Press, *The Gothic: A Very Short Introduction* published in 2012.

Constance G.J. Wagner, writer, poet, and Director of the Writing Program at Saint Peter's University in Jersey City, New Jersey, has spoken regularly on all things Middle-earth at both academic and fan-friendly events nationally and internationally since 2005. Her book *The War Within: Frodo as Sacrificial Hero* is scheduled for release by Oloris Publishing in 2015.

Anna E. Thayer (née Slack), has published a number of essays on the work of J.R.R. Tolkien and regularly contributes to conferences on Tolkien. She is editor of PortalEditions' volume Doors in the Air: C. S. Lewis and the Imaginative World , author of the award winning fantasy trilogy 'The Knight of Eldaran' and co-author to Peter Gladwin's autobiographical apologetic 'Out of the Darkest Place'.

Troels Forchhammer is an active blogger and runs Parma-Kenta as well as contributing to many other Tolkien websites and conferences.

Maureen F. Mann holds a PhD in English literature from the University of Toronto. Her interests include Victorian and medieval literature, fantasy and science fiction, in addition to Tolkien. She is currently editing submissions on 'Humour In and Around the Works of Tolkien' for Walking Tree Press, with Thomas Honegger.

Reuven Naveh was born in 1970 and studied Mathematics and Musicology in the Hebrew University of Jerusalem, receiving a PhD in Musicology in 2005. He is a member of the Israeli Tolkien Society and the Jerusalem Tolkien Group since 2003 and a lecturer on their behalf in several SciFi and Fantasy conferences.

Jim Clarke is a former national newspaper reporter turned academic. His doctoral research examined the fiction of Anthony Burgess at Trinity College Dublin, where he has taught Modernism and Postcolonialism. He has also taught twentieth-century fiction, including Tolkien, at the Free University of Ireland (Saor Ollscoil na hÉireann).

Murray Smith has written widely on Tolkien, contributing articles to online forums and to books. He is also a regular speaker at Tolkien events.

Janet Brennan Croft is head of Access Services and Associate Professor of Bibliography at the University of Oklahoma. Among her contributions to Tolkien research she is author of *Tolkien and Shakespeare: Essays on Shared Themes and Language*. She is also editor of Mythlore and received the Mythopoeic Scholarship Award in Inklings Studies

Chris Barclay is a semi-retired GP who spent several years in Obstetrics and Gynaecology. He has written and lectured extensively on women's health. After reading Tolkien in his teens, he later became interested in combining Tolkien and Women when, while re-reading, he could find just one woman mentioned in *The Hobbit*. This prompted an exploration both the Tolkien's biography and his writings with an eye for the feminine.

Christopher Kreuzer is a long-standing and regular contributor to Tolkien conferences and publications.

Nancy Martsch is the Fan Guest of Honor of RotR, and the editor of 'Beyond Bree', newsletter of the J.R.R. Tolkien Special Interest Group of American Mensa. 'Beyond Bree' celebrated its 31st anniversary in March 2012. Nancy has presented papers at various Tolkien conferences, including *Mythcon*, the Tolkien

Centenary Conference, and Tolkien 2005; published papers in *Tolkien's Poetry*, and in the Tolkien Centenary and Tolkien 2005 conference proceedings, and authored *Basic Quenya*, a primer for Tolkien's Elvish.

Index

D

E

F

G

M

Q

R

About The Tolkien Society

The Tolkien Society is a literary society and educational charity devoted to promoting the life and works of Professor J.R.R. Tolkien CBE. Founded in 1969 as a fan club in the United Kingdom, today the Tolkien Society has over a thousand members worldwide. We are friendly, fun and passionate in our mission to promote Tolkien to as wide an audience as possible while growing our fellowship of people who consider Middle-earth their home.

Membership include a subscription to the Society's two regular publications. *Amon Hen* is our bi-monthly bulletin which includes news, book reviews, short articles, information about events and much more. *Mallorn* is the journal of the Tolkien Society, featuring scholarly articles and in-depth reviews from scholars supplemented by full-colour artwork from some of the best Tolkien artists. In addition to *Amon Hen* and *Mallorn*, we publish one-off publications such as these proceedings together with our 'Peter Roe' booklets which print papers delivered at our annual events.

As well as our wide range of publications, the Society hosts a series of events each year. On 3 January we celebrate the anniversary of Tolkien's birth in 1892 by encouraging fans all over the world to raise a toast to the Professor at 9pm their local time. 3 March is Tolkien Reading Day, marking the date on which the One Ring was destroyed in *The Lord of the Rings*. In the summer we hold our Seminar for serious Tolkien scholarship, usually in early July in Leeds. But the centrepiece of our calendar is Oxonmoot. Held in an Oxford college on a weekend close to Bilbo and Frodo's birthday on 22 September, we gather for a long weekend of talks, discussions, quizzes, food, partying, masquerading and great company. For any Tolkien fan, Oxonmoot is not to be missed.

To learn more and tobecome a member of the Tolkien Society visit our website at www.tolkiensociety.org.

www.ingramcontent.com/pod-product-compliance
Lightning Source LLC
Chambersburg PA
CBHW080851190726
48292CB00011B/2955

* 9 7 8 1 9 1 1 1 4 3 0 3 1 *